Other Titles in the Psychology of Popular Culture Series

*The Psychology of The Simpsons*

*The Psychology of Survivor*

*The Psychology of Superheroes*

*The Psychology of Joss Whedon*

*The Psychology of Dexter*

# The Psychology of The Simpsons

## D'oh!

Edited By Alan Brown, Ph.D.
With Chris Logan

AN IMPRINT OF BENBELLA BOOKS, INC
*Dallas, Texas*

BenBella Books, Inc.
Dallas, Texas

"The Family Simpson: Like Looking in a Mirror?" © 2005 by Misty K. Hook, Ph.D.

"For Better, or Worse? The Love of Homer and Marge" © 2005 by Wind Goodfriend, Ph.D.

"'Which One of Us Is Truly Crazy?' Pop Psychology and the Discourse of Sanity and Normativity in *The Simpsons*" © 2005 by Molly Snodgrass, M.A., and Irene Vlachos-Weber

"Stupid Brain! Homer's Working Memory Odyssey" © 2005 by Nelson Cowan, Michael J. Kane, Andrew R. A. Conway and Alexander J. Ispa-Cowan

"Homer's Soul" © 2005 by Paul Bloom and David Pizarro

"Alcohol—The Cause of, and Solution to, All Life's Problems" © 2005 by Denis M. McCarthy

"The Cafeteria Deep Fryer Is Not a Toy" © 2005 by Mike Byrne

"Righteousness and Relationships: Feminine Fury in *The Simpsons* or How Marge and Lisa Taught Me to Embrace My Anger" © 2005 by Sally D. Stabb, Ph.D.

"Self-Esteem in Springfield: Self and Identity in the Land of D'oh" © 2005 by Robert M. Arkin and Philip J. Mazzocco

"Can Bart or Homer Learn?" © 2005 by W. Robert Batsell, Jr.

"Sex and Gender in Springfield: Male, Female and D'oh" © 2005 by Linda Heath, Ph.D., and Kathryn Brown

"Hope Springs Parental: The Simpsons and Hopefulness" © 2005 by Karin H. Bruckner, M.A., L.P.C.

"Looking for Mr. Smarty Pants: Intelligence and Expertise in *The Simpsons*" © 2005 by Frank C. Keil, Kristi L. Lockhart, Derek C. Keil, Dylan R. Keil and Martin F. Keil

"The Personalities of *The Simpsons*: Simpsons' Big Five" © 2005 by David A. Kenny and Deirdre T. Kenny

"Lyle Lanley, You're My Hero! or The Social Psychology of Group Membership and Influence" © 2005 by Chris Logan

"Springfield—How Not to Buy a Monorail: Decision-Making (Mostly Bad) in *The Simpsons*" © 2005 by David A. Rettinger and James Rettinger

"(a) None of the Below: Psychology Testing on *The Simpsons*" © 2005 by Harris Cooper

Additional Materials © 2005 by Alan Brown, Ph.D.

BenBella Books, Inc.
10300 N. Central Expressway, Suite 400
Dallas, TX 75231
www.benbellabooks.com
www.smartpopbooks.com
Send feedback to feedback@benbellabooks.com

Printed in the United States of America
10 9 8 7 6 5 4

Library of Congress Cataloging-in-Publication Data is available for this title.

ISBN 978-1-932100-70-9

Proofreading by Jessica Keet and Stacia Seaman
Cover design by Todd Michael Bushman
Text design and composition by John Reinhardt Book Design

Distributed by Perseus Distribution
perseusdistribution.com

To place orders through Perseus Distribution:
Tel: (800) 343-4499
Fax: (800) 351-5073
E-mail: orderentry@perseusbooks.com

Significant discounts for bulk sales are available.
Please contact Glenn Yeffeth at glenn@benbellabooks.com or (214) 750-3628.

# Contents

The Family Simpson     1
*Misty K. Hook, Ph.D.*

For Better, or Worse?     21
*Wind Goodfriend, Ph.D.*

"Which One of Us Is Truly Crazy?"     37
*Molly Snodgrass, M.A., and Irene Vlachos-Weber*

Stupid Brain!     49
*Nelson Cowan, Michael J. Kane, Andrew R. A.*
*Conway and Alexander J. Ispa-Cowan*

Homer's Soul     65
*Paul Bloom and David Pizarro*

Alcohol—The Cause of, and Solution to, All Life's Problems     75
*Denis M. McCarthy*

The Cafeteria Deep Fryer Is Not a Toy     95
*Mike Byrne*

Righteousness and Relationships     107
*Sally D. Stabb, Ph.D.*

Self-Esteem in Springfield     121
*Robert M. Arkin and Philip J. Mazzocco*

Can Bart or Homer Learn?     135
*W. Robert Batsell, Jr.*

Sex and Gender in Springfield     147
*Linda Heath, Ph.D., and Kathryn Brown*

Hope Springs Parental     159
*Karin H. Bruckner, M.A., L.P.C.*

Looking for Mr. Smarty Pants     173
*Frank C. Keil, Kristi L. Lockhart, Derek C. Keil,*
*Dylan R. Keil and Martin F. Keil*

The Personalities of *The Simpsons*          *187*
David A. Kenny and Deirdre T. Kenny

Lyle Lanley, You're My Hero!          201
Chris Logan

Springfield—How Not to Buy a Monorail          215
David A. Rettinger and James Rettinger

(a) None of the Below          229
Harris Cooper

# The Family Simpson

## Like Looking in a Mirror?

### Misty K. Hook, Ph.D.

THE UNITED STATES is a country that talks a lot about "family values." That particular phrase is often used as the rationale for major social, political and even business decisions. But what does "family values" mean to individual people? In general, people tend to look at families through two lenses: (a) how their own family operates; and (b) how they think other families operate. We tend to think of our family as "normal," but at the same time we judge the quality of our family life based on what we think other families are like. We form our views of other families based on what other people tell us...and what we see on television.

This can be unfortunate, because we tend to look at other families through rose-colored glasses. We have to rely on what other people tell us—and their accuracy is often in question. After all, who wants to admit that their family is flawed? Family processes are shrouded in secrecy. Gone are the days when we all lived together and could actually see how families talked and played together, what kinds of discipline methods were used, and what roles everyone played. Now we have to guess how it is that other families behave or rely on possibly erroneous self-reports.

Given this secrecy and the reluctance people have to let others into their private lives, where are we to look for examples of family life? Why, TV, of course! By making hits of TV shows like *The Brady Bunch*, *The Waltons* and *The Cosby Show*, we showed ourselves to be fascinated by other families. However, the early television version of families was too sanitized, too perfect. The Bradys didn't even have a toilet and six kids shared a bathroom without maiming or killing each other! Anyone who has ever had to share a bathroom with even one sibling knows that is very optimistic. The Walton and Huxtable parents rarely lost their cool! Clearly these were Stepford parents. We enjoyed these shows because they portrayed families as we wished they were in real life. Of course, it's all too easy to view our own families poorly in comparison.

Into this atmosphere of warm, loving and ideal families came the fledgling network FOX. They had other ideas about families—they could be loud, hostile, deviant and quite dysfunctional—and their programming reflected these notions. Thus, in its early days, FOX brought us two of the most dysfunctional family sitcoms to date: *Married with Children* and *The Simpsons*. The Bundy family depicted in *Married with Children* was too outrageous to be seen by most viewers as anything but a parody. The Simpson family was different. While they too could be rude and insulting, there was a soft core at the center of their dysfunction. This was a family who, at the end of the day, were there for each other. They loved each other and this could clearly be seen through their forgiveness of each other, their unity in the face of external adversity, their sacrifices and their own brand of affection. In many ways they were more like our families than the Bradys or the Cosbys. It was these qualities (along with all the things that the Simpsons get away with) that, in a *TV Guide* poll, made so many people choose the Simpsons as the TV family to which they would most like to belong.

In the Simpsons, we have a family that draws people into their world week after week, year after year. What does their family say about us? Are they the American family? Do they fit into our cultural ideals about families in general? Do they reflect our way of life, our family members, and our family values? Are they truly dysfunctional? In short, we need a deeper analysis of the Simpsons as a family within the larger system of families in the United States.

## General Family Demographics

As a family, the Simpsons accurately reflect a large portion of the families in the United States. They are Caucasian, middle-class and have a typical family structure in that their nuclear family is comprised of two married heterosexual adults, three kids, a cat and a dog. They live near some extended family, including a grandfather, a grandmother (occasionally) and two aunts. Gender roles are somewhat traditional as Homer is the primary breadwinner and Marge, although she dabbles in outside careers, is generally a stay-at-home mother. Homer is allowed to come and go pretty much as he pleases, while Marge volunteers in the community and rules over the domestic domain. Thus, from the outside looking in, it seems as though the Simpsons look like a "normal" middle-class, Caucasian family. However, upon further examination, this is not exactly the case.

## Family Hierarchy

When thinking about families, you usually expect to see a clear hierarchy. When there are grandparents around, they frequently hold considerable influence. They are followed in power by the parental dyad, with the father generally being the most powerful. Directly below the couple are the other adults in the family (like aunts and uncles). At the lowest end of the power spectrum are the children, with the most power being held by the oldest child and the youngest having the least amount of power. At first glance, the Simpson family appears to totally disrupt the traditional power hierarchy...but do they really?

In contrast to what you would expect to find, it seems as if Grandpa Abraham Simpson has the least amount of power in the family. He is treated as little more than a child and is often even ignored. Marge, Homer and the kids frequently laugh at his failing memory and his ineffectual attempts to get what he wants. Even Bart and Lisa do not listen to him. He is left behind, forgotten and rarely invited to spend time with the family (Marge: "Are you really going to ignore Grandpa for the rest of your life?" Homer: "Of course not, Marge. Just for the rest of his life").

However ineffectual he is now, Abraham Simpson had a considerable influence in the formation of Homer's character. Flashbacks repeatedly show what an angry, critical father he was to Homer. He yelled, used corporal punishment and constantly belittled Homer's attempts to have fun, date and excel at various activities (Abe to young Homer: "You president? This is the greatest country in the world. We've got a whole system set up to keep people like you from ever becoming president"). These interactions stick with Homer. Marge has only to remind him of how his father treated him and Homer will change the way he treats Bart, Lisa and Maggie (like the time when he became coach of Bart's football team and forced Bart to be quarterback despite his obvious lack of ability). Homer will become gentler and more supportive because he is determined to avoid being like his father. Homer also tries in vain to repair the relationship with Abraham and continuously seeks his approval. However, Abe continues to be just as critical as ever ("The good Lord allows us to grow old for a reason: so we can find fault in everything he's made"). Grandpa Simpson is not without influence, but he certainly does not play the traditional grandfather role in the family hierarchy.

In most traditionally gendered families, the father holds more power than the mother. Is this true for Homer and Marge? Homer does earn most of the money, tends to the finances (as is shown by his constant loss of wealth), metes out discipline to the children and does little, if any, of the household chores. He also is consulted on all major decisions. In contrast, Marge takes care of all of the household tasks and seems to defer to Homer on most major decisions. So, it seems as though Homer holds more power than Marge. However, Marge makes her desires known. She is good at subtly influencing Homer's decisions and he consistently asks for help. Moreover, whenever Marge gets truly fed up with Homer's behavior, she takes charge and tells him what he needs to do. In an effort to make Marge take him back, he tells her, "I know now what I can offer you that no one else can: complete and utter dependence!" Consequently, although she has to endure a lot to get it, in the end, Marge almost always gets what she wants. As such, it looks as though Marge holds the most power in the family although she lets Homer believe that he has more than he actually does.

For Bart and Lisa, the power equation is a little less clear. Bart tends to bully Lisa until he gets what he wants. He is free to be as insulting and rude to her as he wants to be. That is, until she gets fed up. Then, like Marge, Lisa takes charge and gets her way. Whenever Lisa gets hurt or angry, Bart will almost always suffer until he backs down and apologizes. For example, when Bart was being particularly mean to Lisa on a school field trip, she obtained a restraining order against him. Bart had to live outside the house and be in school with Groundskeeper Willie in order to adhere to the legal requirements of Lisa's order. Bart suffered until he became so wild that Lisa forgave him and he ended up apologizing for his behavior. Consequently, the power is somewhat shared between Bart and Lisa despite Bart being the older child. As a baby, Maggie does indeed have the smallest amount of power.

When analyzing the power differential between the parental dyad and the kids, the situation is a bit more difficult. Like many of today's parents, Marge and Homer do not seem to understand appropriate and consistent discipline. Thus, Bart, Lisa and Maggie (yes, Maggie—how many other babies shoot the local billionaire and get away with it?) do what they want without much parental interference. Marge and Homer rarely get the kind of obedience that they wish to have from their children. As Bart once said, "I can't promise I'll try. But I'll try to try." Thus, it seems that the kids have more power than the adults. However, just as in the parental dyad and the sibling subsystem, the kids have more power until it becomes too much. Then Marge and Homer take charge and the power reverts back to its usual structure. For example, for punishment, Homer once refused to let Bart watch the Itchy & Scratchy movie. Homer dreamt that Bart ended up becoming a Supreme Court Justice as a result of Homer's demonstration of parental power. Similarly, when Marge puts her foot down and exerts her power, the kids fall into line. When Bart was caught stealing, Marge is extremely upset. For once Bart shows remorse: "Mom, I'm really sorry." Marge: "I know you are." Bart: "Is there anything I can do?" Marge: "I dunno (long pause). Why don't you go to bed?" Bart: "Okay." Consequently, Marge and Homer do have more power than the kids when they decide to wield it. This is as it should be.

## Family Roles

Every family has roles for its members to play and these vary by the type and needs of the individual family. Family roles are continuous patterns of behavior through which family members meet the needs of the family as a whole. Each role comes with specific cultural and family expectations for how these roles should be performed. Roles can be anything from something general, like parent or child, to something more specific, like nurturer or family hero. For healthy family functioning, both instrumental and effective roles must be present. Instrumental roles are those that provide physical resources, make decisions and manage the family. In contrast, effective roles provide emotional support and encouragement. Family members usually play more than one role and they can change.

While there are a number of roles possible, there are five general roles that are vital for a healthy family: Provider, Nurturer, Teacher, Maintenance and Sexual Gratifier. Homer fills the role of Provider. He works at the Springfield Power Plant and his salary pays for the house, food and other necessities. Marge is the Nurturer and Teacher. She gives comfort and emotional support for every member of the family and provides the physical, emotional, educational and social development of Homer, Bart, Lisa and Maggie. The Maintenance role involves leadership, decision-making, handling family finances and maintaining appropriate roles with respect to extended family, friends and neighbors. Other responsibilities of this role include maintaining discipline and enforcing behavioral standards. Both Homer and Marge occupy this role to varying degrees. Homer makes some decisions, handles the finances and participates in discipline. However, Marge fulfills the role to a greater degree. She also makes decisions, disciplines the kids and makes sure Homer, Bart, Lisa and Maggie all behave appropriately. She is the one who insists that the family be kind to their neighbors, the Flanderses, when they do not want to do so. She makes certain all members are dressed suitably and behave as well as she can make them. During Lisa's wedding rehearsal dinner, Marge urgently whispers, "Bart! Homer! Maggie! Company eating rules!" Thus, Marge is the primary occupier of the Maintenance role. Indeed, she is the glue that keeps the family together.

However, she does not always have much influence over Homer. He frequently ignores her attempts to keep him within the bounds of correct society, like the time he decided to boycott church or when he decided to gain as much weight as possible in order to be able to work at home. The final role for healthy families, the Sexual Gratifier, involves the parental dyad. Although *The Simpsons* is a family show, it is quite clear that Marge and Homer have a very satisfying sex life. They keep their relationship fresh by taking opportunities for new experiences. They've literally rolled in the hay, made out in a miniature golf windmill, taken a sexual enhancement tonic and had plenty of spicy sexual experiences. As such, both Marge and Homer fulfill this role.

The Simpson kids also have family roles. All families seek balance and attempt to present a good image (whatever it may be) to outsiders. Thus, children choose their roles based on what they think the family needs. The Simpson children fall into some classic roles. Lisa is the family hero, the perfectionist. She is an excellent student and is accomplished in many different areas. As she once exclaimed, "Ugh! I am sick of everyone being so proud of me!" However, despite the successful appearance, the family hero often feels inadequate and their self-worth requires the approval of others. They badly want their families to look good and when they fall short of their goals, they feel like they have failed. Lisa strives desperately to be popular, win Homer's approval and have her family look good. She feels awful when this does not happen. Her lack of popularity, for example, is a constant sore spot. When she was at military school trying to conquer The Eliminator, she says longingly, "If only I was back in Springfield, all my friends would be cheering me on! Oh, God, I'm delirious."

Lisa also plays the Parentified Child role, especially when Homer is in charge. If Marge is not around or refuses to help, everyone turns to Lisa to tell them what to do. This was especially evident when Marge and Homer were having trouble in their marriage. Homer pleads with Lisa, "I know you're only eight years old and I don't want to put a lot of pressure on you, but you've got to save my marriage!" Lisa responds, "You're very lucky to have Mom." Homer (not liking what he hears) tries to put her back in her child role: "That's your advice?! Go to bed!!" During another period of marital discord, Homer takes Lisa's advice and convinces Marge to let him return to the family. Lisa says to him, "I knew you could do it! Now don't screw it up." Lisa's role as the Parentified Child also extends to her attempts to get the family to do the right thing. She tries to convince them of the moral correctness of everything from recycling and vegetarianism to literacy and anti-consumerism.

In direct opposition of Lisa's role, Bart is the classic scapegoat. The scapegoat is the child who acts out for attention. Acting out includes behavior problems, delinquency, or poor school performance. In the classroom, scapegoats often get into trouble because they don't accept authority well. Bart constantly gives his teacher, Mrs. Krabappel, a hard time. Moreover, the list of Bart's delinquent acts is long and cannot be enumerated here. However, suffice it to say that he is blamed for most of the family's problems.

Maggie plays the mascot role. The mascot's job is to be cute and humorous. While mascots are generally older children who can be the clown, Maggie still fits the bill as she diverts attention away from things via sucking on her pacifier or falling down. The roles that Bart, Lisa and Maggie play tend to be complementary versus symmetrical. Instead of acting alike (symmetrical), every member has a particular task to do (complementary). If one person fails to fulfill his or her role, other members are negatively affected and try to make up for it. Consequently, when Lisa is unsuccessful, she may act out (the scapegoat role) while Bart becomes the hero. Similarly, both Bart and Lisa have taken turns being mascot when Maggie is not being cute.

## Family Rules

Just as every family has roles that its members play, every family also has its own rules. Some are overt and are openly discussed. These usually involve things like bedtime, when friends can come over, the timing of family meals and participation in religious activities. However, there are also covert rules. These are rules that exist but are not mentioned out loud; every family member is just expected to know them. These rules have more to do with interpersonal interactions than events or activities. They also are intimately linked with power and the roles that each family member plays.

For the Simpsons, one covert rule is that everyone can ignore and make fun of Grandpa Simpson. However, as befitting his status of holding some power in the family, another rule concerning Grandpa is that he is part of their lives. The family still invites him over to the house and he is involved in many aspects of their lives. When Grandpa is staying with them overnight, they wonder where he should sleep. Marge: "Where are we going to put him?" Homer: "Bart's room." Lisa: "Bart's room." Marge: "Bart's room." Bart: "Dumpster."

Another covert rule is that it is okay to acknowledge Homer's obvious failings. In this way, the power he holds in the family is lessened. When Homer became a food critic, Marge commented to the kids, "Only your father could take a part-time job at a small-town paper and wind up the target of international assassins." When at a company picnic, Mr. Burns tells Homer: "Make yourself at home." Bart responds, "Hear that, Dad? You can lie around in your underwear and scratch yourself." At this same picnic, Homer tells Bart and Lisa, "My boss is gonna be at this picnic, so I want you to show your father some love and/or respect." Lisa: "Tough choice." Bart: "I'm taking respect." In another example, when Homer asks the family if he is slow, all the kids look away in discomfort.

In her role of Nurturer, it is a rule that Marge will always think the best of Bart. She calls him "my special little guy" and is determined to close her eyes to his bad behavior. For example, when Bart was caught shoplifting, Marge refused to believe it. Marge: "I know in my heart that Bart is not a shoplifter…Fine, fine, play the tape and you will see that you have got the wrong boy." She is heartbroken when she discovers that he has indeed stolen from the store. Homer also has a rule concerning Bart: he will yell and threaten bodily harm (and in some of the earlier episodes he even appears to actually strangle him) unless Bart's behavior benefits Homer in some way.

The rule regarding Lisa is that her gifts are frequently ignored and her political beliefs are patronized. When Lisa decided to become a vegetarian, Bart made fun of her concerns while Marge ignored them. Lisa asked, "What's the difference between the lamb I'm eating and the one that kissed me?" Bart mockingly replied, "This one spent two hours in the broiler," and chomped on a lamb chop. Marge said, "Bart, sensible bites." Later, Homer was irritated with Lisa and said to her, "I don't need any serving suggestions from YOU, you barbeque-wrecking, know-nothing, know-it-all!"

The rule for Bart and Lisa has its roots in the quest for power in the sibling subsystem. As they both are rivals for their parents' affection and control of the family, Bart and Lisa constantly fight. Bart bullies Lisa while Lisa gets the best of Bart through her intellect. However, sometimes they just plain bug each other. During one family therapy session, Marge said, "Bart! How could you shock your little sister?!" Bart: "My finger slipped." Lisa: {Shocks Bart} "So did mine!"

While these rules dictate everyday behavior, there are exceptions. While the family belittles Homer, they go out of their way to help him get the things he wants. In accordance with his wishes, Maggie's first word is "Daddy." During Springfield's bicentennial parade, Lisa decides to forego telling the truth about Jebediah Springfield so that Homer can continue being the town crier. Everyone sometimes listens to and appreciates Lisa's political leanings. Lisa and Bart can join together to accomplish a goal. When they both went to military school, Bart faced the ridicule of his classmates to help Lisa surmount a physical challenge.

## Communication and Emotional Patterns

Every family has its distinct ways of communicating with one another. Some families are loud, fast talkers who interrupt constantly while others wait patiently for breaks in the conversation to speak. There are generally rules about who gets to speak first and last, who speaks the most, and what kinds of statements are allowed. Some families communicate solely at a surface level and do not allow members to express emotions or anything truly deep. Other families have very few boundaries surrounding appropriate conversation and talk about everything, including taboo topics like sex and drugs. In larger families, there are also rules about who talks the most to which other member. These are called alignments, coalitions and triangles. Traditionally, alignments occur among the parental dyad and coalitions are found in the sibling subsystem (the kids) but many other variations exist. Triangles occur whenever two people are in conflict and bring in a third person in order to defuse the situation.

The Simpsons appear to have relatively normal communication patterns. Each member of the family gets conversational time, with Marge and Homer usually getting the most. The family members do occasionally interrupt and ignore each other (especially when the TV is on) but not excessively. Homer tends to get the first word but usually not the last. That is reserved for Marge or the kids. In contrast to families in which the children are not allowed to question the adults, every Simpson is allowed to challenge the authority of everyone else. Bart and Lisa can ask questions about the purpose of the adults' behavior or even directly criticize without retribution. However, Marge and Homer do provide structure in conversational rules. They give boundary directions (e.g., "Don't talk when your mouth is full" and "Be polite") and let the kids know when they've crossed the line. Moreover, while the Simpsons are able to talk about anything, Marge and Homer do enforce some limits. For example, they rarely reveal details of their sex life.

In terms of groupings within the family, several are traditional. Marge and Homer are definitely aligned with each other. While each may speak somewhat disparagingly of the other, they obviously are a team. They do not undermine one another's authority and they usually consult with one another before making significant decisions. Similarly, Bart, Lisa and Maggie are in a coalition with one another. Although Bart and Lisa continuously annoy one another, they frequently join in order to get what they want from their parents. In one episode, they decided they wanted a pool. So, they repeatedly asked Homer (in unison), "Dad, can we have a pool?" While Maggie cannot exert much influence, she appears to be in agreement with Bart and Lisa. There also appear to be alignments along gender lines as Marge and Lisa appear particularly close (and they throw Maggie into that mix at times), while Homer and Bart are often in agreement with one another. There also exist some triangles in the Simpson family—but who is in them is dependent upon the situation. If Marge and Homer are having difficulty, Homer will usually consult with Lisa to help him know what to do. Similarly, Homer will sometimes ask the kids' opinions about a particular disagreement he is having with Marge. Bart and Lisa frequently try to get one or both of their parents to intervene in their disputes. However, the triangles within the family are not excessive.

## Parenting

How are Marge and Homer as parents? From flashbacks, we learn that Marge and Homer got married because Marge was pregnant with Bart. As such, they were reluctant parents, at least initially. However, they both agreed to try to build a family and seem to have warmed up to the idea (so much so that they had two additional kids). As parents, Homer and Marge have some obvious failings. Homer has virtually no idea of how to be a parent. His mother left his family when he was young and his father was overly critical and lacked warmth. Homer's own behavior is so outrageous that he has difficulty being aware of the needs of his children. In fact, Homer can barely even take care of himself, much less other people! Consequently, he is the stereotypical clueless father who has to be told what he needs to do as a father.

Both Marge and Homer really need some work on consistent, appropriate and effective discipline. Their methods of teaching the kids right from wrong are erratic, sometimes unacceptable (the implied and overt violence) and often futile. Many of Bart's antics are greeted with humor or avoidance. When Homer returned from being kicked out of the house for a day, Bart told him, "I missed you so much that I couldn't concentrate in school and I got an F." Homer: "This is dated two weeks ago." Bart: "Oh, sorry. Here's a fresh one." Marge then makes suggestive comments to Homer and Bart's poor school grades are ignored. Similarly, when Bart is demoted and Lisa is promoted to the third grade, Homer only becomes aware of this after he sees them on TV. His only comment to this incredible state of affairs is, "They're gonna be in the same class together?" When Bart is actively rude to others (how many kids get away with saying things like, "Don't have a cow, man!" or "Eat my shorts!" — OK, how many kids got away with saying things like that before they became part of the national lexicon?), Marge and Homer do little more than scold. That is, until they get completely fed up and institute punishment like denying Bart the opportunity to watch the Itchy & Scratchy movie. Homer: "Someday, you'll thank me for this, son."

Bart: "Not plenty likely." Homer: "I know my punishment may seem a bit harsh, but I can't go back on it. You're welcome to watch anything you want on TV." Bart: "TV sucks." Homer: "I know you're upset right now, so I'll pretend you didn't say that."

There are other problems with Marge and Homer's parenting skills, including their excessive use of the TV, the patronizing and parentification of Lisa and the lack of attention paid to homework and Maggie's developmental skills (how often is Maggie featured anyway?), yet they also do a lot that is good. In her roles of Nurturer, Teacher and Maintenance, Marge makes certain that the kids have their physical and emotional needs met. The children have a permanent roof over their head, get enough food and sleep and have some material comforts. The kids also know that their parents love them and would do anything for them. As Marge declared, "The only drug I'm on is LSD: Love for my Son and Daughters." Despite Homer having the job of his dreams with the Globex Corporation, he decides to return to his old job when Bart and Lisa are not happy. When Bart and Lisa get lost in Capitol City, Marge and Homer rush to look for them. Similarly, when the kids were sent into foster care with the Flanderses, Marge and Homer attend parenting classes and do whatever they can to get them back. Homer to Judge: "Okay, I'm never going to win Father Of The Year, in fact, I'm probably the last guy in the world to have kids...wait, let me rephrase that. I love my kids. I'd do anything for Bart and Lisa." Judge: "And Margaret?" Homer: "Who? Lady, you must have the wrong file." Marge: "She's taking about Maggie." Homer: "Oh, Maggie. I've got nothing against Maggie." Despite his flippant response, Homer rushes to save Maggie from what he considers a fate worse than death: "Oh, no! In the eyes of God, they'll be Flanderses." Marge and Homer are also affectionate with each other and their children. There are lots of hugs in the Simpson family. Finally, Marge and Homer are active and present parents. They attend their children's events and are there for them when they are needed.

## Conflict Resolution

Even the best of families experience conflict. After all, no one gets along perfectly all of the time. This especially holds true for people who know all of your faults and with whom you spend inordinate amounts of time. Consequently, families tend to have a lot of conflict. There are both good and bad ways to resolve conflict. One good way to resolve conflict is to hold a mature conversation where each member involved in the conflict has a chance to express their feelings and truly listen to the point of view of the other person or people. Another good way to settle conflict is to brainstorm compromises and potential solutions to the problem or, whenever possible, agree to disagree. Bad ways to resolve conflict include violence, yelling and avoiding the problem or the person involved.

Like many people, the Simpsons seem to muddle through conflict without actually having a plan. Sometimes the response is quite childish. When Lisa decided to become a vegetarian, she ruined Homer's barbeque and he was furious with her. Instead of telling her how angry and hurt he was, he decided to give Lisa the silent treatment. Marge foolishly went along with this and even allowed herself to get caught up in their feud. Homer: "Marge, since I'm not talking to Lisa, could you please ask her to pass me the syrup." Marge: "Please pass your father the syrup, Lisa." Lisa: "Bart, tell Dad I'll only pass the syrup if it won't be used on any meat product." Bart: "You dunking your sausages in that syrup, homeboy?" Homer: "Marge, tell Bart I just want to drink a nice glass of syrup like I do every morning." Marge: "Tell him yourself. You're ignoring Lisa, not Bart." Homer: "Bart, thank your mother for pointing that out." Marge: "Homer, you're not not talking to me, and secondly, I heard what you said." Homer: "Lisa, tell your mother to get off my case!" Bart: "Uh, Dad, Lisa's the one you're not talking to." Homer: "Bart, go to your room!"

At other times, the conflict resolution is unacceptable or incredibly inappropriate. First, there is the violence. While the Simpsons are cartoons and, as such, do not get injured the way real human beings would, the violence is still inexcusable. The Simpson children do not get spanked (the "normal" violence toward children seen in the United States) but Bart does get threatened, chased and even strangled. Other methods of conflict resolution are just inappropriate. Homer in particular often says horrible things that are meant to be comforting and distracting. When Lisa and Bart were arguing about whether either of them was capable of shooting Mr. Burns, Homer said soothingly, "Kids, kids, kids. As far as Daddy's concerned, you're both potential murderers."

However, while the Simpsons frequently demonstrate the negative aspects of conflict resolution, they also exhibit the positive ones. Apologies are frequent in the Simpson household. Bart eventually apologizes to Lisa for making her unhappy, Homer apologizes to the children for his poor parenting skills and Marge apologizes to anyone she believes she has wronged. The Simpsons have attempted family therapy and only a curmudgeon would point out that they used electroshocks on one another and ended up getting their money back so they could get a TV (the source of their initial argument). They also try to spend time together in order to connect with one another. Homer goes with Lisa to a sensory deprivation chamber because that is how she wants to spend time with him. Marge and Homer go on weekend retreats and find other ways to spend time alone. The Simpsons also make compromises in order to smooth hurt feelings. When Marge accused Homer of lying to her, in order to prove his love, he lets his obsession (catching General Sherman—the freakishly large catfish) go.

## Social Interaction

Families are connected in some way to the larger community in which they live. However, there are varying degrees of connection. Some families, particularly those with secrets (e.g., abuse, addiction) have a low level of connection to the community. Friends are rarely, if ever, invited to the house, family members have minimal participation in community activities, and they do not talk about their family to outsiders. These types of families are called closed families. In contrast, open families are highly connected. They frequently interact within the community, invite people to the house, and talk freely about their family life. It isn't difficult to guess which is the healthiest way of being.

The Simpsons are clearly an open family. They are intimately involved in the Springfield community. Bart and Lisa participate in sports, plays, musical performances and even a beauty contest, while the whole family turns out for parades, festivals and other community events. Marge and Lisa have even been involved in community governance through Marge's job as a police officer and Lisa's turn as a community elder through Mensa. Marge has even given advice to the community and led the march against the local house of prostitution.

The Simpsons are extremely social. Almost everyone in Springfield has been to their house for one reason or another. Marge and Homer throw disastrous parties (like the one that caused the Van Houtens to divorce or the barbeque that resulted in a pig flying through the air), weddings and other events. They also are well known and accepted within the Springfield community. Homer plays poker with the guys. Marge buys a weekly lottery ticket with the girls. Bart goes on to play with Milhouse. Lisa spontaneously interacts with various adults. However, although the Simpsons tend to get along with most of the citizens of

Springfield, there are exceptions. Homer can't stand Ned Flanders (although that distaste doesn't prevent them from having numerous adventures). And one only has to consider the ominous threat George H. W. Bush made when he moved next door to the Simpsons: "I'll ruin you like a Japanese banquet!" However, Gerald Ford seemed to get along well with Homer.

## A Healthy Family?

After all of this examination, one might ask: are the Simpsons a healthy family? There are several ways to answer this question. One way is to take a look at qualities of healthy families. These include commitment and appreciation of the family, willingness to spend time together, effective communication patterns, the ability to deal with crisis positively, ways to find meaning, encouragement of individuals, clear roles and a growth-producing structure.

The Simpsons clearly have a commitment to and appreciation for the family. When push comes to shove, they choose their family. Homer pretends that he smokes so that Patty and Selma won't lose their promotions, thereby making Marge happy. Marge gives up potentially illustrious careers to be with her family. The kids help each other and their parents. The Simpsons spend a lot of time together as a family and tend to be honest and clear in their communication. They resolve crises, sometimes weekly, and seek meaning in their activities. All members of the family are encouraged to follow their dreams. Bart and Lisa are supported in whatever ventures they attempt, while both Marge and Homer have tried various careers. As mentioned previously, roles are pretty well defined yet are not rigid. There seems to be a lot of potential for growth in the family should anyone actually age. Consequently, based on the qualities of healthy families, the Simpsons basically seem healthy.

A second way to evaluate the healthiness of the Simpson family is to analyze the two overarching family dynamics of family cohesion or togetherness and flexibility. Cohesion is composed of four elements: the I/We balance (how the family balances emphasis on the individual versus emphasis on the family), closeness, loyalty and independence/dependence. Families can be disengaged where the focus is mainly on the I—family members are neither close nor loyal and most are strongly independent. Other families go to the opposite extreme and are enmeshed. This is when the focus is predominantly on the We to the exclusion of the I—family members are excessively close, loyal and dependent. However, there is a middle ground where the family is connected. Connected families maintain a good balance between the I and the We and family members are close, loyal and equally independent and dependent.

The Simpsons focus a lot on the individual until the family becomes in jeopardy. Then the focus reverts back to the We until the crisis has passed. For example, they moved to further Homer's career (the I) but returned to Springfield when the family started to fall apart (the We). Similarly, Bart and Lisa both tried to navigate military school (the I) but joined together to conquer The Eliminator when Lisa was having trouble (the We). They are close to one another and exhibit a high level of family loyalty. Lisa was once upset when she thought that the Simpson genes were destined to make her stupid. Through Marge's help, she was overjoyed to discover that she was a member of an illustrious family, just on the female side. The kids are still dependent on Marge and Homer for the necessities and structure, yet are encouraged to be independent as well. Moreover, while Homer and Marge both profess their dependence on each other, they frequently go off on their own ventures. Thus, the Simpsons appear to be relatively connected with one another.

Family flexibility is comprised of leadership, role shifts, amount of change and discipline strategies. Chaotic families have no leader, roles are shifted dramatically, there is constant change and erratic discipline. On the opposite end of the spectrum are rigid families. They have a domineering leader, static roles, very little change and strict, often harsh, discipline. In contrast to both, flexible families have shared leadership, occasional role shifts, change when necessary and democratic discipline.

It is somewhat difficult to characterize the Simpsons on flexibility. On some dimensions, the Simpson family is very flexible while on others they tend to be a bit more chaotic. Marge is the clear leader in the family yet she is not domineering. While one could make the case for shared leadership with Homer, he cannot be relied upon and Lisa frequently has to give him advice. Thus, leadership is difficult to quantify. Roles are fairly well established yet there are occasional role shifts. Generally, Homer is the breadwinner and Marge the homemaker. However, at times, Marge has taken on a paid position outside of the home and Homer has been able to tend to the kids. Lisa and Bart also intermittently switch roles. So, roles are flexible. The amount of change that occurs is also on the flexible end of the spectrum. Although the Simpson family encounters a lot of different situations (as befits a weekly TV sitcom), there is actually very little change in the overall family structure. Bills get paid, needs get met and the same people are constantly present. However, discipline is another story. As has been discussed previously, discipline in the Simpson household tends to be erratic. Hence, although the Simpsons are mostly flexible, there are chaotic elements. Consequently, based on family dynamics, the Simpsons seem mostly healthy.

A third method of assessing the health of the Simpson family would be to look at the stressors they encounter and the coping strategies they employ to combat the stressors. Healthy families tend to be aware of the potential stressors in life. There are generally two types of stressors: vertical and horizontal. Vertical stressors are ones that bring past and present issues to bear equally on things like family attitudes, expectations, secrets and legacies. They are historical and inherited from previous generations. Types of vertical stressors include all the isms (e.g., racism, sexism, consumerism, ageism, classism), poverty, workplace issues, family emotional patterns, violence, depression and genetics. Horizontal stressors are aspects of our lives that relate to the present; they are developmental and unfolding. Many are predictable (e.g., life cycle transitions) while others are unpredictable. Types of horizontal stressors include moving, accidents, unemployment, war, political climate and natural disasters.

The Simpsons tend to be aware of the stressors they encounter. Like all families, vertical stressors are quite present in their lives. There have been some family secrets that have been brought to life throughout the years (e.g., Mother Simpson's life on the run, Abe Simpson's participation in a secret society with Monty Burns). It also is clear that the family attitude of criticism is alive and well in the current Simpson clan. The isms are also well represented. Marge faced sexism when she was a police officer and Lisa constantly faces sexism in her quest for intellectual stimulation. Grandpa Simpson faces ageism whenever he tries to do anything and Montgomery Burns ensures that the whole family faces classism (Mr. Burns after a company picnic on his estate: "Please get off my property until next year. I suggest you don't dawdle; the hounds will be released in ten minutes"). The Simpson family also faces depression. Marge once became so depressed that they had to hire a nanny, Sherry Bobbins. Lisa has also experienced depression, so much so that she was sent home from school for it (Aside: if that really worked, schools would be a lot emptier!). Horizontal stressors don't seem to affect the Simpson family as much as vertical stressors, primarily because they tend to be developmental (time does not seem to affect the Simpsons) and relatively lacking in humor.

There are a variety of coping strategies that families employ to help them adjust to life situations. Generally speaking, most families cycle through a process of coping. When the crisis first occurs, the family becomes disorganized. They do not know what to do and each member may try something different. A period of dysfunctionality ensues. The crisis then ends and recovery begins. Recovery will depend upon the resources the family has at its disposal and the utilization of these resources. The family itself may change only superficially in order to meet the crisis (known as first-order change) or the family may change its rules and way of being (known as second-order change).

As a general rule, the Simpsons do not engage in much second-order change. They bounce from one crisis to the next without significant modification in family structure or dynamics. For example, when Lisa was so depressed that they sent her home from school, each family member reacted differently. Marge insisted that Lisa needed more attention while Homer responded with dismissal and misunderstanding: Marge: "I don't know ... Bart's such a handful, and Maggie needs attention, but all the while, our little Lisa's becoming a young woman." Homer: "Oh, so that's it, this is some kind of underwear thing." Bart reacts with jokes. Lisa tries to describe her feelings: "Every day at noon a bell rings and they herd us in here to feeding time. So we sit around like cattle, chewing our cud, dreading the inevitable." Bart jokes, "Food fight!" Dysfunctionality reigns as no one knows quite what to do to help her depression go away. However, Lisa is quite resourceful and uses her social and musical talent to forge a relationship with Bleeding Gums Murphy who helps alleviate her feelings of sadness. Consequently, the family did not have to change much to recover from the crisis. This is typical for the Simpsons. However, given that all of their crises are relatively minor (as is the case for most comedies), perhaps major change is not needed. Consequently, based on stressors and coping strategies, the Simpsons appear to be, more often than not, healthy.

A final way to consider the health of the Simpson family is to look at the ways in which they try to stay healthy. Families tend to stay healthy or even get healthier through participation in certain activities, usually in connection with other people. For example, things like family rituals, family dinners, family retreats, interactive cooperative activities, family councils and structured exercises all tend to increase family health.

More so than most families, the Simpsons engage in lots of connective activities. They have a major family ritual that occurs in each episode: they all race for the couch so they can watch TV. They eat meals together and go on family retreats, vacations and do other interactive activities, like farming and playing games. However, they do not usually have family councils or participate in structured exercises. Thus, the Simpsons spend a lot of time together and do fun things but could do more. Consequently, based on active attempts to stay healthy, the Simpsons seem surprisingly healthy.

## The Simpson Family as the Cultural Ideal

So, are the Simpsons the American Family? Can we look to them for information about our family values? The Simpsons do look like many American families (well, sort of—no one is quite that orange). They are a middle-class, Caucasian, heterosexual, two-parent household with the requisite number of kids (mixed gender) and the normal variety of pets. The Simpsons also act like many families. They have a not uncommon hierarchy and typical roles. Some of the Simpson family rules do tend to be a bit cruel. However, for the Simpsons and many other families as well, unkindness seems to be more the result of a lack of awareness of how to be in intimate relationships with others. How do you acknowledge someone's flaws while still loving them? How do you accept the good with the bad? How do you live day after day with people who drive you crazy? In the Simpson family, the solution to these dilemmas lies with humor and mild denigration. In this, they are certainly not alone.

However, despite the unkindness, the heart of the family beats with love, forgiveness and the desire to do what is best for the family. Each member is allowed to talk about what is going on with them and they do so in a mostly clear and effective manner. Many American families have good communication skills but this may not be the norm. We as a culture do not do a good job of dealing with difficult feelings or confronting controversial topics. While the Simpsons have a good foundation with their communication, the kids have not yet reached adolescence. It could all change then.

Marge and Homer's parenting skills, especially those linked with discipline, need work. This is probably true for most parents. As mentioned previously, family dynamics often are cloaked in mystery. Thus, few people have role models much beyond their own parents and grandparents. As such, the skills involved in parenting frequently are unlearned or minimally practiced. Unfortunately, violence toward children is not as rare as we'd like to believe. Again, much of this goes back to the decrease in positive role models and a lack of awareness of other disciplinary options. It also speaks to the overall cultural acceptance of violence, a fact that *The Simpsons* parodies quite effectively. Similarly, the Simpsons appear to find conflict resolution quite difficult. While they are able to eventually settle the argument or work through the hurt feelings, they need to practice more effective solutions. Given our cultural difficulty to resolve conflict on both a national and international scale, it is likely that many families lack the skills necessary to resolve conflict in positive ways. Finally, the Simpsons are quite social and possess many of the qualities, dynamics and activities of a healthy family.

Given all of this, it does indeed appear that the Family Simpson is the American Family. They mirror so many of our flaws and our virtues. Their likeness to our family situations and those we see around us probably goes a long way toward explaining their enduring popularity (the humor probably helps too). So, what are our family values? In short, it looks like we value connection. Let the politicians have fun with that!

Misty K. Hook, Ph.D., was an assistant professor at Texas Woman's University for five years, where she taught courses in family psychology, the psychology of women, social psychology and the psychology of mothering, as well as supervising counselors in training. She is now a licensed psychologist in clinical practice where she sees families who do not bear any resemblance to the Simpsons. She has, however, used *The Simpsons* to illustrate various therapeutic insights.

# For Better, or Worse?

## The Love of Homer and Marge

### Wind Goodfriend, Ph.D.

*"The course of true love never did run smooth."*
—SHAKESPEARE, *A Midsummer Night's Dream,* Act I, scene i

THE MEDIA SEEMS OBSESSED with following the lives of famous couples, watching and commenting as relationships run their course from flirting, through initial dating, perhaps marriage and eventually (most often) a horrific, and captivating, messy breakup. At some point in many relationships there will inevitably be a "tragic turn for the worse," in the language of *The E! True Hollywood Story.* However, most of the relationships that the media focus on seem somehow unrealistic: They are both movie stars, or one is a supermodel or one is just insanely rich. A refreshing change can be found in Homer and Marge Simpson.

Homer and Marge's relationship has many qualities that are common in "typical" American relationships. For example, the family consists of two opposite-sex parents, three children (the oldest being a boy, as preferred by most couples according to a Gallup Poll in 1997) and a variety of pets, consisting of mostly dogs and cats (admittedly, there have been some atypical pets, not found in most households, such as Princess the pony, Stampy the elephant and Pinchy the lobster). Marge is a homemaker and Homer maintains a middle-class job from which he gets little sense of purpose. They have annoying in-laws, go through financial hardships and often question each other's decisions and choices. Although the traditional idea of "family" in America is certainly changing rapidly in the modern world, it is easy to see how Homer and Marge exemplify what many traditionalists envision as an average couple today.

That said, how does psychological theory apply to the analysis of such a normative example of a romantic relationship? The answer comes from Interdependence Theory, one of the most popular and established methods for examining love within psychology.[1]

## Interdependence Theory

Interdependence Theory began with the book *The Social Psychology of Groups* (1959) with the premise that a couple is the smallest group that can be studied by psychologists. The main idea behind the theory was to set up a framework in which interactions between two couple members could be understood. At the base of this theory is the idea that when individuals interact with each other, they will affect and influence each other. Take an example: you and your partner go to the video store to rent something. You want to see a romantic comedy, whereas your partner wants to see something with karate and machine guns. Now, let's say your partner gives in and you rent the movie you wanted. Short term, you're happy, right? But your partner now sulks, and brings up this sacrifice the next day and you end up having dinner at Hooters to make the situation "even." In short, one partner's happiness depends on the other's. This example is brought to life in the episode "Catch 'Em If You Can," where we witness this exchange between Homer and Bart after Marge makes the family rent the movie *Love Story*:

> HOMER: Son, seeing sappy movies with a lady has certain payoffs.
> BART: Like what, they'll do something with you that *they* hate?
> HOMER: Exactly.

Interdependence Theory is complicated (and kind of boring in parts). Entire semesters of college courses are taken up trying to explain just the basics. However, one of the primary purposes of the theory, and the one most relevant to the point here, is the suggestion that we can pre-

[1] Interdependence Theory was originally theorized by John Thibault and Harold "Hal" Kelley in 1959.

dict whether a certain relationship will last over time, or if the couple will eventually break up. In order to make this important prediction, we need to know three vital things: the couple members' *satisfaction,* their *dependence* and their *investment level.* If we know a couple's satisfaction, dependence and investment level, we can diagnose the current state and future fate of any given relationship. The question is: based on these variables, what picture emerges when we focus our lens on the relationship of Homer and Marge Simpson?

## Homer and Marge: Satisfied?

The first of our three key variables is satisfaction. Nicely summarized by Rusbult and Arriaga (1997; 224): "Satisfaction level refers to the degree to which a relationship is experienced as gratifying." So, the question becomes, How does one *know* if he or she is satisfied? Do you simply think about it for a second, and then say "Yep!" to yourself? Not according to Interdependence Theory. The theory says you'll come to a conclusion after two steps. Step One: weigh the good stuff you get from the relationship against the bad stuff. Which weighs more? If you have more positive outcomes than negative, you're on the track to being satisfied. But the theory doesn't stop there. How do you know if your ratio of good to bad is good enough? Step Two: in order to know if you're really satisfied, you compare your own ratio to a "comparison level" (abbreviated CL). Your CL is an abstract standard that is a coming together of all the relationships to which you've been exposed—past partners, your parents' relationship, people you see on TV and in the movies, your friends' relationships, etc. For Homer and Marge, this might include Patty's lesbian relationships, Selma's failed marriages, Principal Skinner's struggle between Mrs. Krabappel and his mother, Apu and Manjula, etc.

So, according to Interdependence Theory, you think about all those relationships, then mentally combine them into what you see as a "typical" relationship, or what you expect from a relationship. For example, let's say that you think a typical relationship has twice as much good stuff (positive outcomes) as bad stuff (negative outcomes). Now, think back to your own relationship ratio—for example, let's say that in your current relationship, you have three times as much good stuff as bad stuff. According to the theory, your ratio is better than your CL, or comparison level—so, you're officially satisfied.

To understand the satisfaction level of Homer and Marge, then, step one is to figure out their good to bad ratio—how much good stuff is in their relationship, compared to bad stuff? Unfortunately, the first things that come to mind seem to be mostly bad. Let's start with Homer: he's fat, just plain stupid and highly accident prone (for example, he indirectly leads to the death of Maude Flanders in "Alone Again Natura-Diddily").

Sometimes, (actually often), Homer makes bad choices. In "The Fat and the Furriest," Homer decides to get revenge on a bear that attacks him. When his friends try to warn him that Marge will be upset when she learns that he snuck out at night to do this, Homer responds, "Gentlemen, sometimes a man must put his marriage at risk, for reasons that are confusing, even to him." Another example of Homer not exactly making good choices is when he photographs Marge while she's asleep, then publishes the photo in *Outlaw Biker* magazine as "This Month's Cycle Slut" ("Take My Wife, Sleaze").

Although he's the sole breadwinner in the family, Homer also seems dismally deficient at his job at the nuclear power plant. In "Missionary Impossible," Bart is filling in for Homer while he's away. Mr. Burns doesn't notice the difference, and tells him that his ten-year performance record is appalling: "In ten short years, you've caused seventeen meltdowns...one is too many! You sold weapons-grade plutonium to the Iraqis—with no markup! Worst of all, you took the Hamburgler's birthday off last Monday AND Wednesday—which is it?!?"

Although Homer certainly has plenty of faults, Marge isn't perfect either. For example, when Homer is kidnapped in "The Computer Wore Menace Shoes" for knowing too much about a secret conspiracy, the kidnappers send a fake Homer to take his place. Marge immediately knows something is up, but the fake Homer says, "Please forgive my unexplained absence. To make it up to you, we will go out to dinner at a sensibly priced restaurant, then have a night of efficient German sex." Instead of continuing to try to look for her missing husband, Marge's response is, "Well, I sure don't feel like cooking. . . ."

However, there is more to a relationship than the individuals—in fact, that's one of the keys to Interdependence Theory: both couple members interact to create the relationship environment. Again unfortunately, Homer and Marge don't seem to be very good at communicating before making important decisions. In "Diatribe of a Mad Housewife" the following exchange occurs:

MARGE: I was hoping you could watch the kids while I work on my novel.

HOMER: Slow down, Picasso! You were going to start a novel without informing me?

MARGE: Homer, you left two jobs and bought an ambulance without even a phone call!

HOMER: I also fed some ducklings.

MARGE: I know. I got your message.

HOMER: Fine. Fine. I'll take the kids tonight, and you go to your precious hair appointment.

MARGE: I'm writing a novel!

HOMER: Whatever. But I think you look great already.

What about the good parts of their relationship? Their intimate life seems relatively healthy. Several times we witness Homer and Marge making love, in situations that seem very representative of other couples. An example is seen in "Beyond Blunderdome," when they get free tickets to a movie screening:

MARGE: They're passes to a test screening of a new movie...starring Mel Gibson!

HOMER: Who else is in it?

MARGE: Who cares?? Mel Gibson!

HOMER: Mel Gibson is just a guy, Marge, no different than me or Lenny.

MARGE: Were you or Lenny ever named "Sexiest Man Alive"?

HOMER: Hmm, I'm not certain about Lenny...

MARGE: Besides, it's not just his chiseled good looks. *People Magazine* says he's a devoted father, goes to church every week, and likes to fix things around the...let's make love.

Of course, later in this same episode when Mel visits them, Homer gets jealous and tells him off: "Listen, Gibson. I'm tired of Hollywood pretty boys like you thinking you can have any woman you want. You see this? [shows Mel the wedding ring on Marge's finger] It symbolizes that she's my property, and I own her!" This response, while perhaps not the most progressive attitude, is certainly a strong display of Homer's love.

Homer does try to display how much he loves Marge, although it might not be in the most eloquent or romantic ways. For example, in "Alone Again Natura-Diddily," Homer and Marge are talking before attending Maude Flanders' funeral. Homer says to Marge, "Poor Ned didn't get a chance to say goodbye...well, from now on I'm never gonna let you leave the room without telling you how much I love you and how truly special...this is really eatin' up a lot of time. Maybe just a pat on the butt."

Although there are a lot of negatives about the relationship between Homer and Marge, there are certainly many positives as well. Based on the ratio of good to bad, they are well on their way to being satisfied. But remember: Step two of the Interdependence Theory definition of relationship satisfaction says that you never really know how you feel about your own relationship until you compare it to your CL (comparison level), which is formed by observing everyone else's relationship. Fortunately, the town of Springfield offers many other relationships for Homer and Marge to observe, which includes quite a range of couples.

One of the most direct comparisons that Homer and Marge make is between their marriage and that of the Van Houtens (Milhouse's parents). The catalyst for this comparison occurs when Marge and Homer decide to throw a dinner party for their couple friends (the Lovejoys, Hibberts and Van Houtens). Unfortunately the Van Houtens end up insulting each other and fighting so much that they decide to divorce. As Interdependence Theory suggests, Homer compares his own marriage to theirs, and decides to get a divorce himself! Of course, in the end we find that he only did this so that he could re-marry Marge and reaffirm their love by planning the elaborate wedding that she always wished for.

One Springfieldian couple that at first seems loving and strong is Apu and Manjula. Although an arranged marriage, Apu is known for being quite a romantic, and things between them seem great at first. In "Eight Misbehavin'" they decide to have children. Unfortunately, too many fertility drugs results in octuplets. When they can't handle it, they agree to let their babies go on display in a zoo (they later take the children back—everybody makes mistakes). But even a seemingly stable relationship like this has its problems. In fact, Homer catches Apu in the Kwik-E-Mart having an affair with the girl who delivers squishee syrup!

Marge's sister Patty comes out of the closet when Springfield legalizes gay marriage ("There's Something About Marrying"), and attempts to marry her girlfriend Veronica. Unfortunately, that doesn't work out when Veronica reveals that she's really a man, causing Patty to immediately break up with her/him. In addition, Marge's other sister Selma is a classic example of someone who can't sustain a relationship at all—she's been married four times!

Finally, in Springfield, even the most unlikely individuals have the chance to find love. In "Worst Episode Ever," Comic Book Guy finds his romantic counterpart in Agnes Skinner. Encountering this couple on the street, Homer and Marge are impressed that they have found each other:

MARGE: Look at you two! You look so couple-y!
COMIC BOOK GUY: Yes, well, we're a perfect match. Her sneer just lights up my day.
AGNES: And we're always finishing each other's insults!

Eventually, this relationship doesn't work out—their large age difference causes the breakup. When Comic Book Guy gets arrested for owning bootleg videos, he asks Agnes if she'll wait for him to get out of prison; her response ends the relationship with, "Are you crazy? My bones are half dust!"

Now remember, the idea from Interdependence Theory is that people who (a) have a decent good to bad ratio and (b) have a better relationship than others around them will be satisfied, and will therefore be more likely to stay in their relationship. Based on the above, we can probably safely say that Homer and Marge are satisfied. But Interdependence Theory doesn't stop there. Surely you can think of relationships where the people don't really seem satisfied, but they stay together anyway. The theory says we can explain those relationships with the second variable, dependence.

## Homer and Marge: Dependent?

Again, nicely summarized by Rusbult and Arriaga (1997; 225), "Dependence level refers to the degree to which an individual relies on a partner for the fulfillment of important needs (i.e., the individual 'needs' a relationship)." So, how do you know if you're dependent on your relationship? According to Interdependence Theory, you must make another comparison. You must think to yourself, *If I weren't in this particular relationship, could my needs be fulfilled elsewhere?* In other words, what are your alternatives? The theory says now you compare your current relationship to your "comparison level for alternatives" (abbreviated CL-alt). Your CL-alt is the *next best* alternative—including other people you could be dating, living with your sister (Patty and Selma), living with your mother (Principal Skinner) or simply being single. Would your next best option fulfill your needs? The theory says if the answer is "yes," then you are not really dependent on this relationship, and thus are likely to leave. If the answer is "no," then you are dependent, and will stay.

The key so far is that these two variables, satisfaction and dependence, are themselves interdependent. In other words, you really need to know *both* variables in order to predict whether a couple will stick together or break up. The members of the couple might honestly not be that satisfied. But if this is their best option (for example, let's say they are both ugly, which explains both the low satisfaction and low alternatives), they'll probably stick together; let's face it, this is the best they're going to get. Alternatively, maybe the couple is doing okay—they're both pretty satisfied. However, the reality is that if something even better comes along, the couple members might split up (for example, trading in someone like Abe Simpson for Monty Burns, as Marge's mother did in "Lady Bouvier's Lover"). So, the question is: Are Homer and Marge dependent? What are their alternatives?

Like many married couples, opportunities eventually arise for either Homer or Marge to have an affair, which is the most direct type of alternative. Surprisingly, other women have found Homer attractive over the years. In "The Last Temptation of Homer," he meets Mindy, a new coworker at the nuclear power plant. They have a lot in common, and even attend a conference together where they have adjoining hotel rooms. Although Homer is greatly tempted to have an affair with Mindy, he finally rejects her advances.

Later, in "Colonel Homer," Homer has the opportunity to have an affair with Lurleen Lumpkin, an up-and-coming country music singer. Even though Lurleen is obviously flirtatious toward Homer, in the end he sacrifices both the sexual opportunity and the money he could make as Lurleen's manager in order to stay loyal to Marge. It seems that in both of these situations, Homer decides that his needs are best met by his own wife.

Marge has also considered other relationships; most memorably, she almost has an affair with her bowling instructor, Jacques, after Homer gives her the infamous gift of a bowling ball with the word "Homer" engraved on it ("Life on the Fast Lane"). Although she is greatly attracted to Jacques and entertains fantasies of what their lives would be like together, Marge also ultimately rejects this potential alternative in favor of staying with Homer. Marge also repeatedly rejects the attentions of Moe, who has always been attracted to her. So far, it seems that both Homer and Marge are dependent on their marriage.

Of course, other relationships are not the only potential alternatives: Another alternative is always the option of being single. If one's needs could be met without any partner at all, then one is not dependent on the relationship, according to Interdependence Theory. We see what life would be like alone, at least temporarily, several times for Homer and Marge. Would either of them be happy without the other?

Homer, at least, does not seem at all eager to live the bachelor's life. In "Take My Wife, Sleaze," Homer has to search for Marge after a biker gang kidnaps her. Just in case he doesn't find her, he instructs Lisa to contact the Korea Love Brides agency, so that he won't have to be alone. This is probably a good call on Homer's part. In "Little Big Mom," Lisa attempts to take over running the household after Marge is injured in a skiing accident. Lisa witnesses what the Simpsons would be without Marge: Homer shows up to breakfast in just his underwear (without Marge there to remind him, he forgot to clothe himself), Homer and Bart try to weasel their way out of doing household chores, Homer buys a bunch of sweets instead of groceries and the list continues.

An important exception to Homer's hesitation to be single is seen in the episode "Three Gays of the Condo." Homer finds an old letter Marge wrote to him that was never delivered, in which she tells him that their dating relationship simply won't work out because they have nothing in common. He also finds a doctor's slip that he interprets as a sign that she only stayed with him because she found out she was pregnant. Hurt, Homer asks her, "So you mean our whole marriage, you've just been resenting me behind my back?" Marge's answer is honest: "A little bit, yeah." Homer is so crushed that he spends time living with two gay roommates. Although Homer has displayed his fair share of homophobia in the past, he seems to flourish in a metrosexual lifestyle and is quite hesitant to return to Marge and the family. Marge doesn't want to apologize; she explains to Lisa, "Lisa, marriage is a beautiful thing. But it's also a constant battle for moral superiority. So I can't apologize."

But the reality is that Homer simply can't live long without Marge. Although he's well dressed and has the softest skin in his life, he's depressed. He tells his roommate, "But it's Marge—my first and only love. I'm like David Spade without Chris Farley: alone and useless." When Dr. Hibbert tells him that Marge decided to stay with him *before* finding out that she was pregnant, Marge and Homer reconcile. Throughout their entire marriage, they fight and have to spend time alone, but they are always drawn back together. Remember, Interdependence Theory says that for two people to be truly dependent on each other, their needs can't be met in any other relationship or situation. We see the true interdependence of Homer and Marge in the episode, "Secrets to a Successful Marriage." After another fight, when Marge has kicked Homer out of house, he appeals to her to let him come back, and begs her in a way that would make John Thibaut and Hal Kelley (the creators of the theory) cry:

> HOMER: Wait a minute...wait, that's it! I know now what I can offer you that no one else can: complete and utter dependence!
> MARGE: Homer, that's not a good thing.
> HOMER: Are you kidding? It's a wondrous, marvelous thing! Marge, I need you more than anyone else on this entire planet could possibly ever need you! I need you to take care of me, to put up with me, and most of all I need you to love me, 'cause I love you.
> MARGE: But how do I know I can trust you?
> HOMER: Marge, look at me: we've been separated for a day, and I'm as dirty as a Frenchman. In another few hours I'll be dead! I can't afford to lose your trust again.

On the other hand, Marge might be a bit better off by herself. Although Homer is certainly the sole breadwinner in the family, Marge has worked various jobs throughout the marriage, and she could probably work full time if necessary. She also has more experience looking after the kids. Yet it is obvious that she depends on Homer to complete the family structure. An example of how things might change without him happens in "Missionary Impossible," when Homer is separated from the family when he's required to complete missionary work. Communicating over the radio, Bart tells Homer that he's not happy. Homer responds, "Mmm...I can see the house is falling apart without me. So, here's the new order: Bart, you're the man of the house. Lisa, I'm promoting you to boy. Maggie's now the brainy girl. The toaster can fill in for Maggie. And Marge, you're a consultant."

Homer sums up the alternatives situation quite nicely himself in "Large Marge," when he reassures Marge that she's the only woman for him: "Why would I want Purina when I've got Fancy Feast right here?"

To summarize so far, Homer and Marge seem satisfied (relatively speaking), and it seems that they are dependent—their needs could not be fulfilled in a different relationship or by being single. The first two variables of Interdependence Theory have been fulfilled; so far we would predict a long future ahead for Homer and Marge.

## Homer and Marge: Invested?

So now you think you've got it: within Interdependence Theory, predictions about relationships are based on satisfaction and dependence. In the 1980s, researcher Caryl Rusbult wanted to explain why some couples are both dissatisfied *and* have reasonable alternatives, but stay together anyway. Picture a couple, Frank and Ruth, who have been married forty years. They fight all the time, never have sex anymore, maintain pretty much separate lives and honestly could probably find someone else to date in their Mah Jong club. Why don't they just get a divorce and get it over with? We can explain these couples with a third and final variable: investments.

The Investment Model (Rusbult, 1980; 172–186) says that we also need to factor in investments, which are the time, effort, money, sacrifices and so on that each couple member has "sunk" into the relationship. In other words, Frank and Ruth have really tied themselves into this relationship. They've had kids together, spent the "best years of their lives" together, own a bunch of stuff together, all their friends are mutual friends—if they broke up now, their lives would be a huge mess. So, they stay together to avoid the loss of these investments, or to avoid wasting all that time and energy.

Investments have proved to be a robust predictor of relationship longevity (Le & Agnew, 2003), and more recent research has found that it even matters what *kind* of investments have gone into the relationship (Goodfriend & Agnew, 2001; 2004). In brief, things like sacrifices and effort or "intangible" investments predict that a couple will stay together better than things like a joint bank account or mutually owned home (tangible investments). Like satisfaction and dependence, the more a couple has invested into a relationship, the more likely they are to stay together.

Even though they may both be satisfied and dependent, investments are certainly a major reason why Homer and Marge are still married—in fact, it's one of the major reasons they got married in the first place! For many couples all over the world, this is the reason to stay together. Perhaps Homer himself best explains the investment of children in "How I Spent My Strummer Vacation" when he tells Bart and Lisa, "Marriage is like a coffin, and each kid is another nail."

In addition to children, one of the most essential investments a member of a couple can make is effort spent on making the relationship work. There are many times when we see both Homer and Marge working toward pleasing each other, or smoothing out the many rough parts of their lives together. In fact, this effort is the point of the marital advice that Marge gives to Becky before she marries Otto (the bus driver) in "It's a Mad, Mad, Mad, Mad Marge." Becky confides to Marge that she's worried about the marriage:

> BECKY: We'll be fine...Otto's got a clean police record, and he doesn't do any needle drugs.
>
> MARGE: Well, the real key, according to "Sexperts," is mutual interest.
>
> BECKY: No prob—we like all the same things...except...don't tell Otto, but I'm not into heavy metal, and he loves it.
>
> MARGE: Oh, you can fix little defects like that with gentle nagging. Make it part of the background noise of your relationship.

Remember, one of the keys to investments, according to the theory, is that they keep you tied to the relationship. We see this concept exemplified in the same episode with Becky and Otto. Right after Otto leaves her at the altar, we see the importance of the investment of time in a relationship. Put simply, it's better to find out that a relationship isn't going to work as early as possible, so that you don't waste the investment of time; the longer you're in a relationship, the more likely you are to stay (even if satisfaction and dependence are low). Homer explains this to Becky when he says, "It's better [to break up] now than when you're too old and fat to get another man."

One investment that all long-term couples must have is working through disagreements. Homer and Marge have certainly done their fair share of this; the theoretical idea is that each time you get over a fight you'll be more committed, as a result of the effort it took to smooth things over. One of the biggest fights between our couple occurs in "Mobile Homer." Marge is upset that Homer spent the family money on an RV and is living in the backyard:

> MARGE: You don't belong on the lawn—you belong in your bed, with your wife.
>
> HOMER: That's no marriage bed. It's a loveless slab of bossiness!
>
> MARGE: Well, you're not perfect, either!
>
> HOMER: Name one way I'm not.
>
> MARGE: You hide food in my hair, you think brushing your teeth is foreplay...

BART: Boy, they're really going at it. Do you think they're going to get divorced?

LISA: No...I don't see Dad doing all that paperwork.

HOMER: I seem to recall you *asked* me to get this fat!!

If a couple stays together long-term they will eventually come to a kind of equilibrium, where the fine balance between trying to fix each other and coming to terms with the fact that people never really change is reached. Homer and Marge have found this peace of mind; in "A Star is Born Again," Homer explains this to Ned: "I used to worry Marge was too good for me. She was always thinking of ways to improve me. But then, part of her died. And she doesn't try anymore. So we're all where we want to be!"

Finally, one of the most important investments that couple members can make is sacrifices—giving up something that would suit their individual, selfish needs for the good of the relationship. One example of Homer making a sacrifice can be seen in "'Tis the Fifteenth Season." At the beginning of the episode, Homer spends all the family Christmas money on a stupid gadget for himself. Eventually he feels guilty and makes a real effort to learn to be unselfish, both to his family (he lets Marge have the last pork chop) and to the entire town. Homer says, "Being unselfish is a natural high—like hiking, or paint thinner!"

Another example of Homer making a sacrifice comes in "The Fat and the Furriest"; Homer must decide to live with either Marge or an eighty-five-pound ball of candy. After debating, Homer chooses Marge (quite a sacrifice for him). Of course Marge makes sacrifices, too. An example is when Homer loses his driver's license in "Brake My Wife, Please." Marge tells him, "I guess I'll have to do all your driving chores. That's what a good wife does—picks up the slack."

In sum, both Homer and Marge are extremely invested in this relationship—if they were to divorce, they would lose everything and their lives would be a complete shambles. This high level of investment is, most definitely, a third reason for them to stay together. In fact, Homer and Marge were destined to be a couple—even though they didn't realize it until years later, they were even each other's first kiss as children at summer camp ("The Way We Weren't"). It's pretty rare for childhood sweethearts to marry, have three kids, and still be in love years later.

The following questions refer to your relationship with your current romantic partner. Please answer every question using the scale below, by writing in the appropriate number. Read each statement *carefully* before giving your response. The higher your total score, the higher your amount of each relationship variable.

```
0    1    2    3    4    5    6    7    8
|____|____|    |____|____|    |____|____|
Do Not Agree   Agree Somewhat      Agree
   at All                       Completely
```

**Satisfaction Questions:**

1. _____ I feel satisfied with our relationship.
2. _____ My relationship is much better than others' relationships.
3. _____ My relationship is close to ideal.
4. _____ Our relationship makes me very happy.
5. _____ Our relationship does a good job of fulfilling my needs for intimacy, companionship, etc.

**Dependence Questions:**

1. _____ The people other than my partner with whom I might become involved are very appealing.
2. _____ My alternatives to our relationship are close to ideal (dating another, spending time with friends, etc.).
3. _____ If I weren't dating my partner, I would do fine—I would find another appealing person to date.
4. _____ My alternatives are attractive to me (dating another, spending time with friends, etc.).
5. _____ My needs for intimacy, companionship, etc. could easily be fulfilled in an alternative relationship.

**Investments Questions:**

1. _____ I have put a great deal into our relationship that I would lose if the relationship were to end.
2. _____ Many aspects of my life have become linked to my partner (recreational activities, etc.), and I would lose all of this if we were to break up.
3. _____ I feel very involved in our relationship—like I have put a great deal into it.
4. _____ My relationships with friends and family members would be complicated if my partner and I were to break up.
5. _____ Compared to other people I know, I have invested a great deal in my relationship with my partner.

Overall Commitment Questions:

1. _____ I want our relationship to last a very long time.
2. _____ I am committed to maintaining my relationship with my partner.
3. _____ I would feel very upset if our relationship were to end in the near future.
4. _____ It is not likely that I will date someone other than my partner within the next year.
5. _____ I feel very attached to our relationship—very strongly linked to my partner.
6. _____ I want our relationship to last forever.
7. _____ I am oriented toward the long-term future of my relationship (for example, I imagine being with my partner several years from now).

## Homer and Marge: For Better, or Worse?

Combined with more recent research, Interdependence Theory is a highly useful and popular method used by psychologists today as a method of assessing the current state and future fate of any given romantic relationship. From this theoretical perspective, it seems that despite all the signs, Homer and Marge really are happy and will probably be married forever. The good seems to outweigh the bad, at least compared to other Springfield couples (which leads to satisfaction), their alternatives really aren't that great (which leads to dependence) and they have spent a Herculean amount of effort, time and sacrifices on maintaining the relationship against all odds (which leads to high investments).

We know what Interdependence Theory says about the love between Homer and Marge. What do they say for themselves? Each couple member has advice to give. Marge offers her view of love to Lisa in "Dude, Where's My Ranch?" when she explains: "Lisa, welcome to love. It's full of doubt, and pain and uncertainty. But then one day, you find a man you love so much it hurts." In turn, Homer offers marital advice to drinking buddies and coworkers Carl and Lenny (in "The Frying Game") with the following three keys to a happy married life: "Make every day a celebration of your love. Surprise her with a pasta salad. Put a mini-beret on your wang."

What does all this mean for the rest of us? It means that no relationship is perfect—we all have to say "D'oh!" every so often. The important thing is to forgive, forget, become truly interdependent and love in spite of everything.

# References

Gallup News Service. "Family values differ sharply around the world." *Gallup News Service*. 7 Nov. 1997. <http://web.lexis-nexis.com>.

Goodfriend, W., and Agnew, C. R. *Clarifying and expanding the investment construct*. Poster presented at the annual meeting for the Society for Personality and Social Psychology (SPSP), San Antonio, TX, Feb. 2001.

Goodfriend, W., and Agnew, C. R. *A factor analytic investigation of the investment construct in romantic relationships*. Poster presented at the Conference on Personal Relationships, Madison, WI, July 2004.

Le, B., and Agnew, C. R. "Commitment and its theorized determinants: A meta-analysis of the investment model." *Personal Relationships, 10*, 2003: 37–57.

Rusbult, C. E. "Commitment and satisfaction in romantic associations: A test of the investment model." *Journal of Experimental and Social Psychology, 16*, 1980: 172–186.

Rusbult, C. E., and Arriaga, X. B. "Interdependence Theory." In S. Duck (Ed.), *Handbook of Personal Relationships: Theory, Research, and Interventions*. Second Edition. Chichester, England UK: John Wiley & Sons, Inc., 1997.

Thibaut, J. W., and Kelley, H. H. *The Social Psychology of Groups*. New York: Wiley, 1959.

# Reference for scale:

Rusbult, C. E., Martz, J. M., & Agnew, C. R. (1998). "The investment model scale: Measuring commitment level, satisfaction level, quality of alternatives, and investment size." *Personal Relationships, 5*, 357–391.

Wind Goodfriend, Ph.D., is an assistant professor of psychology at Boise State University. She earned her Ph.D. in social psychology in 2004 from Purdue University in Indiana. Her areas of research expertise are gender stereotypes and romantic relationships, focusing specifically on positive and negative predictors of relationship stability over time. In her final year of graduate school, Dr. Goodfriend received both the "Outstanding Teacher of the Year Award" and the "Outstanding Graduate Student of the Year Award" for her research.

# "Which One of Us Is Truly Crazy?"

## Pop Psychology and the Discourse of Sanity and Normativity in *The Simpsons*

### Molly Snodgrass, M.A., and Irene Vlachos-Weber

MORE SO THAN ANY recent situation comedy, *The Simpsons* is highly engaged with the discourse of psychology and popular psychology. Whether it is Lisa, who often voices Freudian insights when confronted by absurdity (usually in the form of something that Homer has done), or through direct parodies of the discipline in the figures of Dr. Marvin Monroe or Dr. Zweig, the writers of *The Simpsons* understand the reach of psychology in the popular imagination. It is a show which depends on the familiarity of the American public with various psychological concepts, ranging from the psychoanalytic (e.g., the Oedipal Complex, the Electra Complex, Rorschach therapy, the Id, Ego and Superego), to the diagnostic (e.g., the Rorschach or Ink-blot Test and diagnoses such as ADD and a specific phobia), to the therapeutic (e.g., shock therapy and free association) to the various personality tests that often make appearances in episodes. In its sixteen seasons, *The Simpsons* has found success in part because its premise that its audience is psychologically literate has proven to be true.

And yet, the relationship between psychology and the show's subject matter is often ambivalent. Much of the subtext of the plots that revolve around the psychological deals with the legitimacy of various precepts and the effectiveness or even the value of treatment. In the episode "Marge's Fear of Flying," Homer advises Marge to repress her fears so as not to "bother anyone," whereas Lisa argues for the value of finding the root of her phobia through analysis. This commentary serves as a microcosm of the running debate found in the series: What is the validity of psychology and, as in this example, therapy? Does it help or harm the individual? For while *The Simpsons* often takes the psychology industry to task (including "crack-pot" psychoanalysis and the self-help trends of pop psychology), it often finds itself allied with the main tenet of pop psychology—that an individual is capable of recognizing and understanding the self in better, more effective and fulfilling ways.

Along these lines, *The Simpsons* has worked to expose the enormous role that socialization plays in the process of creating norms and often questions the motives and modes of defining what is "sane" versus what is "insane." The show often critiques pop psychology's sometimes gross oversimplifications and its participation in institutionalizing conformity, which often puts the tenets or stated goals of psychology at odds with the well-being of the individual. In short, *The Simpsons* seeks not simply to deconstruct these tenets and goals, but to engender a conversation that reveals the complexities, contradictions and relevance of pop psychology by seeing it in action (or inaction) in the lives of the most familiar fictional American family.

At first the Simpsons seem to be the archetypal dysfunctional family: a father with a drinking problem, a mother with a gambling addiction and a series of phobias, an angst-filled daughter and a hellion of a son with ADD and oppositional-defiant disorder combine in hilarious but troubled ways. But upon closer examination, the Simpsons are actually quite functional. The family has endured sixteen seasons of marital problems, money problems, personal problems and literally hundreds of misadventures. It is because of their problematic lives that the show has resonated with its millions of viewers. The show brazenly throws the concept of "normality" into serious doubt; anything that can be considered "normal" is examined with great skepticism as *The Simpsons* explores the establishment and maintenance of social order. Again and again, the sitcom questions the role of pop psychology and clinical therapy in the maintenance of a healthy family and a healthy self. Oftentimes we find a shared sensibility between some of the basic aims of counseling and the show's precepts about the importance of communication and self-awareness. Above all, the family manages to find channels of communication that are central to its survival.

In "There's No Disgrace Like Home," the third episode of the first season of *The Simpsons*, the family seeks therapy after Homer decides that his is not a "happy" or "healthy" family. Embarrassed by his family at the family picnic staged at the Burns Estate, Homer decides that his family is dysfunctional: His children are ill-behaved; Marge gets drunk; and most embarrassing, Mr. Burns sees through Homer's brazenly insincere attempt to curry favor with his boss when he sees Homer paying Bart to show him affection. Homer investigates the practice of "healthy" families by taking his family on a voyeuristic trip through their neighborhood where they peep through windows only to find that their family fares poorly in comparison. His solution turns up in the form of an advertisement for Dr. Marvin Monroe's Family Therapy, in which the doctor guarantees healthy functioning or "double your money back." After pawning the family television in order to afford the treatment, the family engages in several hilarious techniques, all of which fail, as an increasingly frustrated Dr. Monroe continues to ratchet up the level of "interaction." At first the family is asked to draw the source of their problems. Predictably, the image of Homer appears in each of their drawings. When Monroe asks them to take out their mutual aggression using foam-covered bats, the family finds that their anger and frustration is not sufficiently expressed with such flimsy accoutrements. In desperation, Dr. Monroe offers his most radical technique: mutual electric shock.

Strapped into individual chairs, electric wires taped to foreheads and arms, paradoxically, the Simpsons are promised that they will create mutual aversions to the insensitivity they have shown toward each other through the use of electric shock. As is typical with the Simpson family, the treatment turns into a fiasco, as the family immediately engages in pre-emptive shocking. Ostensibly, the family therapy is a huge failure, but upon closer inspection we find quite a different result. In the end, due to the "double your money back guarantee," they are able to buy a new, better TV and the family is happy again. The TV that brings the family back together in one loving "group hug" moment may be criticized as being an empty, even idiotic, solution. It is a comic solution, suggesting that the numbing distraction of television is central to the family's ability to tolerate itself.

But on second look, the solution revolves not around television or any "professional" cure, but upon the practice of a technique common to all forms of psychotherapy: open and clear communication. The closing scene is behavioral therapy at its best: the family is reinforced and rewarded for working together. There is but one TV in the Simpson household and more often than not the family engages in useful and oftentimes insightful conversation as they watch television. Rather than being a simple diversion, television provides the stimulus for healthy exchanges, becoming, in a sense, a kind of therapy (or therapist) itself. What this episode demonstrates is that the idea of "normalcy" is often an impossible standard; that intense self-reflection is at once necessary and ugly, useful and self-defeating; that coping mechanisms are legitimate and useful; that the best therapy is often already at hand and not necessarily dispensed by a "professional." And while Dr. Monroe's one-approach-fits-all fails miserably and exposes him as a quack, the episode endorses several precepts that encourage healthful communication and honesty in the maintenance of the family.

Perhaps one of the areas in which *The Simpsons* finds itself in direct alliance with the tenets of pop psychology is in its assertion that everyone has problems and that the individual can rise above those problems. For if everyone is crazy or neurotic (and in Springfield everyone is) then at least there's no shame in it. Perhaps, even, being "crazy" or "neurotic" is really what is normative after all. A roll call of the various psychopathologies displayed or diagnosed among the characters of *The Simpsons* reads like a checklist of the most common Axis I and II disorders listed in the DSM-IV. Just about every major character on the show could meet the criteria for some psychopathology or psychological anomaly. Bart is diagnosed with and prescribed medication for attention deficit disorder (ADD). He also qualifies as oppositional-defiant and perhaps a myriad of other behavioral disorders. In one episode, he begins taking Focusyn, a "radical, untested, potentially dangerous new drug," to treat his ADD, which results in extreme paranoia and psychotic thoughts and behavior. Homer has addictions to both alcohol and food. These, in fact, make up the essence of his character. Lisa shows signs of obsessive-compulsive personality disorder in her zealous commitment to schoolwork, social crusades and the Corey Hotline. She also suffers from a neurotic fear of failure and develops an eating disorder in season fifteen, which develops after shopping for clothes in the mall (where a wafer-thin young model is working the runway, and Lisa overhears one girl say, "I hear she's down to her birth weight!" As the girl turns on the catwalk, she becomes so thin, her silhouette disappears). Marge suffers from various incapacitating phobias including aviophobia (the fear of flying) and agoraphobia. In various episodes she develops a taste for alcohol when the family moves to the perfect corporate community for Homer's new job and overcomes a gambling addiction when Springfield introduces a casino to raise money for the schools. She also averts mental crises through at least two trips to Rancho Relaxo: once after she suffers a nervous breakdown at the hands of her taxing family, and again in a later episode after the onset of delusional paranoia when she comes to believe Otto's ex-fiancée, Becky, is trying to kill her.

Lisa, Homer and Marge all go through bouts of depression at different points, and Homer even contemplates suicide in "Hello Gutter, Hello Fadder." Even the reliably cheerful Ned Flanders is institutionalized in one episode for an uncontrollable, if unexpected, rage. Principal Skinner's unhealthy attachment to his mother makes him a textbook case of dependent personality disorder, while the evil Mr. Burns is both narcissistic and antisocial. And speaking of antisocial personalities, we mustn't leave out Springfield's favorite sociopath: Sideshow Bob, a murderous but elegantly rational character voiced by Kelsey Grammer (not coincidentally, instantly recognizable as Dr. Frasier Crane, pop psychologist extraordinaire).

And yet, the ubiquity of mental and personality disorders renders neither psychological categorizations nor treatments meaningless in the world of The Simpsons. Characters and their problems are most often taken seriously. The brilliance of the show inheres in its insistence that while categorization and diagnosis are relevant, mental health issues are complex. The Simpsons insists that while categorization may be helpful and even necessary, the act of diagnosis is often incomplete and always a matter of nuance and complexity. The Simpsons is willing to explore—in all its absurd glory—the precepts of psychology that are often rendered simplistically or one-dimensionally when represented by pop psychology.

None of Springfield's characters fit neatly into a single diagnostic category. The show insists that each character is more than a cluster of symptoms, more than just a one-dimensional character. They are more than the sum of their diagnoses: their personalities transcend the categories into which a therapist would assign them. While the real world may be sharpening the distinctions between "crazy" and "sane" or "good" and "evil," The Simpsons revels in the ambiguities and ambivalence kept alive in Springfield. We find ourselves empathizing or even identifying with the most unlikable characters. Even the impulses of two of Springfield's most unattractive characters, the greedy Mr. Burns and the murderous Sideshow Bob, are given their due in past episodes. The portrayals are so nuanced that there is a sympathetic element to Homer's nemesis, Monty Burns, when as a child he loses his beloved "Bobo." The writers ask the audience for a measure of empathy, for who at one time hasn't wanted to "set loose the hounds" on an irritating solicitor or, as is often the case with Sideshow Bob, destroy what one sees as the root of all evil in a town? What *The Simpsons* does effectively is to insist on the complexity of each character. In particular it explores what exactly is meant by "sanity" and "insanity" in the bizarre but surprisingly familiar land of the three-eyed fish; Krusty, the beloved maniacal, unfunny clown; and the overtly promiscuous mayor. Most provocatively, *The Simpsons* asks, "Who defines what is normal?" and "How is 'normal' defined in our own society?"

Self-reflection is one aspect of pop psychology that appears in each episode of *The Simpsons*. Each of the characters at one time or another undergoes bouts of intense self-reflection that lead them forward, toward a solution to the problem of the day. The characters in *The Simpsons* engage in an inordinate amount of intense self-reflection; even the oft-clueless Homer has examined his role as a father, a worker, a man and a friend in such classic episodes as "Hello Gutter, Hello Fadder." But while *The Simpsons* finds itself in agreement with some aspects of the mission of psychology, the show expresses no qualms about exposing and exploiting the more suspect aspects and uses (and abuses) of the discipline. *The Simpsons*, unlike many situation comedies, plays with the sitcom convention of serving up a ready-made solution that will remedy life's overwhelming problems in thirty minutes or less. And while the show often sardonically posits such quick solutions, it manages to mock, question and undermine those very conventions. By mocking the sitcom convention of the quick fix, it also mocks the pop psychology trend of treating serious personal issues on the air or through the popular press. The quick diagnosis and cure offered by Dr. Phil or Dr. Laura is often parodied as having the precision and sensitivity of a dull hatchet. From a clinical perspective, many of the psychological issues tackled by the characters in the show might in reality take years of treatment to sort out (or at least require efficacy-based treatment with proven outcomes). But in Springfield, even when issues like Marge's fear of flying surface, wreak havoc on daily life and are remedied in the course of a single episode, the message is that mental and emotional problems need to be confronted and understood.

In Springfield, the psyche of the individual is always a complex issue. The cookie cutter analysis, the Dr. Phil/Dr. Laura speed diagnosis and lowest common denominator advice is present and is practiced, but does not work. In the sixteen seasons of *The Simpsons*, viewers have learned that every character has a complex and nuanced story. It will not do to simply label the characters "sane" or "insane"; there are equal parts sanity and insanity in each of these characters.

While the pop psychology approach is parodied in episodes in which the quack Dr. Monroe appears, there are also episodes in which the psychologist is a conduit to better self-awareness, and treatment is seen as useful and even necessary. Dr. Zweig (voiced by Anne Bancroft) in the episode "Marge's Fear of Flying" is portrayed as competent and understanding. While the revelation that Marge's aviophobia has its source in her childhood discovery that her father was not a pilot but an airline "stewardess," is comical, Dr. Zweig's assistance in delving into the source of her irrational fear is seen as useful self-revelation.

If the answer to the running debate between Lisa and Homer in "Marge's Fear of Flying" is that psychological counseling is a useful undertaking in the cause of self-knowledge and self-recognition, the episode, like many others, also posits that the absurd, rather than being simply denied or repressed, must be examined and understood. While Homer fears that Marge's therapy will lead to her realization that he is the source of her problems (Homer fears that therapy "turns wives against husbands, children against parents, neighbors against me."), Marge learns that the solution is to confront rather than to avoid. Lisa's argument that problems should be confronted directly is ultimately reinforced by Marge's progress. In this sense, psychological treatment is endorsed in *The Simpsons* when it serves the individual in finding ways to deal with the absurd, the painful, the maddening. *The Simpsons* suggests that an appropriate role of psychology, whether in its pop form or in its clinical incarnation, is to provide a useful conduit for the individual to engage root problems, to ferret out causes and most of all, to understand the self.

*The Simpsons*, like psychology, affirms the need to communicate and emphasizes the central role of context and complexity in the making and understanding of the self. In essence, *The Simpsons* endorses the psychological mission when it sees psychology serving to disrupt and question the definition of normalcy. It is when the show sees the role of psychology in collaborating with the various institutions of power to create conformity and to deny or regulate individuality that it offers its most withering critique of the discourse of psychology.

In one such episode, "Stark Raving Dad," Homer is deemed "insane" and is institutionalized. Homer is first singled out when he is caught by Mr. Burns' surveillance cameras wearing a pink shirt. This immediately results in an investigation which includes a "full body cavity search," and in Homer being subjected to Dr. Monroe's comically brief and specious personality test: amongst other things, the questions query whether Homer wets his pants or hears voices. After Homer has Bart fill out the form, the doctors determine that Homer is mentally ill and cart him off to the psychiatric ward. When inquiring how the staff "knows" who is sane and who is insane, Homer is given his answer in the form of a rubber stamp which prints the word "Insane" on his hand in red ink.

In the words of Michael Jackson/Leon Kompowsky in "Stark Raving Dad" The Simpsons asks, "To make a tired point, which one of us is truly crazy?" When faced with the powers of Mr. Burns and the corporatist mentality that he represents, with the dictates of mores and practices and definitions of "normalcy" as prescribed by the media or by one's social circles, how does one come to understand the forces allied against seeing oneself as a functioning individual? If one argues that The Simpsons is fundamentally concerned with critiquing the practice and definition of "order," then The Simpsons argues that norms and conventions, ideologies and practices are most often defined by the powerful, the elite. The individual is most often at odds with the institution because the institution wishes to grind individuals down, to have them comport themselves in a manner most useful to the efficient operation of the organization. This is often at odds with what is best for the individual. Hence, The Simpsons, rather than ignoring or disposing of the abnormal, tends to embrace the absurd and the oddity as a useful disruption to the workings of a crushing order.

The narrative coherence of a Simpsons' episode is often disturbed through surreal or unusual occurrences. Examples from various episodes include talking monkeys, extraterrestrial observers who kidnap the family and doppelgangers who tread in and out of the screen. While such narrative disruptions seem to serve as puzzling non sequitors, they serve a far more philosophical role. Such absurdities serve to confound expectation, disrupt conventional narrative frameworks, and seek ultimately to endorse the role of nonconformity and quirkiness as a way of dealing with the forces allied against the individual's ability to know and understand him/herself uniquely.

Homer's place of employment, the Springfield Nuclear Power Plant, is ruled with an iron fist by the malicious Mr. Burns, a man who depends upon surveillance and fear to keep his employees in line. Mr. Burns wants to snuff out any individualistic self-expression (Homer's pink shirt marks him as a "free-thinking anarchist"). His plant's smooth operation rests on keeping an eye out for "troublemakers." Singled out by the watchful Burns, Homer is seen as a potential threat. That Dr. Monroe, and later the psychologists at the mental institution, collaborate with Mr. Burns is a most disturbing partnership for *The Simpsons*. In corporate America, the CEO must maintain order and that begins with ferreting out the potential rabble-rouser. One of Dr. Monroe's main tasks in "Stark Raving Dad" seems to be to assist Mr. Burns in keeping the individual faceless, bland, un-opinionated and in essence, the perfectly conformed worker. The standardized test given to Homer, while absurd in its transparently facile and insipid questions, has the intended effect of keeping the individual in fear of being different (understanding the risks of being perceived as a nonconformist, Homer tells Marge that he "is not popular enough to be different").

The writers behind the show are well aware that wild conspiracy theories and paranoid fantasies often have roots in the real world. This is comically rendered in episodes like "Brother's Little Helper," where Bart's prescription to Focusyn has him believing that his every move is being monitored by satellites operated by Major League Baseball. Leading him to drive a tank through town with the barrel of the gun pointed skyward, his paranoid fantasy winds up being true (Mark McGuire stealthily stashes the market research information being spit out by the satellite Bart has shot out of the sky). In "It's a Mad, Mad, Mad, Mad Marge," extreme, even psychotic, paranoia proves to be warranted when Marge discovers that Becky, Otto's ex-fiancée, really is out to kill her in order to assume Marge's role in the Simpson family.

Thus, the absurd, the abnormal and even the insane must not only be confronted but understood. *The Simpsons* suggests that they serve useful purposes in confronting power and its dictates. Dr. Marvin Monroe, unlike Dr. Zweig, might be understood as a parody of the Dr. Lauras and Dr. Phils of the world, of a pop psychology which seeks not to create deeper and more complex understanding of the self, but instead serves the interests of the powers that be; snake oil salesmen who offer one simple prescription for all life's problems, who seek to facilitate a mindless conformity, an acceptance of the status quo, and seek to end useful skepticism and disruptive questioning. Just attend this seminar. Just read this book. Just follow this advice. Such pat answers treat individuals and families as if there were one cure for all the ills of the world.

Dr. Monroe and his colleagues have inverted Tolstoy's notion that "every happy family is the same, every unhappy family is unique." At the root of this problem is the inherent understanding that some families are "happy" and others are "unhappy" and those that are happy all look and act alike and those that are unhappy are all making the same mistakes. But *The Simpsons* is never more critical of psychology than when it critiques the use of psychology to institutionalize normality.

Here psychological intervention is seen not as a benefit to the individual's sense of self or his/her role in the community, but in the service of the institution of power. Dr. Monroe, in "Stark Raving Dad," serves to assist Mr. Burns to ferret out the "problem" worker so that the institution can function even more ruthlessly. Here the hand stamps of "Sane" and "Insane" are applied arbitrarily and unscrupulously. While the distinction between who is "sane" and "insane" is ostensibly black and white in these scenes, *The Simpsons* is nothing if not a skeptical critique of pop psychology's gross oversimplification of the complex inner workings of the human mind. What might be lost in the comic situation of Homer landing in an insane asylum only to bring home an imposter of the King of Pop, is the relation between norms, conformity and, most damning, the cozy relationship between the psychologists and Mr. Burns.

The deep engagement of *The Simpsons* with psychology revolves around asking questions about who controls the definitions of sanity and insanity; how these categories are policed; how psychology has moved toward a partnership with government, corporate and military power instead of being used to "free" the individual. And yet, finally, *The Simpsons* leaves room for the possibility that while pop psychology, like the King of Pop Michael Jackson, might sometimes be artificial and facile, it can serve a useful purpose. At the end of "Stark Raving Dad," prompted and guided by the faux Jackson, Bart is able to reach out to his sister Lisa by expressing his "true feelings" for her in song. But lest we forget the potential misuses of the discourse of sanity and insanity in which some practitioners of psychology participate, we are left with the image of Homer trying desperately, but with no success, to erase the red stamp from his hand that labels him as "insane."

The irony here is that this observation is being made in a pop psychology text. Just as *The Simpsons* never fails to parody its own sitcom foibles, a collection of pop psychology essays on *The Simpsons* would be incomplete without an exploration of what the show itself is saying about popular psychology. The same debates occurring in *The Simpsons* are taking place in the discipline of psychology—difficulty of defining diagnoses, quantifying a qualitative condition, a questioning of the use of psychology in the management of various social and political and economic institutions. *The Simpsons* might not merely be both critiquing and bolstering the tenets of psychology, but rather also mimicking the contentious discourse of the discipline itself.

Molly Snodgrass, M.A., is a freelance writer and the study coordinator for the Longitudinal Assessment of Manic Symptoms (LAMS) study in the psychiatry department at the Ohio State University. Molly earned her B.A. in English and psychology and her M.A. in English at Indiana University. She has taught at both Indiana University and the University of Texas at San Antonio. She plans to pursue a Ph.D. in clinical psychology.

Irene Vlachos-Weber is a lecturer in psychology at Indiana University. She received her B.S. from Colorado State University and is completing her Ph.D. in clinical psychology at Indiana University. Irene has received several teaching awards, including a 2005 Student Choice Award for Outstanding Faculty.

# Stupid Brain!

## Homer's Working Memory Odyssey

Nelson Cowan,
Michael J. Kane,
Andrew R. A. Conway and
Alexander J. Ispa-Cowan

**JANUARY 6:** Today the doctors pulled a crayon out of my nose, taking pressure off of my brain, and almost at once I felt a kind of awakening of my mind for the first time since I was a young child.

**JANUARY 7:** Homer. What did my parents have in mind when they assigned me that moniker? Was it the blind Greek bard of *The Iliad* and *The Odyssey*, or slang for the act of propelling a baseball over the wall and out of the playing field? . . . I was leafing through the dictionary today and only now, I believe, have I mastered the words *assign, moniker, propel, slang* and *manifestation* (see the following), as well as Homer in its ancient Greek manifestation; and until now I have not questioned the meaning of my name at all. I have plenty of time to ponder such questions, now that I've lost my job at the Springfield Nuclear Power Plant. Of course, this is not the first time I've been terminated. Mr. Burns was rather upset the time that I caused a meltdown, but he was happy to have me back when I ended my push for public safety in the nuclear power industry. This time seemed different, though. Mr. Burns seemed more than just angry. In the past he's been upset by the ridiculous problems I've caused—quite a few—but this time he just seemed threatened and a bit frightened as if he imagined, let's say, that I would eventually take control of his company. Mr. Smithers didn't defend me in any noticeable way, either. I found it appalling, and below my dignity to fight their fabricated accusations. Oh, Marge and Bart just came in and I smell some fresh-baked doughn—

JANUARY 8: Dear Diary: Two days ago I stole you from Lisa's closet floor but it's for an important cause. Now I know that *I am so smart!* I am so s-m-A-r-t! (I used to leave out that A). Diary, you were blank except for three pages written several years ago, and I really needed to tell my story. I'm tempted to throw about some of the marvelous new words I've learned (like *marvelous*), but I must remember that someday I may be unable to read these words anymore and I will want to reflect upon this period of my life. Homer of the future, if you're reading this, good for you, pal! (Why did I just write "If you're reading this?" You only need the rest of the sentence if you ARE reading it. Well, I do go on too long sometimes now. Ciao!!)

It all began with our trip to the animation convention last month. I lost my life savings in a bad investment and had to sell my body for medical testing to make money. The x-ray turned up something so unexpected that I never would have dreamed of it. There was a crayon lodged in my brain! I do vaguely recall shoving it up my nose when I was a kid to see what would happen, but I cannot be sure that the memory is authentic. At any rate, the doctors removed the crayon and, as it seems, within several minutes I was noticeably smarter. Within about fifteen minutes, I grew ashamed of many of the things I've done during my life, all while unaware of what I was really doing.

The doctors explained it all to me and so now, Dear Diary for Homer of the New Brain, I want to explain it to you. The human brain includes many different systems of nerve cells working together. We know about it from people with brain damage, from new equipment that watches the brain in action (like one they call functional magnetic resonance imaging, or fMRI), and now from the new field of "neurocrayonology" announced in a recent publication reporting the study of my own case. It seems that there is a large piece of neural real estate called the frontal lobe that is just behind the forehead, and my crayon was pressing up against that part of my brain, limiting the blood flow. It's the part of the brain that does many active things. Human things! When people have severe damage to the frontal lobes, they often seem like vegetables. They can still hear, see, feel, smell, move around, and pick up things, mind you. You can tell them stuff and they may remember, but they often don't react much. This is what happened to all those troublesome mental patients who got frontal lobotomies years ago.

This reminds me of something. Bart, if you ever read this diary: I am very sorry I told you that "if something's hard, then it's not worth doing," or that when you try your best and fail, the lesson you should take is never to try. Shame on my crayon-cracked former frontal lobes! Oh, and one more lesson. Despite all the little lines, your frontal lobe is not a coloring book.

Even a little frontal lobe damage goes a long way. You often can't get people with a few frontal lobe problems to plan their schedules, or much of anything else. If one of them is in a restaurant, they may not be able to order by themselves because they think there are so many choices that they can't decide. Or they may get completely stuck on just one choice and not be able to consider the others at all. (Mmm, food choices....). It's called "perseveration." (And all of this depends on exactly which parts of the frontal lobes are damaged, you understand. It's a complex system in itself). I remember the perseveration I had one time when I played blackjack at the casino....

DEALER: 19.
ME: Hit me!
DEALER: 20.
ME: Hit me!
DEALER: 21.
ME: Hit me!
DEALER: 22.
ME: D'oh!

D'oh indeed. How humiliating.

At the same time, someone with damage to the frontal lobes may do something rash, on an impulse that doesn't require much thinking; in other words, they may let their stomach think for them, or they may let their base animal instincts think for them, or they may just do what they feel, physically or emotionally. Like the time I saw a billboard for doughnuts and Duff Beer, and rubbernecked it until I slammed into the truck in front of me. Or the time I was driving through a storm with Ned Flanders, and I forgot who my passenger was. When he told me that I just hit something I said, "I hope it was Flanders." Or the time I spent Springfield's entire annual sanitation budget during my first week in charge. N'ooooh....

And come to think of it, with frontal lobe damage your memory often isn't so great, either. You can remember your past experiences pretty well, and the facts you learned (if any), but you really can't keep track of new stuff. It's like if your wife told you a short grocery list but you didn't bother to say the words to yourself. So, later, you might remember being asked to buy bread if you happen to pass it in the store or, then again, you still might not. Also, you might remember meeting someone but you might not remember exactly who they are or where you met them even though they seem familiar, which isn't too helpful. Of course, everybody has these problems to some degree, I'm told. Look at how many times old Mr. Burns has failed to recognize me! But people with frontal lobe problems tend to have them much worse. Again, all of these problems really do hit home when I reflect on the stupid things I've done throughout my life, apparently because of the fateful crayon. You'll pay for this, Magenta!

JANUARY 9: I realize that my true sins and blunders must have been even worse than I recall, because my brain would not have been able to form very smart or detailed memories of them. It's just like when you don't recall what you did when you were drunk. Wow, come to think of it, drunk + crayon in the frontal lobe = the Homer that the folks at Moe's Tavern knew and loved. (I guess loved.) That is almost unfathomable, but, Ha! I guess if everyone else at Moe's was as drunk as I was, then they may not remember much, either. Even so, I feel so humiliated. What must they have thought of me? I didn't used to worry about stuff like that, but now I do all the time. The psychologists say that I have a theory of mind now and that I didn't have one before. What this means is that I think about what other people are thinking. I hope my appointment with the doctors tomorrow goes all right.

JANUARY 10: Had another trip to the hospital today, and another brain scan. They said that the operation to remove the crayon was only ninety percent successful and that the other ten percent is still in there. They explained in more depth about parts of the frontal lobe. Most of the complicated thinking seems to happen in the outer part that they call the *cortex*. That part seems normal now, from what they can tell. The inner part of the frontal lobe is related to some other circuits that are more primitive. Apparently, a small particle of crayon is still affecting those more primitive circuits. What they call the limbic system affects my memory, but also my emotions and appetite. They seem to think that there may be something wrong with those things still, making me overemotional and overhungry, though I don't see it myself. I'm

FIGURE 1
The Human Brain and Its Functions

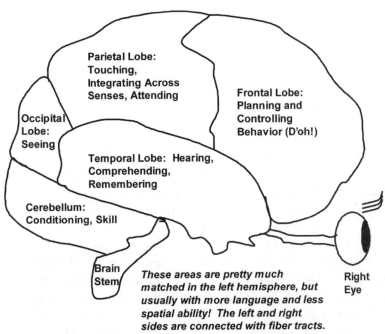

Parietal Lobe: Touching, Integrating Across Senses, Attending

Frontal Lobe: Planning and Controlling Behavior (D'oh!)

Occipital Lobe: Seeing

Temporal Lobe: Hearing, Comprehending, Remembering

Cerebellum: Conditioning, Skill

Brain Stem

*These areas are pretty much matched in the left hemisphere, but usually with more language and less spatial ability! The left and right sides are connected with fiber tracts.*

Right Eye

the American ideal! Sure, I understand now about the danger of trans fat in doughnuts, but we can't let our intellects govern our whole lives, can we?

JANUARY 13: I've been so busy that I didn't have time to write in the past few days. I want to document what's been happening in great detail so that others can learn from my travails and I can remember them. Well, of course the theme is: Damn that Bart! To explain what he did—D'oh!, I gotta go, the painters and the roof repair people both just arrived, and so did the principal. To think that Bart could practically demolish the school and our house in the same day with so little effort. I can't afford to reimburse the school system so I'm just going to try to act stupid about the whole Bart incident. I'm going to act like the old stupid Homer, until the principal gives up and leaves.

JANUARY 17: It's getting harder and harder to write, what with so many people asking for my advice these days. I bet they wonder why I've changed. They probably just think I stopped drinking (there I go with that "theory of mind" again!). Anyway, I've been reading a lot about intelligence. It all started in the early 1900s when the French school system was made available for all children. Imagine, a single school system for the poor and also the rich. We should try that in Springfield (just kidding). Well, they wanted to know which kids should go to school with which other ones. Now, they could have decided that in several ways. They could have just done it by age as we do now in the good old U.S. But children of the same age can be quite different. Did you ever see the hallway in a junior high school, when the big ones just push the small ones aside? Well, I think they probably should have separated the kids according to some combination of height and weight. That way, at least, we wouldn't have the small ones getting the skit picked out of them. (You know what I'm trying to say, Mr. Censor!) But so the French decided they wanted to combine children who were at the same level of mental capability. You know: Which children can succeed at long division? Who can read Descartes? Who can spell? And so on. This was the birth of the idea of the intelligence quotient, or IQ.

JANUARY 17, 2:00 P.M: To continue: The psychologists really didn't have a very good idea of who could do what, except by asking them. But a guy named Alfred Binet came up with a brilliant scheme, the idea of a mental age. Say you're a seven-year-old but you can answer questions just like the typical nine-year-old. Sort of like Lisa. Then they would say that you have a mental age of nine. So they could put you in with the other smart seven and eight-year-olds, and with the average nine-year-olds, and with the dumb ten-year-olds, and call it a classroom. I still think that would lead to the small ones getting the skit picked out of them. Unless they use their smarts to avoid that. I guess they'd have to tell a lot of jokes. I heard that's how Jon Stewart got by when he was a kid. Anyway, we must not use the smart-dumb method very much in the USA; Lisa is in class with Ralph Wiggum, and he makes the old me look like the new me!

JANUARY 18: The more I read about intelligence the less satisfied I am with the concept. You know, it isn't measured by questions that make a lot of sense in an organized or principled way. The questions that are used are just "whatever." Namely, whatever works. To invent the intelligence test, the psychologists made up a bunch of questions that sounded like they might be good. If a question was pretty reliably answered correctly more often by older kids than by younger kids, they would keep that question in the test. But if a question didn't distinguish between the older and younger ones, the question would be dropped....But what if the younger kids remembered something that the older ones didn't, like, for example, the details about some nursery rhyme? I don't think the psychologists could answer that. So the test depended on their assuming certain things. The tests don't necessarily show that older children are smarter; the tests are based on that assumption! The test-makers could have focused on more well-defined abilities, but to do that I guess they would have needed more of a theory of mind!

They also made up IQ tests for adults. They did it first for the U.S. army, to see who should be in charge of aiming the rockets and who should be peeling potatoes (mmm...potatoes). So, here, the thing they used to decide how good a question is, was called the criterion. If a soldier had really good performance on a lot of different jobs, even the complex ones, they called him smart. The criterion was job performance. Any question that those smart guys could answer more often than the screw-ups was considered a good question, and it was kept in the test. But...it's hard work to compare how the answers to lots and lots of questions relate to soldiers' work performance, so after a while they just started comparing newer tests to the older tests. I hope that after so many years, the test scores still relate to job performance, even though jobs have changed so much over time!

As I said, though, the questions on intelligence tests often seemed kind of arbitrary and I'm not very satisfied with them. For one thing, they failed Maggie on her first intelligence test because she couldn't talk, but when we realized that she could communicate through playing blocks, they re-tested her and found out she's even smarter than Lisa (although it turned out she was cheating)! Actually, some of the psychologists aren't very happy with the tests, either. They keep arguing over whether there's just one basic kind of intelligence, which they call $g$ for general intelligence, or whether there are several different types. They use really complicated math to investigate this. Some people say that what you already know—the facts and skills—make up your *crystallized intelligence*, and that that's different from how well you use what you know to figure out new ideas and new ways to do things, your *fluid intelligence*. Anyway, the tests they use to decide who gets into college were once more like fluid intelligence tests but now, these past few years, they're a bit more like crystallized intelligence tests.

**JANUARY 19**: To continue: Where was I? Oh yes, crystallized and fluid intelligence. They are very closely related, I'm told. People with high crystallized intelligence also tend to have high fluid intelligence. I guess that's because, after a while, people who can learn the best and figure out new things will obviously end up knowing the most. Just like, as I was reading the other day, the stars that are traveling the fastest are also the farthest away from Earth. I'm the exception because I haven't been smart long enough to know all that much; you might say that I'm the only close star traveling fast. . . . Anyway, some people say there are many different kinds of intelligence, like verbal, spatial, musical, athletic, emotional and social intelligence, just to name a few. But everything they measure seems to be somewhat related to everything else, in that people who are high on one intelligence also tend to be high on others, so this g idea of a general intelligence doesn't seem like something to be ignored. They also say that identical twins tend to have g's very similar to each other, but the way you're treated matters also, if it's extreme. So if one twin lives well, like us in Springfield, and the other twin is sent to the poorhouse, like that town I won't mention by name, they don't end up thinking alike after all.

JANUARY 25: All right, I'm definitely getting interested in this "smart" thing. I've enrolled in a course at the community college in what's called cognitive psychology. It means psychology about the way people see, listen, perceive, think, imagine, remember and act out. That's a lot to consider, and I wanted to get a good value for my tuition money. Actually, I got a scholarship from the Kwik-E-Mart "Always-Open Minds" Foundation and I want to get the most value for that.

Cognitive psychology is a lot to cover in just one course. It's as if your mind is a whole committee and each guy in the committee needs a whole course of his own about him. Like that first time I met Marge. The perception guy told the impulse guy to go right up and kiss her, but then the imagination guy figured that Marge wouldn't take it too well and we might just get slapped. So he told that to the think guy, who decided that it would be better just to, say, ask her to tutor him in French to get to know her (even though we weren't taking French). Then when we knew her better, we could ask her to the prom. So that's the final decision we gave to the action guy and thankfully he listened to the think guy instead of the impulse guy. Of course, these guys didn't do as well when the impulse guy convinced the action guy to admit that we weren't taking French, but later the emotion guy acted up on his own and Marge forgave us. And it worked out happily ever after for the whole committee! Judging from what I've seen at Moe's, it's lucky that the beer-drinking guy wasn't too involved in this one.

FEBRUARY 4: My instructor is interested in something he calls "working memory." That's what I have from the power plant—working memory, meaning memory of when I used to work. Heh, heh. No,

I'm joking. Working memory refers to the small amount of ideas that you can use and keep track of at one time. We all have tons and tons of stuff in our head. Well, not literal tons, but lots of ideas and memories, built up over a lifetime. (They're quite lightweight, literally speaking, at least.) But we can't think about all of them at once. The small part that we can think about is called working memory. There are lots of ways to measure it. For example, in intelligence tests they use something called digit span, which is when they say a series of numbers to you out loud and you have to say them all back in the right order. The more you can repeat in a series without a mistake, the better your score is. This is important stuff. For example, suppose someone tells you a telephone number that you have to call and then leaves, and you don't have paper. If you forget the number, you can't make the call. You have to just re-member the number in your head. It could be important, like calling for a taxi or a pizza (or maybe even a taxi with a pizza in it). You might try strategies like imagining that you are saying the number over and over until you finish pressing buttons. I think I read that they invented the digit span test not long after they invented telephone numbers!

**FEBRUARY 6**: So, I was thinking. I never really had much trouble remembering telephone numbers, except for that time I had to ask the operator the number for 911. Oh, and the time they made us dial an area code every time we made a call. Hmmm. Well, anyway, some other kinds of working memory made me look really, REALLY stupid. Think about what I did after I met that great guy who was a roofer. (I think his name was Ray, and people thought he was my imaginary buddy.) I was told to watch CBS Monday night at 9 P.M. I recall that I kept ask-ing stuff and the guy kept answering. "...and what day would that be?" "Monday." "On what channel?" "Channel 9." "If I were to watch this show, what time would I watch it?" "9 P.M." "Really? What channel is showing it?" And so on, like that, over and over. Yikes, how many times have I said something like, "Uh-huh, uh-huh. Okay. Um, can you re-peat the part of the stuff where you said all about uhhh, the things?" I never would have realized how stupid I sounded if Bart hadn't secretly tape-recorded me, and if Lisa hadn't stolen the tape from his tree house, and if Maggie hadn't put it in her mouth and crawled into my bedroom with it. So why was this so much harder than telephone numbers? I suppose it was because I wasn't saying the information to myself, like I sometimes do with telephone numbers. And some of the other working memory tests, the ones that really seem to predict how intelligent you are, make you do two things at once, like counting some dots and remembering the sum; counting some more and remembering that sum; and after several sets of dots, you have to repeat all of the sums. You really have to be smart to succeed at a list of four or five of those at a time. People who do are usually really good at lots of other complicated stuff like solving problems, understanding what they read, and reasoning. That's why some people think that working memory is what makes you intelligent!

**FEBRUARY 8:** I asked my cognitive psychology professor about working memory today. He said that using your working memory often requires that you pay attention. If you say the words over and over, you don't have to pay attention much. But if you don't say them like that, you do have to pay attention or you'll lose them. And it depends on the brain. It depends on the frontal lobes, as we've been saying, and the parietal lobes doing a different job. The professor said the parietal lobes are farther back in the brain, on the left and the right. (The frontal lobes have a left and the right too, but they come together in the center.) More intelligent people seem to have better frontal lobes and maybe better parietal lobes, too. But behaviors can be deceiving. If intelligent people are upset or bored and unmotivated and thinking about something else, they won't do well on your test because they aren't using their frontal lobes in the right way. They won't do well if they're tired or drunk, either.

The frontal and parietal lobes work together as a team, in a network. So, with a crayon stuck in my frontal lobe, I wasn't able to control my attention very well. The Duff Beer and doughnut billboard just captured my attention away from driving like nothing, and I couldn't stop it. But if I had the crayon in my parietal lobe somehow (though it couldn't get there through my nose), I would have different problems. Then I wouldn't be able to see or imagine things the right way. If it was stuck in the left side, I wouldn't be able to notice things on the right side of the world, like the billboard. If it was stuck in the right side, I wouldn't be able to notice things on the left. That's called unilateral neglect and a lot of folks Dad's age get it from a stroke. Maybe that's what was wrong with his golf game, when he kept hitting the ball to the right of the hole. (His stroke made him add strokes! Hee hee, I'm hilarious sometimes!) Also, some parietal lobe patients don't know that there is anything wrong with them, and they deny it. Then they just seem so unaware. But also, without your parietal lobes you wouldn't be able to keep very many things in mind. You wouldn't remember the time, the place, and the channel all at once. (I don't think that the crayon could affect my parietal lobe but, since the frontal lobe helps to control what the parietal lobe emphasizes, maybe they work together enough that they gave me the problem in paying attention. That seems to be why I didn't do too well on intelligence tests. Actually, my golf score was much higher than my IQ until recently).

I have been doing really well in my cognitive psychology class. Part of the reason is that I have been using information that I learn in class to improve my study habits. I learned that we remember information better if we study it a little bit every day, rather than trying to cram it in all the night before the exam. Also, that allows better sleep before the exam, which is important for working memory and retrieving information for the exam. Woo hoo!

**MARCH 20**: It is too bad that I haven't written in a long time. I haven't felt like it at all. I've been depressed. It's just been a little disconcerting to have an IQ of maybe 140 and a whole life history of a guy with an IQ of maybe 85. I just don't feel like I know who I am. The people around me don't seem to know who I am either. I'm not sure that being smart is everything I hoped it would be. Also, it makes me practically ineligible for some jobs with the government. I'm seriously toying with the idea of doing away with Smart Homer. All it would take is another crayon back up the nose....

**APRIL 3**: Dear Diary: This is Lisa. I am carrying on for Dad. He hasn't felt like writing in a while but I was fascinated and touched by his personal Odyssey documented in these pages. The trouble was, being smart made him depressed for some reason. Apparently, there was some friction with Mom because she felt like he wasn't the man she married. She couldn't explain it and was crying a lot. Also, he wasn't getting along with any of his old friends. So, against my counsel, Dad decided to put the crayon back in his nose. Actually, I think Moe helped. I have to admit that I am relieved, having the old Dad back again. But I hereby swear to transcribe something he says every day, because I pledged to him that I would do that. I love him very much and it's the least I can do. Every day I'm going to ask him to tell me about his day and, in the interests of science, I'll write down exactly what he says, verbatim.

**APRIL 4**: H.S., transcribed by L.S. Well, Lisa, today I went to my class in cogitative psychology. That's where the guy talks about stuff and it helps me to figure out why we are the way we are. He asked if anyone ever lost brain cells and he told us about a study on somebody who did.... So, Lisa, you really think I messed up my brain once? Uh-oh, me lose brain cells? I don't remember that. Oh well, what's important is to treat the brain cells you've got to beer and TV! (Note from L.S.—Today, to impress us with his continuing education, Dad is wearing a leather jacket onto which he sewed tweed elbow patches. When I told him that professors actually wear leather patches on a tweed jacket, not the reverse, and that he ruined a perfectly good jacket, he said, "Incorrect, Lisa. TWO perfectly good jackets!").

APRIL 5, 5:30 P.M: H.S., transcribed by L.S. I heard about this crazy experiment in class today where the not-so-smart people with bad working memories noticed things better than the smart people with good working memories. Woo hoo! They gave some people a message in one ear in headphones, and they were supposed to repeat that message out loud. At the same time, in the other ear there was a message they were supposed to ignore. What was very sneaky was that they said each guy's own name in the ear that was supposed to be ignored. Guess what? Most of the not-so-smart people noticed their names, and most of the smart people didn't notice. The teacher said something about smart people with good working memory focusing their attention better, blah, blah, blah. But I say that the not-so-smart people are smarter than the smart people! I am so smart! S-M-R-T! Why are you looking at me like that? Oh, look at that bird at the window. What do you think is for dinner? Wait, I think Marge is talking about me on the phone and I want to go spy on her.

APRIL 5, 6:30 P.M: H.S., transcribed by L.S. Hey, Lisa, in class today I heard about this funny experiment where the low working memory people noticed things better than the smart people. Woo hoo! They gave some people a message in one ear in headphones, and…Huh? What do you mean I told you this already? Lisa, don't you think I know whether I've told you something or not? Hey, was that your stomach I just heard or mine? Okay, good. Anyway, Lisa, don't you think your daddy knows when he's told you something or not?

APRIL 6: H.S., transcribed by L.S. Well, Lisa, I heard about another crazy experiment today. They said you could only remember about three to five different things. Like I can remember all three of the people in our family: me, Marge, and Maggie….Didn't I say you? You, Mart, and Barge. I mean, Bart and Marge. And you. And, oh yeah, Maggie. And me. Anyway, you can remember more if you make chunks out of them (mmm…chunks…). Okay, so if you and Bart tied your legs together and Mom and I tied our legs together, then I'd be able to remember all four of us: you and Bart, me and Marge, so the whole family would be remembered….What do you mean? I said Maggie. Didn't I? D'oh! Anyway, the smart people think they're so GREAT because they can remember MORE things, and make larger CHUNKS. Well, I showed them. I made a huge chunk out of six doughnuts by squooshing them together into a paper cup, and when I got to Moe's I remembered to take all six of them in with me for a snack. I'm like that guy who built a rocket from scratch and blasted into orbit! What was his name? Apollo Creed?

APRIL 7: H.S., transcribed by L.S. I'm so glad that I got my job back! The interview was a cinch. I knew just how to answer every question without even thinking! I knew that vampires are make-believe, just like elves, gremlins and Eskimos! And I owe it all to a little crayon. Let's go out tonight to celebrate... you all can wait in the car while I stop at Moe's for a few minutes, and then we'll go to dinner.

APRIL 8: H.S., transcribed by L.S. I played a really good trick on Mr. Smithers. It was all from an experiment that I learned from my Cognatorial Psyching class. They showed us that people who can't remember many things in their working memory also look the wrong way. Or, actually, they look the right way when they're told to look the wrong way. Anyway, you tell them that when a light flashes on the left, they are supposed to look right, and if it flashes on the right, they are supposed to look left. The professor did this on a computer screen, but later when I got to the power plant I managed to get the lights on the console to blink that way, too. Anyway, the not-so-smart people look at the blinking light even though they were told that they were supposed to look the other way. Heh, heh, heh. Silly not-so-smart people! So, I told Mr. Smithers he had to look away from the light when it blinked or he'd get a surprise. And when he looked at the light, I shot him in the eye with a squirt gun. Then he was sort of mad but I told him he could do it to me. But before we could get that far, more lights started blinking. I'm not sure what all of the blinking lights meant. Maybe I shouldn't have messed with the first one. But we've never had any safety troubles at the power plant because they hire watchmen. I'm a watchman, actually. Anyway, so I'm glad I have my job back.

APRIL 9: H.S., transcribed by L.S. Well, I took my final exam today in Cogitative Scatology. Yep, we graded it right in class. I flunked the exam but I got a C in the class. Woo hoo! My first two exam grades were great but somehow I blew the final. It had a lot of good questions on it but they made me think of other things. I don't understand why I blew it after I pulled an all-nighter to read the textbook and the notes. I thought I could take short naps between questions in the exam, but the professor didn't like me setting an alarm clock in the classroom. But it's still the best class grade I ever got. So maybe that crayon stabbed me right in the "stupid gene" that all the male Simpsons are supposed to have. You never can tell.

# References

Baddeley, A. (2000). "The episodic buffer: a new component of working memory?" *Trends in cognitive sciences*, 4, 417–423.

Baddeley, A., & Hitch, G. J. (1974). "Working memory." In G. Bower (ed.), *Recent advances in learning and motivation*, Vol. VIII. New York: Academic Press.

Conway, A. R. A., Cowan, N., & Bunting, M. F. (2001). "The cocktail party phenomenon revisited: The importance of working memory capacity." *Psychonomic Bulletin & Review*, 8, 331–335.

Conway, A. R. A., Kane, M. J., & Engle, R. W.(2003). "Working memory capacity and its relation to general intelligence." *Trends in Cognitive Sciences*, 7, 547–552.

Cowan, N. (2005). "Working-memory capacity limits in a theoretical context." In C. Izawa & N. Ohta (eds.), *Human learning and memory: Advances In theory and applications*. The 4th Tsukuba international conference on memory. Erlbaum, 155–175.

Cowan, N. (2005). *Working memory capacity*. New York, NY: Psychology Press.

Kane, M. J., & Engle, R. W.(2002). "The role of prefrontal cortex in working-memory capacity, executive attention, and general fluid intelligence: An individual-differences perspective." *Psychonomic Bulletin & Review*, 9, 637–671.

Kane, M. J., & Engle, R. W. (2003). "Working-memory capacity and the control of attention: The contributions of goal neglect, response competition, and task set to Stroop interference." *Journal of Experimental Psychology: General*, 132, 47–70.

Miyake, A., & Shah, P. (eds.) (1999). *Models of Working Memory: Mechanisms of active maintenance and executive control*. Cambridge, U.K.: Cambridge University Press.

Neisser, U., Boodoo, G., Bouchard, T., Brody, N., Ceci, S. J., Halpern, D., Loehlin, J., Perloff, R., Sternberg, R. J., & Urbina, S. (1996). "Intelligence: Knowns and unknowns." *American Psychologist*, 51, 1–25.

## Acknowledgments

We thank Christopher Barona, Angela Currie, William Lockhart, Tina Miyake, Adam Moore and Bradley Poole for ments. This work was supported by NIH Grant R01 HD-213. ̨cu to Nelson Cowan.

Nelson Cowan is a cognitive and developmental psychologist with research interests in working memory, attention, intelligence, individual differences and their development across the life span. He earned his B.S. from the University of Michigan in 1973 with an independent major in the neurosciences, and his Ph.D. in psychology at the University of Wisconsin in 1980. He is currently Curators' Professor of Psychology at the University of Missouri at Columbia and an associate editor of the *European Journal of Cognitive Psychology*. In the past he has served as associate editor of the *Journal of Experimental Psychology: Learning, Memory, and Cognition* and of the *Quarterly Journal of Experimental Psychology*. In addition to research articles, he has written two books: *Attention and Memory: An Integrated Framework* (Oxford Press, 1995) and *Working Memory Capacity* (Psychology Press), and he has edited *The Development of Memory in Childhood* (Psychology Press, 1997). He is married with a son in high school and an older stepson and stepdaughter.

Michael J. Kane is a cognitive psychologist with research interests in memory, attention, intelligence, cognitive control and individual differences. He earned his B.A. in psychology from Haverford College in 1989, and his Ph.D. in cognitive psychology in 1995. He is currently an associate professor of psychology at the University of North Carolina at Greensboro and serves on the editorial boards of two scientific journals, as associate editor for *Memory & Cognition* and consulting editor for *Journal of Experimental Psychology: General*. He is also the father of two and the husband of one.

Andrew R. A. Conway is a cognitive neuroscientist who conducts research on individual differences in memory capacity, cognitive control and intelligence. He earned his B.S. in computer science and psychology from Union College (Schenectady, NY) in 1991, and his M.A. and Ph.D. in experimental psychology from the University of South Carolina in 1993 and 1996, respectively. He is currently a lecturer in the psychology department at Princeton University, where he teaches courses on statistics for psychologists. He also serves on the editorial board of the scientific journal *Memory & Cognition*. He is single (with no legal right to marriage in his state) and resides in Manhattan.

Alexander J. Ispa-Cowan is a high school student who enjoys playing guitar and piano, working with lasers, electronics and the physical sciences generally, playing soccer, watching *The Simpsons* and its animated competitors, picking up political information from *The Daily Show* with Jon Stewart and, sometimes, reading and creative writing.

# Homer's Soul

### Paul Bloom and David Pizarro

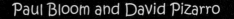

THE DEEPEST QUESTION in psychology—perhaps the deepest question that humans have ever faced—concerns the very existence of mental life. We know that our minds are the products of our brains. We can even use methods such as fMRI to localize certain sorts of mental events, such as the concentration involved in reading a difficult passage of text, the nervousness that many whites feel while looking at a black male face, or the anger at being cheated while playing a simple game. But we remain mystified by what the philosopher David Chalmers has called "The hard problem": How is it that a physical object (and not a fancy one at that, a bloody lump of grey meat) gives rise to pain, love, morality and consciousness?

Fortunately, scientists can make considerable progress without solving this problem. Viewing the mind as a computer, for instance, has given rise to detailed and intricate models of language learning, visual perception and logical reasoning—all without a theory of how computation can give rise to conscious experience. Similarly, clinical psychologists don't need to solve the mind-body problem to ascertain the causes of specific mental disorders, or to assess potential treatments. Scientists were able to invent Prozac and Viagra without an explanation of how a material brain can produce the experience of sadness and lust. But, still, solving the mind-body problem remains a major preoccupation of both psychologists and philosophers; no science of the mind can be complete without it.

What does *The Simpsons* have to say about this issue? Most likely, absolutely nothing. *The Simpsons* is a fine television show, but it's not where to look for innovative ideas in cognitive neuroscience or the philosophy of mind. We think, however, that it can help give us insight into a related, and extremely important, issue. We might learn through this show something about common-sense metaphysics, about how people naturally think about consciousness, the brain and the soul.

This is a question that really matters. For one thing, such notions are intimately related to our religious beliefs, and if we wish to answer the question of what all religions have in common (and why religion is a human universal), we would do well to understand how people think about bodies and souls. Furthermore, our folk conception of the mind is implicated in all sorts of social and political issues, including stem-cell research, cloning, abortion and euthanasia. Common-sense beliefs, for instance, about what counts as a morally significant being—a fetus, a chimpanzee, or someone with brain damage, such as the controversial case of Theresa Schiavo in 2005—rest in part on our beliefs about the nature of mental life. Like many fictional creations, the world of the *Simpsons* embodies our intuitive assumptions about the nature of things, and so the study of this world might teach us something about what these assumptions really are.

Consider, in this regard, Homer Simpson. In the earliest shows, he was portrayed in a fairly realistic manner, as a flawed, but loving, father and husband, but—in line with the general evolution of the show—he has become increasingly fantastical, often bizarrely stupid and criminally indifferent to his family. More than any other character, his traits have been exaggerated. But this sort of exaggeration can be valuable from a psychological perspective; it might bring to light facts and distinctions that are more subtle, and hard to appreciate, in the actual world.

Homer has at least three parts. There is Homer himself, an experiencing conscious being. There is his brain. And there is his soul. The implicit metaphysics of *The Simpsons* provides a striking illustration of how we naturally draw these distinctions in the real world—not only for the American television viewer, but for all humans.

# Homer and His Brain

In the 1640s, René Descartes asked what one can know for sure. He concluded: Not much. It seems like you have been around for a while, for instance, but you have to admit that it is possible (not likely, but possible) that you were created five minutes ago, and all your memories are illusions. (Consider the fate of the androids in the movie *Blade Runner*). You can wonder if you don't really have a body; as Descartes pointed out, your sensory experience could be an illusion created by an evil deity. The modern version of this concern is nicely portrayed by the makers of *The Matrix*, who depicted a world where our experiences are created by malevolent computers.

But, as Descartes famously concluded, there is one thing that you cannot doubt:

> …I have just convinced myself that nothing whatsoever existed in the world, that there was no sky, no earth, no minds, and no bodies; have I not thereby convinced myself that I did not exist? Not at all…Even though there may be a deceiver of some sort, very powerful and very tricky, who bends all his efforts to keep me perpetually deceived, there can be no slightest doubt that I exist, since he deceives me; and let him deceive me as much as he will, he can never make me nothing as long as I think I am something.

Cogito ergo sum. I think therefore I am. My body is different from my self; I can doubt the existence of my body; I cannot doubt the existence of my self. What follows from this, for Descartes, is that the two are genuinely different. There are two distinct "substances"—a body, which Descartes was perfectly content to think of as a "well-made clock"—and Descartes himself, which is immaterial and intangible.

If you tell this to a philosopher or scientist, the response you will get is that Descartes was wrong. Philosophically, his method is suspect—just because one can imagine a self without a body does not mean that this state of affairs is actually possible. One can easily imagine, after all, that something can travel faster than light, but it does not follow that it could actually occur. And there is abundant positive evidence that, in fact, Descartes' mental life is the product of his brain.

But it doesn't feel that way, not to Descartes and not to the rest of us either. When people in our culture are taught the scientific mainstream view that the brain is involved in thinking, we tend to reject this, and distort it into something more palpable. We do not take the brain as the source of conscious experience; we do not identity it with our *selves*. Instead we think of the brain as a cognitive prosthesis—there is the person, and then there is the brain, which the person uses to solve problems just as he might use a computer. The psychologist Steven Pinker describes this common-sense conception of the brain as "a pocket PC for the soul."

This is certainly the conception that is implicit in *The Simpsons*. Homer's brain is not Homer. It's more like Homer's smarter sidekick—a handy, albeit limited, reference book, calculator and occasional source of decent advice. Homer's brain provides a great running gag, because, of all the characters (save perhaps Ralph Wiggum), Homer's wits leave the most to be desired. He could very much *use* a good brain, and there is even some evidence that he had one at one point. Once Homer removed the crayon lodged in his brain as a child and his cognitive abilities saw a drastic improvement, only to cram the crayon back up his nose at the end of the episode. (Or consider the Intel commercial where Homer's brain has received a hardware upgrade, as evident by the "Intel Inside" logo on the back of his head). But for the most part, Homer's brain is still the low-end model as far as brains go.

Still, even though Homer's personality and judgment have been in steady decline over the years, his brain sometimes kicks in to offer useful social advice, solve difficult problems and present him with a variety of behavioral options. This process is usually depicted by showing Homer engaged in a dialogue with his Brain—sometimes even striking bargains with it, as can be seen here, as Homer is trying to determine the excessive long-distance charges on his phone bill:

HOMER: Burkina Faso? Disputed Zone? Who called all these weird places?
HOMER'S BRAIN: Quiet, it might be you! I can't remember.
HOMER: Naw, I'm going to ask Marge.
HOMER'S BRAIN: No, no! Why embarrass us both? Just write a check and I'll release some more endorphins.
[*Homer scribbles a check, then sighs with pleasure.*]

Of course, Homer isn't required to take the advice given to him by his brain. In line with the view of the brain as a prosthesis and not as the true self, Homer can reject or accept its advice. As in this case, when Homer pays a visit to the "Bigger Brothers" office:

ADMINISTRATOR: And what are your reasons for wanting a Little Brother?

HOMER'S BRAIN: Don't say revenge! Don't say revenge!

HOMER: Uh, revenge?

HOMER'S BRAIN: That's it, I'm gettin' outta here.

[*Footsteps, and a door slam*]

At other times, Homer's brain provides knowledge and information that is apparently not generally available to Homer himself. When Homer is in doubt, his brain is much like the "phone-a-friend" option in the popular game show *Who Wants to be a Millionaire*. In one episode, for instance, Homer is eating peanuts on the couch. Homer tips his head back, closes his eyes, opens his mouth, and tosses the peanut toward his head, missing his mouth. The peanut clatters behind the couch, and after a couple of seconds, Homer observes, "Something's wrong." He gets down on his hands and knees in front of the couch and reaches underneath.

[*Homer searches under the couch for a peanut.*]

HOMER: Hmm…ow, pointy! Eww, slimy. Oh, moving! Aha! [*looks, then says remorsefully*] Ohhh, twenty dollars…I wanted a peanut!

HOMER'S BRAIN: Twenty dollars can buy many peanuts!

HOMER: Explain how.

HOMER'S BRAIN: Money can be exchanged for goods and services.

If the notion that "Homer" is not the same thing as "Homer's Brain" didn't jibe well with our intuitions, the viewer would have a hard time making sense of any of the above examples. The dialogue might instead seem like the confused ramblings of a person suffering from hallucinations. But Homer's conversations with his brain don't pose any particular problem for us. *The Simpsons* viewers have had to accept some strange premises—e.g., that NASA would allow Homer to fly in the Space Shuttle—but this is not one of them. It is no stretch to assume that people's thoughts are not entirely the product of their brains.

This is the same understanding of mental life that young children have. Five-year-olds know where the brain is and what it is for, and they know that animals cannot think and remember without a brain. But they do not usually understand that the brain is needed for physical action, such as hopping or brushing your teeth, and they do not think the brain is needed for an activity like pretending to be a kangaroo. And if you tell these children a story in which a child's brain is successfully transplanted into the head of a pig, children agree that the pig would now be as smart as a person, but they think that it would still keep the memories, personality and identity of the pig.

Even highly educated scientists and journalists often have difficulty shaking this intuition. Modern brain imaging techniques provide us with the opportunity to observe the brain changing in (almost) real time. What this means is that we can bring people into a laboratory, provide them with a specific task (e.g., multiplication problems), and watch the brain "in action." But the next time you read the latest write-up of one of these studies in the popular press, make careful note of the language used to describe the studies. It often sounds something like this: "we observed that when participants thought about triangles, the brain was activated in brain region x." But from what we know about the brain, the "thinking" about triangles doesn't "activate" the brain region. The "activation" *is* the "thinking." As we are writing this chapter, a particularly stark example of common-sense dualism has appeared in *The New York Times* Science section (August 2, 2005), with an article titled "Discovering that denial of paralysis is not just a problem of the brain." The article includes the revealing passage, "But in a new study, Dr. Berti and her colleagues have shown that denial is not a problem of the mind. Rather, it is a neurological condition...."

If the self is not material, this leaves open the appealing possibility that we can survive the destruction of our bodies. We might ascend to Heaven, descend to Hell, go off into some sort of parallel world, or occupy some other body, human or animal. Mark Pinsky, in his book *The Gospel According to The Simpsons*, has an extended discussion of how *The Simpsons* treats the afterlife. The main theme is simple: after death, the person leaves the body. And the person then goes to...well, this isn't entirely clear. In one episode, Homer regains consciousness after a heart attack, and tells the doctor about his experience:

> HOMER: [It was] a wonderful place filled with fire and brimstone, and there were all these guys in red pajamas sticking pitchforks in my butt.

In another episode, the characters explicitly debate the Cartesian puzzle of which entities are merely bodies, and hence cannot survive physical destruction. What about ventriloquists, Bart asks. Their dummies?

Robots with human brains? As for the Cartesian—and Christian—conclusion that only humans have selves, and other animals hence cannot enter Heaven, Homer is rightly skeptical:

> HOMER: I can understand how they wouldn't want to let in those wild jungle apes, but what about those really smart ones who live among us, who roller skate and smoke cigars?

## Homer's Soul

Up to now, the notions that *The Simpsons* draw upon are universal: a common-sense dualism, a belief that we occupy our brains/bodies, but we are not ourselves physical. But there is something more. We also believe in something like a soul, distinct from ourselves and our brains.

Unlike the body/self distinction, this is less likely to be universal. The common-sense conception of the soul differs from society to society. (If *The Simpsons* were made in India or Japan, one would find very different episodes.) Even within the United States there are a variety of beliefs about the nature of the soul. While of course most Atheists reject the notion of an immaterial soul, as do many scientists, even some Christians (such as Seventh Day Adventists) are reluctant to believe in the soul as a separate entity. But most Christians—well over ninety percent according to recent polls—do believe in the soul.

Even children seem to believe in the soul. The psychologists Paul Harris and Rebekah Richert asked children various questions and found that they tended to distinguish the soul from both the mind and the brain. Most four- to twelve-year-olds, for instance, claimed that a religious ritual such as baptism changes the soul—but not the mind or the brain. They think of the mind and brain, but not the soul, as important for mental life, and they think that the mind and brain grow and change over time, but they are less likely to say this about the soul. For a child, the soul's role is limited to mostly spiritual functions, having to do with morality, love, the afterlife and some sort of contact with God.

And, not surprisingly, this is the view of the Soul most evident in *The Simpsons*. In line with Christian doctrine, the Simpsonian Soul is clearly the part of you that goes to Heaven or Hell after death, such as when Homer sells his soul for a doughnut and has to endure a trial to prevent eternal damnation ("The Devil and Homer Simpson"). But the soul is also that part of you that is sensitive to morality, and can be affected by your moral actions. The official song of Springfield is, aptly, "Embiggen your Soul," an exhortation to improve one's moral standing (a sort of Manifest Destiny for the individual).

"Hitch that team up, Jebediah Springfield,
whip them horses, let them wagons roll.
That a people might embiggen America,
that a man might embiggen his soul."

In the episode entitled "Bart Sells His Soul" Lisa elegantly expresses her intuition about what a soul is. Despite her healthy religious skepticism, Lisa seems to believe in an immaterial, eternal soul:

LISA: Where'd you get five dollars?
BART: I sold my soul to Milhouse.
LISA: How could you do that? Your soul is the most valuable part of you.
BART: You believe in that junk?
LISA: Well, whether or not the soul is physically real it represents everything fine inside us...your soul is the only part of you that lasts forever.

But in the same episode even Lisa backs away a bit from this claim, viewing the soul as the seat of morality rather than as an explicit metaphysical entity:

LISA: ...But you know, Bart, some philosophers believe that no one is born with a soul, you have to earn one through suffering, thought and prayer like you did last night.

Indeed, some philosophers and theologians say that without a belief in a soul, one cannot make sense of the social concepts on which we rely, such as personal responsibility and freedom of the will. There is a lot at stake here.

## A Trickle-Down Understanding of the Mind:

One explanation for the view assumed in *The Simpsons* is that it is trickle-down theology. An understanding of souls, and of a distinction between a person and his body, has deep roots in religion, and especially in Christian tradition. The writers of the show, and those of us who watch it, are exposed to this tradition, and therefore can make sense of the multifaceted nature of Homer Simpson. But this theory fails to explain the *naturalness* of this way of understanding people, its universality across cultures and its early emergence in young children. A better explanation is that this type of understanding of people is common sense, part of how we have evolved to see the world. We naturally believe in bodies and minds and souls, and this shapes religion, culture, morality and *The Simpsons*.

In this domain, as in so many others, common sense clashes with science. While we have not solved the mind-body problem, and perhaps might never solve it, there are certain things that psychologists and neuroscientists do know. The brain is the source of mental life; our consciousness, emotions and will are the product of neural processes. As the claim is sometimes put, *the mind is what the brain does*. Our minds are the products of our physical brains, not separable from them, and there are no souls to sell.

But this view is like certain other positions put forth by scientists, such as evolution by natural selection. While it is possible for people to adopt such views and give up on common sense (every child does this when learning that the Earth is not flat), this learning process is slow and effortful, intellectually and emotionally challenging. Those who hope to effect such a shift away from common sense—whether toward science, a progressive theology, or some combination of the two—should not be surprised at how much resistance they will get. It would be like getting Homer to reject the Devil's Doughnut.

Paul Bloom is a professor of psychology at Yale University who does research on language and development. He is the author of *Descartes' Baby: How the Science of Child Development Explains What Makes Us Human*.

David Pizarro is an assistant professor of psychology at Cornell University. His research interests include moral judgment and the influence of emotion on judgment.

# Alcohol—The Cause of, and Solution to, All Life's Problems

## Denis M. McCarthy

I T'S FAIR TO SAY that we are of two minds about alcohol. In the U.S. about half of the population over twelve report being current drinkers (1). Alcohol abuse is a serious health problem, and is estimated to cost the U.S. over $184 billion a year in health care, lost productivity, accidents and other effects (2). On the other hand, recent research has demonstrated health benefits from regular moderate use of alcohol (3). Increasing legal limits on cigarettes in public places have raised some eyebrows, such as the recent move in New Jersey to ban smoking in cars. However, cigarette smoking is permitted at earlier ages and in more places than alcohol consumption. Alcohol is also the only product that has been the cause of two U.S. Constitutional amendments. The fact that one of these amendments repealed the other illustrates my point. We may be "Listening to Prozac" (4), but our culture is having a discussion with alcohol.

The people of Springfield have as complicated a relationship with alcohol as the citizens of any U.S. town, fictional or not. Alcohol has played a central role in many individual episodes, as well as influencing the lives and behaviors of many Simpsons characters. As satire, *The*

*Simpsons* should not only make us laugh, but also give us some insight into our own lives. What can we learn about alcohol use from the seventeen seasons of *The Simpsons*?

This essay will focus on two important alcohol-related issues. The first issue concerns what constitutes an "alcohol problem." Three *Simpsons* characters at some point have been identified as having a problem with their alcohol use: Homer, Barney and Ned (yes, Ned Flanders). What do the very different drinking patterns of these three characters say about when alcohol use should be considered a problem?

A second issue is determining who is at risk for developing alcohol problems. Are Bart, Lisa or Maggie likely to develop alcohol problems later in life? From what we know about their parents, home environment and behavior, what level of risk, if any, do the three Simpson children have of developing alcohol dependence?

## Defining Alcohol Use Disorders: Do Homer, Barney and Ned Have the Same Problem?

At what point does the use of alcohol become a problem? When does normal drinking turn into alcoholism or alcohol dependence (5)? We have long recognized that alcohol use can be more problematic for some people than for others. But locating the line between recreational use of alcohol and an alcohol problem is not easy. Are there a certain number of drinks per week that define dependence, or do the number or severity of problems from alcohol that someone experiences define it?

As a psychologist who studies alcohol use behavior, I am particularly concerned with how the scientific and professional field defines alcohol dependence, and the criteria for a formal diagnosis of this disorder. However, the majority of people who have alcohol problems do not consult professionals. Millions of people are members of Alcoholics Anonymous, a nonprofessional society dedicated to helping people stay sober. There is also evidence that a large proportion of people who use alcohol heavily reduce or discontinue use without any assistance (6). So while a considerable amount of research and theory has gone into determining a professional definition of alcohol dependence, this definition is only applied in a minority of cases.

At least three *Simpsons* characters have at some point determined that they have a problem with alcohol—Barney, Ned and Homer. How was this determination made, and what does it say about our perception of alcohol problems? Barney and Ned are two ends of a single continuum. Barney's drinking is so problematic that everyone (including him) agrees he has a problem. Ned's drinking, and his problems from it, are so minor that only he thinks he has a problem. Homer is somewhere in the middle. Both he and his family seem undecided about his alcohol use—sometimes treating it as a problem, other times not. For Barney and Ned, I want to talk about two different types of subjective standards for alcohol problems—consensus opinion and personal decision. For Homer, since his own and his family's judgment are unclear, I will see whether he meets an objective definition of alcohol abuse or dependence.

> LISA: Mr. Gumble, this is a Girl Scout meeting.
> BARNEY: Is it? Or is it that you girls can't admit you have a problem?

Barney Gumble is an example of someone whose struggles with alcohol are considered a problem by consensus—when everyone, including Barney, agrees that his use of alcohol causes significant problems. Barney is a satirical/extreme example of this—he drank beer from the tap in Moe's until his heart stopped, and had a Duff Beer truck hooked to an IV. But in the real world there are times when someone's problems with alcohol use are so clear that there is no question in anyone's mind that they have a problem. We don't have to decide where the line is between normal alcohol use and problem use with Barney, since we know that wherever it is, he has crossed it.

A common problem with this "common sense" definition is that very often everyone agrees except the one with the problem. As many who have been close to someone with alcohol dependence can tell you, people often don't recognize their alcohol use as a problem, even when it is extreme. This is often referred to as denial. Barney himself does not seem to truly experience denial. He accepts his alcohol use is a problem, but is only intermittently motivated to do something about it, and is unable to maintain sobriety when he does. Although people sometimes view denial as unique to alcohol or substance dependence, failing to recognize that you have a problem happens with other mental disorders as well. For example, both Ted Kaczynski and Colin Ferguson denied having mental disorders despite overwhelming evidence to the contrary. Kaczynski, "the Unabomber," refused to use the insanity defense despite being diagnosed with paranoid schizophrenia. Ferguson, the gunman who shot twenty-five people on the Long Island Railroad, also refused the insanity defense. Despite being apprehended during the shooting, he insisted he was framed, defended himself and compared himself with John the Baptist during closing arguments.

A common-sense standard may seem intellectually lazy or simplistic. But it is not an unreasonable standard for difficult-to-define concepts. The U.S. Supreme Court has often struggled with an explicit definition of obscenity. One justice famously concluded that such an explicit definition was not necessary, since he said, "I know it when I see it" (7). But not everyone knew it when they saw it, since cases were brought to the Court only when there was a disagreement over whether something was obscene or not. Like obscenity, alcohol dependence does not always meet the standard of being clear by consensus.

NED: Ann Landers is a boring old biddy.

Ned Flanders is an example of someone who made a personal decision that he has a problem with alcohol. Again, he is a satirical or extreme version of this—he most likely would not be thought to have a problem by any other standard. In some ways, defining alcohol problems through personal decision is very appealing—who better to decide whether someone has a problem with alcohol than the person him/herself? He or she is the only one who is present every time they drink, and the only one to observe and understand the full consequences of their use.

There are two difficulties with this standard. The most obvious I already mentioned—many people are reluctant or unable to see they have a problem with alcohol. This can be thought of as a "false negative," or deciding that an alcohol problem does not exist when it in fact does.

But what about the flip side of false negatives—false positives? False positives are when we identify a problem as present when it is not. Is Ned a false positive? The basis for his decision that he had an alcohol problem was after his "first and last blackberry schnapps," which resulted in the outburst about Ann Landers. Ned described himself as "more animal than man" while under the influence of a single drink.

It is easy to dismiss Ned's self-definition as a false positive—as an overreaction by a somewhat uptight man. However, it raises the interesting question of whether false positives are possible by a personal standard. Can you define yourself as having a problem with alcohol and be incorrect? Compare this to physical disorders—it does not matter if you think you have a broken leg or emphysema, if your leg is intact or your lungs are in fact healthy (well, it does matter, but only in the sense that you may have a different type of problem, rather than the one you think you have). Does the same hold true for alcohol problems? If someone believes that alcohol use has caused them significant problems, in what way can their decision be deemed incorrect? If they believe they need help to refrain from using again, by what criteria can someone else decide they do not need this help?

In Ned's case, his decision seems to indicate a fair degree of insight into himself. Following the death of his wife, Ned's infrequent experiences with alcohol caused him some significant problems, including getting married to a Vegas showgirl during an alcohol-induced blackout. Ned's insight into his own potential for problems from alcohol make the argument that, while false negatives are possible by the personal standard, false positives are not. People can be mistaken when they deny they have an alcohol problem, but maybe they cannot be mistaken when they decide that they do have a problem.

> MOVEMENTARIAN WOMAN: Would you rather have beer, or complete and utter contentment?
> HOMER: What kind of beer?

So we don't need to define alcohol dependence for Barney, since he obviously has a problem with alcohol. It is also probably safe to allow people like Ned to subjectively define themselves as having an alcohol problem. But in Homer's case, such judgment calls are not sufficient. If there is a line between normal use and dependence, Homer and his family are not always clear about which side of it he is on. In such cases, it is useful to rely on an objective standard that specifies characteristics, behaviors, or symptoms that define when someone has an alcohol problem. In the field of mental health, objective evaluation using formal diagnostic criteria has increasingly become the standard for determining when someone has a mental disorder, including alcohol and substance use disorders. Working as a researcher, I am admittedly biased toward this method, as explicit and objective diagnostic criteria are essential to the scientific study of alcohol use disorders.

A great deal of time and energy has been spent on deciding what explicit criteria should be used for mental health disorders. Today the American Psychiatric Association's *Diagnostic and Statistical Manual* (DSM) is by far the most often used and well-studied set of diagnostic criteria for mental disorders in the U.S. Coming up with the criteria for these disorders has been a long process. As many as thirty-nine different diagnostic systems were proposed prior to 1940 for alcohol use disorders (8). The DSM is currently in its fourth revision, and work has begun on a fifth.

The current DSM criteria are the same for all substance use disorders, from alcohol to nicotine to opiates. These diagnoses are based on Edwards & Gross' (9) conceptualization of the dependence syndrome. Most people think of someone as being "dependent" on a substance when they have a physiological need for it, demonstrated by symptoms like tolerance to the substance, and withdrawal if use is discontinued. But the dependence syndrome is not based only on physiology. Instead, the syndrome reflects a progressive problem where use of the substance becomes increasingly important in the person's life and leads to the exclusion of other important activities. A distinction is also made between dependence and a lower level of problematic involvement, which is labeled abuse. This distinction allows for differentiating between people with full dependence and a lower level of problems that might still require treatment. The current diagnostic criteria for dependence and abuse are presented in Table 1.

No one argues that these criteria for alcohol dependence are perfect. Instead, the symptoms are designed to serve as "fallible indicators" of the disorder (10). What do I mean by fallible indicators? Again, an example from physical illness is illustrative. Multiple Sclerosis (MS) has a large number of possible symptoms, such as vision problems, pain, fatigue and dizziness. Not everyone with MS will exhibit all of these symptoms, and conversely not everyone with these symptoms has MS. These symptoms instead serve as potential indicators of MS. However, MS is also defined by its etiology or cause—myelin loss (what causes the myelin loss is a different question). The symptoms might indicate the disorder, but a clear demonstration of myelin loss is conclusive evidence of MS.

Unfortunately, alcohol dependence and other mental health disorders are not currently definable by their etiology. Instead, we are wholly reliant on the fallible indicators themselves, without any conclusive test we can administer. These indicators, like the judgment standards for Barney and Ned, can incorrectly identify someone as dependent who is not, and can also fail to identify dependence when it is there.

Diagnosis is particularly difficult in Homer's case. DSM symptoms are not a "checklist," like the "Is your spouse a souse?" test that Homer failed. A true diagnostic evaluation would involve an extensive clinical interview conducted by a trained professional, which unfortunately I

## TABLE 1
### DSM-IV Substance Use Disorders Criteria

*Substance Abuse (1 of 4)*

1. Recurrent substance use resulting in failure to fulfill major role obligations.
2. Recurrent substance use in situations in which it is physically hazardous.
3. Recurrent substance-related legal problems.
4. Continued use despite social or interpersonal problems caused or exacerbated by use.

*Substance Dependence (3 or more)*

1. Tolerance—increase in amount needed for intoxication or diminished effect of the same amount.
2. Withdrawal—experiencing physical symptoms after discontinued use, or use of similar substance to avoid these symptoms.
3. Taking the substance in larger amounts or longer than intended.
4. Persistent desire or unsuccessful attempts to cut down or control use.
5. Great deal of time spent obtaining, using, or recovering from the substance.
6. Important social, occupational, or recreational activities are given up or reduced because of use.
7. Use despite having a physical or psychological problem that is caused or exacerbated by use.

Source: American Psychiatric Association (1994). *Diagnostic and Statistical Manual of Mental Disorders* (4th ed.). Washington, DC: American Psychiatric Association.

was not able to conduct with Homer. The diagnostic criteria for dependence also require that symptoms be exhibited within the same twelve-month period. Since it is unclear how much time each season entails, or how much time elapses between episodes, I will be using observations from all of *The Simpsons* seasons. Due to fluctuations in drinking behavior over time, it is possible that Homer would not exhibit any three criteria over any specific twelve-month period.

So, with these caveats in mind, let's see how Homer compares to the diagnostic criteria for alcohol abuse and dependence:

First, let's get alcohol abuse out of the way. Homer certainly meets criteria for alcohol abuse. If nothing else, his repeated DUI troubles warrant symptom two. In a formal interview, I would not spend much time on deciding whether he has alcohol abuse or not, but would move right to dependence.

1. **Tolerance—Yes.** From flashbacks to his adolescence, we know Homer is able to drink larger amounts of alcohol than before. Part of this may be due to his increased weight, but we have enough evidence to show that this is at least in part due to his body developing tolerance to alcohol.

2. **Withdrawal—Maybe.** Withdrawal symptoms vary by substance. For alcohol, they include anxiety, hand tremor, sweating, nausea and transient hallucinations. When Homer did not drink for thirty days, he experienced transient hallucinations of Duff bottles falling from the sky. However, these did not show up until near the end of the thirty-day period. Withdrawal symptoms usually appear within hours or days of stopping use.

3. **Larger/Longer—Yes.** To cite one example of this, when Homer and Marge were estranged, he was late for their reunion date because he continued drinking margaritas with his gay roommates.

4. **Persistent Desire/Unsuccessful Control—Maybe.** Again, Homer has been able to stop drinking. However, he did experience some desire to drink during this period. Whether this desire was persistent or strong enough to merit this symptom is unclear. While he did run to Moe's at the end of the thirty-day period, he also decided not to drink and went bike riding with Marge.

5. **Great Deal of Time—Yes.** Homer spends only slightly less time at Moe's than Barney.

6. **Social/Occupational/Recreational Activities Given up or Reduced—Yes.** One example is that Homer left work early to drink with Larry Burns (Mr. Burns' son, voiced by Rodney Dangerfield), leaving a "Gone Drinkin'" sign at his desk.

7. **Use Despite Exacerbating Problems—Maybe.** Homer does not have an ulcer or a liver problem that his drinking exacerbates. You might argue that his weight problem is increased by his drinking, although I think his eating is more the issue there.

Based on this analysis, Homer meets at least four of the criteria for alcohol dependence. Like twelve percent of U.S. males (1), he would be diagnosable with alcohol dependence.

## Dependence Risk in the Simpson Children

For any disorder, one of the more interesting and important questions is what causes it. Understanding the etiology of something allows us to predict when and for whom it will occur, and possibly reduce or eliminate the disorder by removing the cause or interrupting the causal process in some way. Think of all the benefits modern society has gained from understanding that many diseases are caused by microorganisms (rather than evil spirits or an imbalance of body humors). Vaccines, hospital sterilization and improved sanitation have all been directed at interrupting the causal processes of diseases, with great effect. We could reap similar benefits if we had a complete understanding of the causal process by which someone develops alcohol use disorders.

However, as I mentioned earlier, most mental health problems are not definable by their etiology. For alcohol dependence, the only thing that all alcohol dependent individuals have in common is that they consume alcohol. While on one level alcohol consumption is the primary "cause" of alcohol disorders, it is not very helpful or informative to know this. It is the equivalent of saying that cancer is caused by certain tumors. The etiology of many disorders, such as many types of cancer, Parkinson's disease and most mental illnesses, cannot be defined by a single etiological factor. In these cases, the study of the etiology of the disorder is not deterministic, but rather involves examining probabilities—factors that increase the likelihood of the disorder developing.

A wide range of factors have been found to be associated with alcohol dependence. Some factors make relatively minor changes in liability to the disorder. Others have a large effect on this likelihood, as smoking cigarettes does for many forms of cancer. Research has identified genetic, biological, environmental and behavioral factors that affect the probability of alcohol dependence. In the rest of this essay, I will use this research in an examination of the Simpson family. This is not an exhaustive review of alcohol dependence risk factors. Instead, my goal is to see what light research findings can shed on Bart, Lisa and Maggie's chances of developing alcohol dependence later in life. I will start by reviewing two general factors that apply to all the Simpson children—genetics and familial modeling of alcohol use. I will then contrast risk and protective factors between the Simpson children.

## General Risk Factors

*"Genetics is not an excuse."*
—written on blackboard by Bart

Given that we have decided that Homer meets criteria for alcohol dependence, one contributor to his children's risk for alcohol dependence is genetics. Twin and adoption studies have demonstrated fairly clearly that there is an increase in risk for alcohol dependence from genetic factors (11). Homer's children have a "family history" of alcohol dependence, which makes them more likely than other people to develop alcohol dependence in turn. But the question of what specific genetic factors Homer might have passed to his children that increases their risk is a bit more difficult to determine.

Some human traits and diseases are controlled by single genes. Such traits are often referred to as Mendelian traits, named after the nineteenth-century monk Gregor Mendel. You may remember him from such things as high school or the Discovery Channel. Mendel's work with peas helped form the rules of heredity (one gene from each parent) and expression (dominant/recessive) with which most people are familiar. When a trait is due to a single gene, it mostly follows the rules Mendel laid out. It is relatively easy to discover when something is due to a single gene, and whether it is dominant or recessive, by examining its inheritance patterns. Examples of phenomena due to a single gene include hemophilia, Huntington's disease and the Hapsburg lip (12).

Unfortunately, most diseases are not this simple. Instead they are most often influenced by multiple genes (polygenic). Even characteristics that may be due to one or only a few genes can have their expression (phenotype) so influenced by other genes that they do not behave in Mendelian ways (13). So despite knowing that there is a genetic basis for alcohol dependence, it is not (yet) accurate to say there is a gene (or even a set of genes) for alcohol dependence that Homer has passed on to his children (14).

So what can we say about genetic contributions to the Simpson children's alcohol dependence risk? In the absence of specific genetic data, we can examine two things—density of alcohol dependence in the Simpson-Bouvier family tree, and the presence in that tree of heritable phenotypes or characteristics associated with alcohol dependence. A simple schematic of these factors is presented in Figure 1.

Since Homer has alcohol dependence, we can infer that the Simpson

FIGURE 1
Simpson-Bouvier Family Tree: Alcohol Dependence

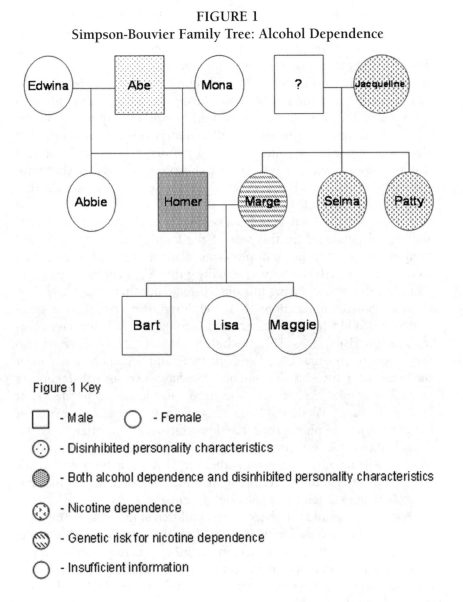

Figure 1 Key

☐ - Male      ◯ - Female

⊙ - Disinhibited personality characteristics

⬤ - Both alcohol dependence and disinhibited personality characteristics

◎ - Nicotine dependence

◍ - Genetic risk for nicotine dependence

◯ - Insufficient information

children have some increase in risk. We would be more convinced that there was a genetic component to Homer's alcohol dependence if there was a high prevalence of alcohol dependence in Homer's ancestors. Abe Simpson does not appear to have had a problem with alcohol. However, in his youth he did exhibit disinhibited personality characteristics such as risk-taking/sensation-seeking. These traits are associated with dependence risk, and we have some evidence that he passed these traits on to Homer (more on personality later). There is circumstantial evidence that Mona Simpson, Homer's mother, may have abused substances. This evidence is flimsy, however, and based only on her background as a radical hippie, and her behavior during the few episodes in which she appears. Of particular interest would be Homer's supposed half-sister, Abbie. Given that she was raised separately from Homer, if she has alcohol dependence, and her biological mother, Edwina, did not, this would be strong evidence for a genetic contribution to risk in the Simpson side of the family. However, we do not have sufficient information about her to determine this.

What about the Bouvier side? There is no real evidence of alcohol abuse or dependence on this side of the family. Although Marge has been in treatment for alcohol problems, she was sent following a DUI conviction of which Homer was actually guilty. She may have met criteria for alcohol abuse during this one episode, but that most likely does not have genetic implications for her children. However, there is some evidence that alcohol dependence and nicotine dependence have common genetic risk factors (15). Alcohol and nicotine dependence are also very likely to co-occur (16, 17). Both Patty and Selma obviously meet the criteria for nicotine dependence. We have also seen their mother Jacqueline smoke. So she may also have had nicotine dependence, at least at one point. We do not know enough about Marge's father (except that he was a baby photographer and possibly an airline attendant). Although Marge does not smoke, it is possible that the Bouvier family has some genetic liability to nicotine addiction. This would increase the risk of the Simpson children developing nicotine addiction later in life, and possibly increase their risk of alcohol dependence.

Overall, this would put the Simpson children at moderate to high genetic risk. They have a family history of alcohol dependence from one side, and of nicotine dependence on the other. There is also some evidence of disinhibited personality traits on the Simpson side. If we could confirm that either Abbie or Mona had a problem with alcohol, their genetic risk would be high.

> "Marge, I'm going to Moe's. Send the kids to the neighbors,
> I'm coming back loaded!"

Because the Simpson children are not only biologically related to someone with alcohol dependence, but are also raised by him, their family environment can also increase their alcohol dependence risk. One way parents with alcohol dependence can influence their children's risk is through familial modeling. Children exposed to higher levels of parental alcohol use are more likely to drink at an early age and to develop problems with alcohol.

Most interpretations of this effect are based on social learning theory (18), which posits that a behavior can be learned through vicarious exposure to it. At early ages, children can learn what positive and negative consequences are associated with a behavior by observing the behavior in others. Studies have shown that children who are exposed to high levels of drinking in their home learn to associate more positive reinforcement with alcohol, and this association increases their likelihood of using alcohol (19).

Despite the quote heading this section, Homer often drinks or is drunk in front of his children, thereby modeling excessive alcohol use for his kids. Such parental modeling of alcohol use is a significant risk factor for his children's early initiation into use, and potential later problems with alcohol.

## Specific Factors:
## Bart the Musician and President Lisa

So the Simpson children in general have a few strikes against them so far. But Bart and Lisa are so different. Why is this? Are their differences indicative of differential risk for alcohol dependence? You of course are guessing that Bart is more likely to develop dependence than Lisa, and you would be right. First, males are statistically almost twice as likely to develop dependence (1). Second, differences in parental treatment, personality characteristics, passive-avoidance learning and possibly IQ increase Bart's risk for alcohol dependence. But all is not lost for Bart—there are some positive signs as well, including his relationship with Marge, his peer relationships and the type of delinquent behavior he displays.

*"I am the Lizard Queen!"*

One risk factor for the development of alcohol dependence is early initiation of use. None of the Simpson children have as yet started using substances. True, there has been some substance use by them—Bart drank one St. Patrick's Day and Lisa took a hallucinogen. Studies have shown that those who use alcohol prior to age fourteen are much more likely to develop dependence (20), so it is possible that this early use is a bad sign. However, it's not clear that either of these episodes really count as risk events, as they were both accidents. Research has not been conducted on accidental use of substances in children, and whether such accidental use influences risk.

*"Inside every hardened criminal beats the heart of a ten-year-old boy."*

One of the strongest predictors of alcohol dependence is childhood delinquency. Some theories hypothesize that use of substances and delinquent behavior are part of a family of behaviors with similar underlying causes (21). There is also evidence that delinquent behavior and alcohol use share common genetic vulnerability (22), which may be due to heritable personality characteristics associated with both.

It is therefore useful to examine current delinquent behavior as a risk factor for later alcohol use, as well as common risk and protective factors for future delinquent/addictive behavior. Bart displays many of the signs of early conduct problems, and has several risk factors that may indicate he is at risk for later disruptive and addictive behavior. Bart's conduct problems are many—from harassing Principal Skinner to playing pranks on as many adults as possible. He also seems to be in trouble at school during the opening credits of every episode. Lisa on the other hand has almost no disruptive behavior.

Personality differences between Bart and Lisa are also illustrative. People have long had interest in whether there is such a thing as an "addictive personality." While there is no current scientific basis for a true addictive personality type, there are some personality traits, such as high impulsivity, sensation seeking and behavior undercontrol, that are related to alcohol dependence (23). Bart's desire to be a daredevil is indicative of behavioral undercontrol or high sensation seeking. These personality traits are also heritable (24). As we can see in Figure 1, there is evidence that this personality characteristic is common to Simpson males. Abe was a Hellfish in his youth, and appears to have had high levels of risk taking and sensation seeking. Homer does not display risk-taking behavior per se. However, he does have a high degree of impulsivity (that sometimes leads him to take risks). He also exhibits high sensation seeking, even if most of it is food-related, such as eating chili. If this personality characteristic has a genetic basis, it may be sex-linked in the Simpson family, as Lisa would appear to be low on disinhibited personality characteristics. Instead, her dominant personality traits are most likely conscientiousness or agreeableness—such characteristics as getting along with others and attention to detail are not associated with risk for alcohol dependence.

### "Why, you little...."

Another risk factor for Bart is parental maltreatment. Particularly for boys, childhood maltreatment has been found to be associated with later conduct problems and disruptive behavior (25). Bart has received more frequent and harsher punishment from Homer than the other Simpson children. Homer's treatment of Bart shows signs of neglect (calling him "the boy" for several seasons instead of using his name) and overly punitive punishment (frequent choking at a level that is physically impossible with non-animated children). Lisa is treated quite differently by Homer. Although she is sometimes punished, she is never choked. She is rarely yelled at, unless she goes so far as to make a perpetual motion machine.

### "I am so smart, I am so smart, S-M-R-T...."

Another difference between Bart and Lisa that is related to dependence risk is neurocognitive functioning. Neurocognitive factors, such as IQ, have been found to be negatively correlated with delinquent behavior—lower IQ is related to higher delinquency (26). Lisa obviously has a high IQ, which would lower her risk. However, there is some contradictory evidence about IQ for Bart. On the one hand, Bart is purported to have the Simpson gene for stupidity. To Lisa's relief, this gene is Y-linked (males only). However, we also know that Homer is in fact quite intelligent. The fact that he exhibits such low IQ in most *Simpsons* episodes is due to a crayon he stuck up his nose which presses on his brain. This means that Homer's genotype is for high IQ, while his current phenotype is for low IQ, due to brain damage. Since it is the genotype, not the phenotype, which is passed on to his children, this could imply a potential genetic basis for high IQ in his children. While this is already demonstrably true for Lisa, it is unclear what the future holds for Bart's IQ. To my knowledge, the only test of Bart's IQ was taken by Martin.

### "Is my brother dumber than a hamster?"

But Bart also displays another neurocognitive risk factor—deficits in passive-avoidance learning (27). Passive avoidance is the ability to refrain from responding when punishment is indicated. For example, when children learn to avoid touching a stove when it is hot, they are learning to avoid a behavior (touching) when punishment cues are present (hot stove). A more complex passive-avoidance task would involve a mixed-incentive condition, where both punishment and reward cues are presented at different times. In mixed-incentive tasks, the goal is to learn the cues associated with reward and punishment, to respond when reward cues are present, and to avoid responding when punishment cues are present. Risk for alcohol disorders and conduct problems are associated with deficits in learning to avoid punishment in mixed-incentive conditions. Alcohol consumption can be thought of as a mixed-incentive task—there are both rewards and punishments associated with use. There is some evidence that those who have difficulty learning passive avoidance in mixed-incentive tasks may be more likely to attend to the rewards of alcohol use, and less likely to notice the negative consequences of use (28). This attentional bias, in turn, can increase alcohol use.

Lisa gave Bart just such a mixed-incentive task, wiring a cupcake to an electric shock. Bart displayed significant deficits on this task, like repeated responding in search of reward (cupcake) despite repeated punishment (shock). Although we do not have a quantitative measure of Bart's passive-avoidance deficits, the fact that it was lower than the hamster is not a positive sign.

## Bart the Musician or Bart the Policeman?

Bart has a number of serious risk factors for later acting-out and addictive behaviors, while Lisa does not. Given the combination of general risk in the family, and specific risk for him personally, it is likely that Bart is at risk for developing later problems with alcohol. Professionals working with the Simpson family would likely recommend Bart for early intervention, focusing on both his conduct problems and potentially preventive work concerning substance use.

However, there are three factors that might moderate Bart's risk. First, maternal expressed emotion has been found to be associated with lower problem behaviors (29). Marge appears to express a good deal of emotional warmth toward Bart, her "special little guy." This emotional attachment between Bart and Marge may offer him some degree of protection against later problems.

Peer factors can also play a role in the development of alcohol dependence and acting-out behavior. Having peers who become involved with alcohol use behavior can increase the risk of early initiation and the development of dependence (30). Bart's closest friend, Milhouse, does not appear at significant risk for early initiation or for other acting-out behaviors. Although he does play pranks on others with Bart, he is usually a follower, not a leader in this. It is unlikely for Milhouse to facilitate Bart's initiation into alcohol use.

The type of conduct problems Bart displays may also be of lower concern than other types of disruptive behavior. Bart's delinquent behavior is a mix of authority conflict (with Homer or Principal Skinner) and covert aggression (destruction of property). He almost never displays overt physical aggression, which is associated with more long-term disruptive behavior (31).

These factors may help limit Bart's risk. Although he has a number of strikes against him, his relationship with Marge and his friendship with Milhouse may offer him resources to resist early initiation of use and potentially help him cope with or mature out of possible alcohol or conduct problems later on.

## The Evidence of "Simpson DNA"

The Simpson I am most worried about is Maggie. Like Bart and Lisa, she has both genetic risk and environmental exposure to parental modeling of alcohol use. Although she does not suffer parental maltreatment, she is exposed to the maltreatment of Bart at a younger age than Lisa. You may think that Maggie, because she is female, is more likely to grow up like Lisa, as so many of the Simpson risk factors seem to be more present in males. But due to her age, we do not have much information regarding her neurocognitive functioning or personality characteristics.

But most importantly, Maggie is the only Simpson child to engage in overt, extreme physical aggression. At her tender age, she has already shot Mr. Burns and gunned down a Mafia hit squad. She is also physically threatening of her rival, the uni-brow baby. As noted, early physical aggression has been found to be a unique predictor of later disruptive behavior problems. Maggie appears to be exhibiting this behavior at a very early age.

But aren't females less likely to develop these problems? Yes. However, there is evidence for a "gender paradox" for disorders with an unequal sex ratio (32). What this means is that for problems less prevalent in females, the presence of a risk factor is more strongly associated with later disorder. For a female of her age, Maggie's propensity to shoot adults represents a very significant risk factor. This behavior should raise alarm bells in her family that she is at serious risk for conduct problems and alcohol/substance dependence later in life. And in my opinion, her remorseless wink when she got away with shooting Mr. Burns should keep Homer and the rest of Springfield awake at night.

# References

1. Substance Abuse and Mental Health Services Administration. (2004). *Results from the 2003 National Survey on Drug Use and Health: National Findings* (Office of Applied Studies, NSDUH Series H—25, DHHS Publication No. SMA 04—3964). Rockville, MD.
2. Estimate is for the year 1998, taken from Harwood, H. (2000). *Updating Estimates of the Economic Costs of Alcohol Abuse in the United States: Estimates, Update Methods, and Data*, report prepared by the Lewin Group for the National Institute on Alcohol Abuse and Alcoholism.
3. Klatsky, A. L. (1999). "Moderate Drinking and Reduced Risk of Heart Disease." *Alcohol Research and Health, 23,* 15–24.
4. Kramer, P. D. (1997). *Listening to Prozac: The Landmark Book About Antidepressants and the Remaking of the Self, Revised Edition.* New York: Penguin Books.
5. A note on terminology: In the U.S., the term 'alcoholism' has traditionally been used to describe severe alcohol problems, and it remains in frequent use in both the public and professional arenas. For many purposes, the term 'alcoholism' and the DSM diagnostic category of alcohol dependence are thought to be equivalent. For sake of clarity, in this essay I use the terminology of alcohol dependence and alcohol abuse from the current DSM.
6. Dawson, D. A., Grant, B. F., Stinson, F. S., Chou, P. S., Huang, B., & Ruan, W. J. (2005). "Recovery from DSM-IV alcohol dependence: United States, 2001–2002." *Addiction, 100,* 281–292.
7. *Jacobellis v. Ohio,* 378 U.S. 184 (1964).
8. Schuckit, M. A. (1994). "DSM-IV: Was it Worth All the Fuss?" *Alcohol and Alcoholism, suppl 2,* 459–469.
9. Edwards, G., & Gross, M. M. (1976). "Alcohol Dependence: Provisional Description of a Clinical Syndrome." *British Medical Journal, 1,* 1058–1061.
10. Frances, A. J., First, M. B., Widiger, T. A, Miele, G. M. et al. (1991). "An A to Z Guide to DSM-IV Conundrums." *Journal of Abnormal Psychology. 100,* 407–412.
11. Heath, A. C. (1995) "Genetic Influences on Alcoholism Risk? A Review of Adoption and Twin Studies." *Alcohol Health and Research World, 19,* 166–171.
12. Watson, J. D. & Berry, A. (2003) *DNA.* Knopf, New York, p. 312.
13. Glazier, A. M., Nadeau, J. H., Aitman, T. J. (2002). "Finding Genes that Underlie Complex Traits." *Science, 298,* 2345–2349.

14. For an interesting, easy-to-follow discussion of what it means to say we have a "gene for" something, see Kendler, K. S. (2005). "'A gene for…': The Nature of Gene Action in Psychiatric Disorders." *American Journal of Psychiatry, 162,* 1243–1252.

15. True, W. R. et al. (1999). "Common Genetic Vulnerability for Nicotine and Alcohol Dependence in Men." *Archives of General Psychiatry, 56,* 655–661.

16. Breslau, N. (1995). "Psychiatric Comorbidity of Smoking and Nicotine Dependence." *Behavior Genetics, 25,* 95–101.

17. Knight, J. R., Wechsler, H., Kuo, M., Seibring, M., Weitzman, E. R., Schuckit, M. A. (2002). "Alcohol Abuse and Dependence Among U.S. College Students." *Journal of Studies on Alcohol, 63,* 263–270.

18. Bandura, A. (1977). *Social Learning Theory.* Englewood Cliffs, NJ: Prentice Hall.

19. Brown, S. A., Tate, S. R., Vik, P. W., Haas, A. L., & Aarons, G.A. (1999). "Modeling of Alcohol Use Mediates the Effect of Family History of Alcoholism on Adolescent Alcohol Expectancies." *Experimental Clinical Psychopharmacology, 7,* 20–27.

20. Grant, B. F., Dawson, D. A., Stinson, F. S., Chou, S. P., Dufour, M. C., & Pickering, R. P. (2004). "The 12-Month Prevalence and Trends in DSM-IV Alcohol Abuse and Dependence: United States, 1991–1992 and 2001–2002." *Drug and Alcohol Dependence, 74,* 223–234.

21. Donovan, J. E., Jessor, R., Costa, F. M. (1988). "Syndrome of Problem Behavior in Adolescence: A Replication." *Journal of Consulting & Clinical Psychology, 56,* 762–765.

22. Slutske, W. S., Heath, A. C., Dinwiddie, S. H., Madden, P. A. F., Bucholz, K. K., Dunne, M. P., Statham, D. J., Martin, N. G. (1998). "Common Genetic Risk Factors for Conduct Disorder and Alcohol Dependence." *Journal of Abnormal Psychology, 107,* 363–374.

23. Sher, K. J., & Trull, T. J. (2004). "Personality and Disinhibitory Psychopathology: Alcoholism and Antisocial Personality Disorder." *Journal of Abnormal Psychology, 103,* 92–102.

24. Slutske, W. S., Heath, A. C., Madden, P. A. F., Bucholz, K. K.; Statham, D. J., Martin, N. G. (2002). "Personality and the Genetic Risk for Alcohol Dependence." *Journal of Abnormal Psychology. 111,* 124–133.

25. Widom, C. S. (1989). "The Cycle of Violence." *Science, 244,* 160–166.

26. Lynam, D., Moffitt, T., & Stouthamer-Loeber, M. (1993). "Explaining the Relation Between IQ and Delinquency: Class, Race, Test Motivation, School Failure or Self-Control?" *Journal of Abnormal Psychology, 102,* 187–196.

27. Lynam, D. R. (1996). "Early Identification of Chronic Offenders: Who is the Fledgling Psychopath?" *Psychological Bulletin, 120,* 209–234.

28. McCarthy, D. M., Kroll, L. S., & Smith, G. T. (2001). "Integrating Disinhibition and Learning Risk for Alcohol Use." *Experimental and Clinical Psychopharmacology, 9,* 4, 389–398.

29. Caspi, A., Moffitt, T. E., Morgan, J., Rutter, M., Taylor, A., Arseneault, L. et al. (2004). "Maternal Expressed Emotion Predicts Children's Antisocial Behavior Problems: Using Monozygotic-Twin Differences to Identify Environmental Effects on Behavioral Development." *Developmental Psychology, 40,* 149–161.
30. Curran, P. J., Chassin, L., & Stice, E. (1997). "The Relation Between Adolescent Alcohol Use and Peer Alcohol Use: A Longitudinal Random Coefficients Model." *Journal of Consulting & Clinical Psychology, 65,* 130–140.
31. White, H. R., Bates, M. E., Buyske, S. (2001). "Adolescence-Limited Versus Persistent Delinquency: Extending Moffitt's Hypothesis into Adulthood." *Journal of Abnormal Psychology, 110,* 600–609.
32. Loeber, R. & Keenan, K. (1994). "The Interaction Between Conduct Disorder and its Comorbid Conditions: Effects of Age and Gender." *Clinical Psychology Review, 14,* 497–523.

Denis M. McCarthy is originally from Long Island, NY. He received his bachelor's degree in psychology and philosophy from the University of Notre Dame and his Ph.D. in clinical psychology from the University of Kentucky. His research focuses on examining factors (e.g., personality traits, genetic differences) that influence what people learn about alcohol use and alcohol-related behavior. He is currently an assistant professor in the Department of Psychological Sciences at the University of Missouri.

# The Cafeteria Deep Fryer Is Not a Toy

### Mike Byrne

**M**URPHY'S LAW is usually stated as "if anything can go wrong, it will."[1] Yet somehow, Murphy is not a major character on *The Simpsons*. This seems surprising (he could at least be an occasional patron at Moe's or an irregular customer at the Kwik-E-Mart) since mishaps involving, well, just about everything are a long-standing tradition in *The Simpsons*. In this essay I want to focus on mishaps involving technology, or more precisely, artifacts that were designed by people to be used by other people. This obviously includes a wide array of things, from dolls to trains to nuclear power plants. It does exclude a great many other classes of misadventure, though, such as those involving elephants, mobsters, lightning strikes, sexy coworkers, deals with Sa-

---

[1] It turns out this isn't what Murphy actually said. Murphy was an Air Force engineer and he had discovered that a technician had made a mistake installing a part and said, "If there is any way to do it wrong, he'll find it." How it evolved into its current form is not entirely clear.

tan for a doughnut[2] and the like. The discipline devoted to the study of human interaction with technology is termed *human factors*. People in human factors are, as often as not, psychologists. Obviously—or maybe not so obviously based on some of the e-mail I get—these psychologists are not of the "lie on the couch and tell me about your mother" variety. Human factors professionals are concerned with understanding human capabilities and limitations and applying that understanding to the design and operation of technological systems. This involves everything from biomechanics (i.e., the physics of muscles and bones) to human cognition, including perception, memory, decision-making and so on. The dominant backgrounds of human factors people are therefore in psychology and engineering (generally industrial engineering). Many human factors-oriented programs in psychology go by the name *engineering psychology*. Because computers have become such a dominant technology, a particularly rich domain in human factors is focused there and is termed *human-computer interaction* (HCI for short), and also involves computer scientists.[3] Human factors is not merely an academic discipline; human factors specialists work in a variety of industries and large corporations, government agencies, consulting firms and elsewhere.

All well and good, but what does this have to do with *The Simpsons*? There are numerous connections, but the most obvious one is Homer's place of employment, the nuclear power plant. The nuclear power industry has long been a consumer of human factors knowledge, as accidents and errors in the operation of such plants have the potential for truly spectacular consequences (much more than simply a green glow, as often seen on the show). This was first made clear with the incident at Three Mile Island and firmly reinforced with the Chernobyl accident.[4] A not dissimilar disaster occurred at the Union Carbide plant in Bhopal, India, which resulted in many more fatalities than the two nuclear

---

[2] All of which were, in fact, mishaps encountered by the Simpsons, mostly in the fourth and fifth seasons. I'm going to focus on those seasons for several reasons. First, because seasons four through eight are regarded by many as the golden years; second, because of those seasons, only seasons four and five are available in their entirety on DVD so readers can easily see them; and third, because those episodes aired in the early part of my graduate career when I had time to do things like watch cartoons on TV, so I actually saw many of them pre-syndication.

[3] I have degrees in engineering, computer science and psychology. This is wholly unnecessary—training in just one area is generally sufficient. All a record like mine is good for is keeping document framers in business.

[4] For readers too young to recollect either of these events (both of which happened before most current university students could possibly remember), I highly recommend asking your parents. OK, seriously, try Google.

events.[5] All of these high-profile events occurred because of a rare confluence of physical plant failures (i.e., a stuck valve) and human error.

Of course, on *The Simpsons*, such events are not so rare, but they do illustrate some of the principles which actually contributed to the real events. One of them is the complexity of the power plant environment itself. Homer's workstation is always portrayed as a huge bank of mostly undifferentiated buttons, knobs, dials, gauges, indicators, etc. In fact, this is not far from real control rooms. These displays have traditionally been designed by engineers more concerned with space efficiency than how well the displays map onto human capabilities. For example, people find monitoring of multiple changing values fairly difficult even when those values are all on displays which are right next to each other. Imagine a screen with six dials on it, all of them changing, and trying to watch for various configurations, like "dial A over 300 with dial B between 50 and 125 and dial C less than 475." Now imagine trying to keep track of ten such configurations. Now imagine the dials are not all next to each other, but on completely different panels—sometimes even in different rooms! Humans have limits, and such environments supremely tax both the perceptual and memory systems of the plant operators. So Homer's confoundingly complex control room is not an exaggeration at all.

In fact, I have often wondered whether the synergy between Homer and nuclear power is based on a real incident from a nuclear power plant. One of the properties of people is that we are highly sensitive to what is called *stimulus-response compatibility*. Imagine that you're looking at a blank screen and you're holding onto a joystick or some similar control. A light comes on. If the light is on the left side of the screen, move the joystick to the left, and if it's on the right, move it to the right. Easy, right? Here, the stimulus (the light) and the response (the joystick) match, or are compatible. Now consider what happens if the task is changed such that if the light appears on the left, you are to move the joystick right, not left. This task—the incompatible task—is harder, and people are much slower at it. In fact, even after thousands of trials of practice, people still find this harder than the compatible task. Furthermore, in complex situations where some controls have compatible movements and some incompatible, remembering which is which can

---

[5] In 1984 the Union Carbide plant in Bhopal released a cloud of highly toxic gas, methyl isocyanate, killing at least 3,800 people and since implicated in numerous other health problems in the region, such as increased cancer rates. The exact causes are to this day the subject of legal proceedings (the CEO of Union Carbide is under indictment in India for homicide but has not been extradited by the U.S.), but it has been widely suggested that things like poor maintenance, incomplete safety procedures, and staff reductions were significant contributors.

be very difficult. This difficulty is amplified if all the relevant controls lack any kind of perceptual differentiation.

And this has what to do with Homer Simpson and nuclear power? As it turns out, in one actual nuclear power plant control room, there were too many identical levers which required different movements and the operators had trouble remembering which was which and in which direction to move them. So they replaced the tops of the levers with...beer taps![6] What could possibly be more Homer-esque?

Homer managed to illustrate, albeit indirectly, another reason why power plants (and many other large complex systems, for that matter) are so dangerous when he managed to miss his morning doughnut at work, and went off in desperate search of one. He retrieved a truly enormous tome labeled "Emergency Procedures."[7] Fortunately there wasn't a plant emergency (only a doughnut emergency), but this points to exactly the kind of problem that real operators have on their hands when things go wrong. Consulting a book about what to do is not the same as knowing what to do; in psychology, this is often referred to as the distinction between *declarative* knowledge (knowing what) and *procedural* knowledge (knowing how). For example, you can go read as many books as you like on how to ride a bike, but at the end of it, you still won't really know how to ride a bike. The same is true for complex problem-solving. Resorting to procedures in a manual is just not the same as knowing what to do. Of course, plant operators have a great deal of training and many have years of real experience. The problem is that the kinds of situations that lead to serious mishaps are intrinsically unusual. In fact, in the interests of safety, the plant designers certainly do everything they can to make such situations uncommon. But it is exactly the unfamiliarity of the situation which makes it difficult for the operators to figure out what to do to fix it. High-fidelity simulation, which is a relatively recent development, can certainly help expose operators to unusual situations without endangering the plant, but because the simulators themselves are highly complex and expensive, such training is not easy to come by, at least in the nuclear power industry. So operators are often at something of a loss as to what to do, and experimentation can be dangerous. Homer illustrated this nicely[8] when his competence

---

[6] Really. I did not make that up.

[7] This was in the episode "Treehouse of Horror IV" right before Homer sells his soul to the devil (who turns out to be Flanders).

[8] This was in the episode "Homer Goes to College." The first third or so of this episode is a human factors tour de force.

was tested by a government agency in a simulator. They simulated an emergency event, and Homer panicked. His response? "Just poke blindly at the controls until they let you go." Somehow Homer managed to cause a meltdown in the simulator—quite a feat considering that it had no nuclear material, being just a simulator.

One of my other favorite Homer-at-work moments comes from the same episode. Homer was dozing in the control room and accidentally hit a big red button labeled "PLANT DESTRUCT DO NOT PUSH." To the best of my knowledge, nuclear power plants do not have such buttons. However, what may be surprising are the number of lights and buttons in everything from nuclear power plants to everyday devices which have unusual, useless, dangerous or misleading functions. I'd be willing to wager that more than half of the readers of this chapter have at least one remote control which has at least one button on it that has no apparent use. To go back to the nuclear power plant, a contributing factor to the Three Mile Island disaster was an indicator light for a water flow valve. This valve was stuck open and allowing coolant to drain from the reactor. Plant operators mistakenly believed that a part of the reactor was dangerously close to overflowing so they cut back on emergency coolant, when in fact the reactor was overheating and needed more coolant—largely because of one indicator light.

What would be the obvious thing for an indicator light on a valve to indicate? Most would answer "whether the valve is open or closed." That's what the Three Mile Island operators thought as well. In fact, what the light indicated was whether or not the valve had been *commanded* shut, not whether it was *actually* shut. It took plant operators considerable time to realize that while the light suggested that the valve was shut, it was actually stuck open. I can just imagine one of the plant operators, using the "whining Homer" voice, saying "But the light says it's shut."

Returning to Homer's accidental pressing of that button, pressing this button raises the obvious question: how were Homer and the rest of the plant saved? Fortunately for everyone, there was a dog asleep at Homer's feet. The dog awoke and pulled a lever on the console, causing the P.A. to announce "meltdown averted, good boy." Now wait, I can hear some readers wondering, do human factors people also study the psychology of dogs? Generally speaking, no. But there is a joke involving a dog that gets told from time to time in the aviation psychology community, which is of course made up primarily of human factors people in the aviation industry. Aviation has a special relationship with human factors, because to a large degree, aviation is where human factors was born. Anyway, as technology has progressed, more and more of the job a pilot does, particularly a commercial pilot flying something like a 757, could be automated by the engineers. This trend is so pervasive it has led to this joke: In the cockpit of the future, there will be a pilot and a dog. The pilot's job will be to pet the dog, feed the dog, and generally make sure the dog is happy and comfortable. The dog's job, of course, will be to bite the pilot if he tries to touch anything. This is another situation which isn't hard to imagine making an appearance in a *Simpsons'* episode.

Of course, there is no shortage of human factors problems and Simpsons mishaps involving transportation. An excellent episode which showcases this is "Marge vs. the Monorail." Poor Homer won the job of monorail conductor and was at the controls when the inevitable disaster struck. Homer even did the right thing by pulling on the brake lever, but he was greeted by the message "The lever you have pulled is not in service" over the P.A. This time it really was not Homer's fault, but rather the fault of the shady Lyle Lanley, who sold the monorail to Springfield and cut every corner possible in building it.[9] Overzealous corner-cutting seems like an obvious thing to avoid in safety-critical systems such as transportation, but this problem is not limited to *The Simpsons*.

Consider the story of the English cross-Channel car ferry *Herald of Free Enterprise*. This ferry had large doors on the bow to allow cars to drive into the ship. However, it was impossible to see from the bridge whether or not the bow doors were open. After an incident of a similar ship going to sea with doors open, one ship captain had requested that an indicator light be installed so the bridge crew could tell if the door was open. It is estimated that this would have cost somewhere in the £400–500 range (about a thousand U.S. dollars) to fit the ships with such a light, but in a move which would make Mr. Burns proud, the company's management chose not to do so. The *Herald* set off across the Channel with bow doors open, took on too much water, and capsized. Fortunately, she came to rest on a sandbank and "only" 189 of the 459 people aboard perished.

Of course, this disaster was not driven entirely by the lack of a warning light; substantial Homer-like human error was involved as well. In particular, the assistant bosun, whose job it was to actually close the bow doors, went to sleep in his cabin without first closing the bow doors. There were various other crew members who might have noticed

---

[9] The picture of the famous Hindenburg disaster on the wall on the inside of the monorail train should have been a subtle clue to the residents of Springfield.

the problem and reported it to the captain, but none did, in part because it was not clearly laid out in the procedures exactly whose job it was to do so. Again, it's not hard to imagine any number of Springfield residents failing to perform a safety check because they weren't sure that was in their job description. In fact, that's not far from what happened in "Bart's Inner Child": the grandstand collapsed and the ferris wheel came loose because people failed to do their safety-critical jobs.[10]

More mundane than monorails and ferris wheels is the humble automobile. The safety issues with cars are not to be sneezed at, as the annual death toll in the United States for automobile accidents typically numbers around 40,000.[11] In 2002, motor vehicle accidents were the leading cause of death in the U.S. for ages 4–34.[12] Most people tend to underestimate this risk,[13] perhaps in part because it usually claims only a few lives at a time, as opposed to the big-headline disasters. The Simpsons and their fellow Springfieldians are certainly no strangers to automobile accidents, though somehow the "fatality" part is usually omitted. The number of cars wrecked over the decade-plus years the show has been on is surely impressive.[14] While of course there are numerous moments of comic negligence, there are also some interestingly accurate incidents. One thing most people are surprised to learn is that some thirty percent of the total motor vehicle fatalities come from *single-vehicle* accidents, such as driving into ditches, collisions with medians, and so on.[15] Poor Homer wasn't even being negligent[16] when he totaled his

---

[10] In this case, it was because they were listening to their inner children and "didn't feel like it," rather than because of job role confusion, but the results were similar.

[11] Different agencies and organizations report somewhat different numbers for this. Not surprisingly, transportation industry groups almost always use a more stringent criterion for inclusion and report smaller numbers.

[12] NHTSA report January 2005. "Motor vehicle traffic crashes as a leading cause of death in the United States, 2002." Available at www-nrd.nhtsa.dot.gov/pdf/nrd-30/NCSA/RNotes/2005/809831.pdf.

[13] I'm always amused by the irony when someone drops me off at the airport and says "Have a safe trip," since the drive back from the airport is substantially more dangerous than any flight I'm likely to take.

[14] Though probably still less than in the movie *The Blues Brothers*. See it if you haven't yet and you enjoy car wrecks. Actually, see it even if you don't—it's funny.

[15] In fact, there is a feature now available on many cars which substantially reduces the risk of single-vehicle accidents. Different manufacturers use different names for it, usually something like "stability control." The Insurance Institute for Highway Safety estimates that approximately 7,000 lives per year would be saved in the U.S. if all cars and light trucks (which includes SUVs) had this feature. Mr. Burns, of course, would oppose such a feature being mandatory if he owned a car company because it might cut into his bottom line.

[16] Well, OK, not that negligent. For Homer.

car in his own driveway in "Mr. Snow," it was simply that in the blizzard conditions the poor visibility made avoiding an accident very difficult. Homer is not alone in having this problem: Poor visibility is a contributing factor in many car crashes, especially at night.

To take the spotlight off Homer for a moment, one of my favorite Bart pranks involves automobiles, although no crashes were involved. In "The Last Temptation of Homer" Bart repainted the lines in the staff parking lot, creating especially narrow spaces. All of the school staff, of course, became very irate with one another because they'd all parked too close. Besides being fiendishly clever, this prank relies on one of the features of the human perceptual system which is often unappreciated but is critical to understand in designing for use by people. It is this: people are generally very bad at judging absolute magnitudes. This is true for all kinds of dimensions such as size, distance, loudness, etc. When shown a scene with two objects in it, people usually do not have a hard time judging which object is closer. However, judgment of the absolute distance to either object is likely to be poor. It turns out even relative judgment has its quirks, but these quirks are systematic. If you show people two lines, one 1" long and the other 1.25" long and ask them which is larger, people can do this task fairly quickly and accurately. But that same difference of 0.25" is much harder to get right (that is, people are slower and make more errors) if the two lines are 10" and 10.25" long. To get the same speed and accuracy out of people, the two lines would have to be 10" and 12.5" inches long. The fact that the difference required scales in proportion to the absolute size is called Weber's Law. The lesson here for future Barts is that for this prank to work, all the new spaces need to be the same size, because people are good at picking out the differences (but won't notice the absolute change until after the fact), and the smaller the spaces, the more accurately they have to match.

The final frontier in transportation is, in fact, the final frontier: space travel. Space flight raises all kinds of human factors issues, some of which have even been faced by (who else?) Homer. One of many special problems faced by people traveling in space is microgravity, often called "zero-g." For example, there is a group of human factors professionals at NASA's Johnson Space Center who spend a fair amount of time worrying about foot restraints.[17] Why? Because astronauts have returned

---

[17] My wife happens to work in this group. Based on what she deals with at work, you won't see me signing up to become an astronaut. Example: shuttle astronauts have been known to go on liquid diets before and during missions just to avoid the issues generated by the need to pass solids in microgravity. (thankfully, this aspect has not been explored in a Simpsons episode—yet.) You've been warned.

home with blisters on their feet from wedging them into places they shouldn't, so that they can remain still while trying to get things done with both hands. In microgravity, things simply float away. Things like human bodies, even when simply pushing on a latch to a door, but also things like potato chips and ants, as illustrated in "Deep Space Homer."[18] One thing left out in that episode, however, is what happens upon returning to earth. Because of potential hazards like radiation, muscle atrophy and disruption of circadian rhythms, one of the fist things astronauts have to do upon their return to earth is receive a thorough medical evaluation.

Maybe this wasn't included in "Deep Space Homer" because medical mishaps happen in numerous other episodes. Medicine is presently a very "hot" area within human factors, spurred on by an Institute of Medicine report which estimated that some 98,000 fatalities per year could actually be attributed to preventable medical errors.[19] Doctors haven't gotten to the point where treadmill stress tests include flaming hoops and crocodile pits,[20] nor is it routine for ambulance paramedics to inject themselves with morphine and subsequently shock themselves with the defibrillator,[21] but hospitals are dangerous places. Healthcare has become incredibly complex and the people receiving care are obviously not at their peak health. One of the more common and dangerous errors is mis-delivery of medication, either the wrong medicine or the wrong dosage. This is possibly the source of Bart's "I will not prescribe medication" chalkboard duty in "Lisa the Beauty Queen." This problem is certainly exacerbated by failure to understand perceptual confusions people make, such as movements of small perceptual items (such as decimal points) or transposition of letters or syllables (numerous medications have surprisingly similar names). Anesthesiology is another particularly perilous activity that doesn't always leave everyone laughing as they are at the end of "Last Exit to Springfield," when the dentist accidentally leaves open the valve on the laughing gas.

---

[18] This episode is also the source of the classic line "I for one welcome our new insect overlords." I haven't figured out how to put a human factors spin on that one yet, but I couldn't not include it, especially for those fans of fark.com out there.

[19] The report is "To Err Is Human: Building a Safer Health System" by Linda T. Kohn, Janet M. Corrigan, and Molla S. Donaldson, Editors; Committee on Quality of Health Care in America, Institute of Medicine, 2000.

[20] As Dr. Itchy does to patient Scratchy in "Kitty-kill Condition" in the episode entitled "The Heartbroke Kid."

[21] Which Homer does to himself in "Diatribe of a Mad Housewife." Yes, these last two references aren't from the fourth or fifth seasons; I said I would focus on those, not use them exclusively.

As I see my limit on length is looming, I'll cover one final issue, warnings. Sometimes it is indeed very difficult to design systems to make them less error-prone, and many human activities (such as deep frying) are inherently dangerous. A complicating factor is that people do a great deal of learning, especially in problem-solving contexts, by just kind of wandering around and trying things, without necessarily having a clear goal in mind. This leads people to choose behaviors which, in hindsight, can seem amazingly negligent, but which when taken in the context in which they occurred are in fact quite reasonable. One approach designers have taken to help deal with this problem is to put warnings on things. Some warnings are simply bizarre attempts to protect the manufacturer from highly frivolous lawsuits,[22] but others are intended to help people deal with their environment. Of course, the warnings themselves can be horribly botched, as is often illustrated in the Simpsons' universe. For example, Homer put up a "Caution" sign in his yard, unfortunately *after* many people were injured jumping on his new trampoline.[23] My favorite after-the-fact warning came after a particularly grisly Itchy & Scratchy cartoon: "The preceding program contained scenes of extreme violence and should not be viewed by young children."[24] A lot of good that did Homer, who saw the warning after Bart and Lisa had already seen the cartoon. Many of the jokes in *The Simpsons* are simple throwaways, such as the mottos which appear on various institutions, but some of them are actually insightful warnings, such as the motto of Monstromart: "Where shopping is a baffling experience."[25] There's a warning I would really appreciate, when the system designer realizes that the system is horrible and at least warns the consumer. I wonder how many remote controls would merit the same warning.

I can't believe I'm very nearly out of space, because there is so much more great material in *The Simpsons* that I want to cover, like the Bobo-replacement robot (programmed to be just as cuddly as Bobo) which attacks Mr. Burns in "Rosebud," the Ultrahouse 3000, Apu's ninety-six-hour work shift, the implied misadventures in chalkboard discipline, such as the title "silly string is not a nasal spray," and "next time it could

---

[22] My personal favorite is on the back of the sunshade I put inside the windshield of my car when it's parked in the hot Texas sun: Do not drive with shade obstructing view. Really?

[23] In the episode "Bart's Inner Child."

[24] In "Deep Space Homer."

[25] In "Homer and Apu."

be me on the scaffolding," the sleep disruption in "Kamp
many others. If the next time you're watching the show
ber that many of the misadventures are only mild exagger
problems caused by mismatches of technology to the rea.  ....
and limitations of humans, I will have done my job.

## Recommended Further Reading

These are two excellent books which provide a clear and detailed,
though non-technical, introduction to the issues in human factors and
why those issues are important. I start my undergraduate human factors course with these, and student response has been almost univer-
sally positive.

Don Norman's *The Design of Everyday Things* (1988) published by Doubleday/
Basic Books, ISBN 0465067107. Includes a photograph of the beer taps in
the nuclear power plant control room.
Steve Casey's *Set Phasers on Stun* (2nd edition, 1998), published by Aegean,
ISBN 0963617885. This includes an interesting speculative account of the
*Herald of Free Enterprise* accident.

Mike Byrne is an assistant (but hopefully associate by the
time you read this) professor of psychology at Rice University in Houston, Texas, though he grew up in Minneapolis,
Minnesota. He has an advanced love-hate relationship with
all forms of technology, particularly computers. Mike's research is focused on computer simulation of human cognition and performance, in order to better understand how to
design technology which more effectively meshes with human capabilities. When not working, Mike spends most of
his time with his wife and two boys (ages one-and-a-half and
five at the time of this writing), neither of whom will hopefully turn out too much like Bart.

# Righteousness and Relationships

## Feminine Fury in *The Simpsons* or How Marge and Lisa Taught Me to Embrace My Anger

### Sally D. Stabb, Ph.D.

*"The two most dangerous words in the English language are 'Marge Simpson.'"*
—MARGE, "Bart after Dark"

THIS OPENING LINE brings me back to the old saying "Hell hath no fury like a woman scorned." Why is it that a woman's anger is so dreaded? Why is it that girls are told "anger isn't pretty?" Maybe it's because anger works! Marge and Lisa can show you how, but it takes some doing. Compared to many of us, they have really arrived.

First of all, you and I were probably socialized pretty much the same way: People of the feminine persuasion were supposed to be nice and quiet and pretty; those of the masculine ilk could be rougher around the edges and were allowed to stomp around, raise their voices and maybe even throw things or take a slap at someone if they were upset. Anger was a sign of power in a man, but an indicator of being out of control, bitchy and—the ultimate insult—"unladylike" in a woman. And we were threatened with the ultimate consequence: Boys wouldn't like us and we'd never find a husband. (I can just hear Malibu Stacy saying "Let's buy make-up so boys will like us!") Men who were not assertive and competitive were shamed from boyhood by being called "wimp," "wuss," or "gay" (or anything else alluding to homosexuality); they were verbally and physically pushed around or beaten up.

Of course there were also influences from our immediate families, our religions, our cultures. These affect the basic, gendered script for anger and tweak it a little bit. In some cultures, anger and other so-called "negative" emotions are freely expressed and considered part and parcel of a complete life. In some religious perspectives anger is a sin, or at least dangerous and evil. Some families teach all members to suppress anger; others rage.

But in its most simplistic form, the following rules for men and women tend to apply: Women should not show anger. Vulnerable and soft emotions like love, sharing and caring, fear and sadness are all acceptable. Men should show no girly emotions; the one allowable emotion is anger. Happiness is all right for everyone but it must be expressed in keeping with your gender role (no squealing with delight, guys!). This is not to say that aggressive women don't exist or that gentle men who are even ashamed of their angry outbursts are figments of our imagination. However, they are exceptions to what are, perhaps sadly, still very strongly socialized scripts for masculine and feminine behavior.

And since we're talking about anger here, I should tell you that there are some things about anger that are universal, so it's not just a gender thing. Keep in mind that women and girls absolutely do get angry! Anger is the emotion that is most clearly recognized across cultures. Of course there are things that would make anyone angry. These prototypical anger scenarios include being betrayed, being insulted and being treated unfairly. Make no mistake: These are also at the heart of anger in the Simpson family. Research also shows that internally, men and women think angry thoughts at roughly equal frequencies, and experience anger in their bodies in similar ways; it is in the outward expression of anger that the differences between the genders can be seen. So here's a short list from my analysis of Lisa and Marge in their angriest episodes, and many of the topics appear multiple times in the show's history. Most of them fit well into the universal themes of betrayal, insult and injustice:

| Lisa | Marge |
|------|-------|
| Bart's destruction of her work | Treating women as sex objects |
| Congressional bribery and lying | Lying |
| Being used by Bart | Being publicly humiliated |
| Sexism | Violence in the media |
| Being controlled by teachers | Lack of support from Homer |
| Corporate corruption | Being insulted |
| Cruelty to animals | Inconsiderate houseguests |
| Inconsiderate brother and dad | Being tricked |

Yet women are hampered in dealing with these and countless other situations by having internalized many myths about anger. Here are five of the worst ones:

1. Anger always messes up relationships and is always bad
2. Anger destroys your health
3. Anger means you're a weak, emotionally unstable person
4. You can permanently steer clear of anger
5. Anger makes you stupid and makes it difficult to think rationally

One of the reasons these myths have gained such strength is that we tend to confuse two things that are actually different: Anger and aggression. Anger is an emotion. It can't "do" anything. You can be mad as hell and take no action whatsoever. Anger doesn't "make" you do anything. Aggression is a behavior. It is an action. It is anything you do, verbally or physically, with the intention to harm another person (or animal or someone's property). You can be aggressive without being angry. Someone who mugs you is certainly being aggressive, but he or she is not angry at you: You just happened to have an available wallet or purse.

All emotions, anger included, are adaptive in the evolutionary sense; they convey critical social information in split seconds. Human beings are exquisitely tuned to each other's voice tones, micro-facial expressions and body language. An angry scowl tells you in a moment what someone might spend half an hour explaining. The moral of the story is this: There are no bad or negative emotions—it's all in what you choose to do with them.

So what do the women of the *Simpsons* do with *their* anger? Let's take a look at Lisa and Marge and explore some of the mistaken ideas about anger along the way.

## 1. Anger Always Messes up Relationships and Is Always Bad

Well, let's face it. If anger ended all relationships, *The Simpsons* couldn't exist. There'd be nothing to write about. And think about your own relationships—most of the time we have conflict with those closest to us (such as our family and our romantic partners) and we don't inevitably end those relationships. Even the idea that anger is bad, per se, can be debunked. Anger brings essential energy for change—correcting injustice, making life choices and re-aligning relationships that may have been off-track. Marge and Lisa are often angry, and realistically, their bonds with others survive these emotional upheavals. Sometimes their connections to others are even strengthened. Here are some examples:

In "Lisa the Vegetarian," Lisa stops eating meat after imagining the cuddly lamb she played with at the petting zoo becoming her dinner. When Homer ignores her preferences and decides to throw a huge barbeque ("You don't entertain friends with salad!"), Lisa becomes enraged and crashes the party with the riding lawn mower, scattering people, furniture and food everywhere, shouting, "I can't live with this prehistoric carnivore!" After driving the lawn mower into town, Lisa goes into the Kwik-E-Mart and encounters Apu's stash of vegetarian goodies, as well as his rooftop garden, complete with Paul and Linda McCartney. They reassure her that her food preferences are valued, but also encourage her to be more tolerant. Homer, who is now desperate to find his daughter, sees Lisa on the street outside the Kwik-E-Mart. Homer, guilt stricken, says, "It's all my fault!" Lisa counters, "Not this time—it's both of us. I still stand by my beliefs, but I can't defend what I did. Sorry for ruining your barbeque."

Marge, in "Secrets of a Successful Marriage" is livid when Homer, who is teaching a class on how to make relationships work, starts divulging personal information about him and Marge, including details of their sex life. She demands that he stop. When he doesn't, and in fact invites his entire class over to their home for dinner, Marge explodes: "I want this to end! GET OUT! I can't trust you!" Bart says, "I've never seen Mom so mad at Dad!" Homer goes to live in the tree house, becoming progressively more pathetic, disheveled and delusional. Marge holds firm to her anger, but misses Homer at the same time. It is only when Homer comes groveling back, apologizing and claiming that, "I *don't deserve to live without you!" and admitting that all he can give her is "complete and utter dependence" that Marge relents and they make up.*

In both of these scenarios, women use their anger to make an important point, then get into conflict with Homer and end up resolving the conflict when both parties come around to an acceptable agreement.

## 2. Anger Destroys Your Health

This one is a bit trickier, because research actually supports this claim, but only under specific circumstances. Repressed anger and long-term hostile attitudes (always thinking someone is out to get you, interpreting others' behavior as a personal attack) are both related to a host of physical ailments. So is chronic raging, which floods your body with a biochemical downpour and causes stress. However, people who express their anger appropriately and regularly—and don't let it build up—are healthy. This balance between "x" and "y" takes skill and an understanding that emotions wash over us like a wave and then depart if we let them, leaving us freer to make choices informed by those emotions. People feel better when they get their anger out, but a regular pattern of holding it in tight and then exploding wreaks havoc on one's body. See how this gets played out for the Simpson gals:

*Marge unravels on a number of levels in "Brake my Wife, Please." In this episode a series of events leaves Homer without a driver's license, so he either walks everywhere or has to have Marge chauffer him; she is left with all the duties of driving the kids around (with Bart and his buddy and their Peruvian fighting frogs in the backseat). She is furious, but tries to squelch it and be a good mom. As the load of duties becomes increasingly aggravating, Marge is depicted as tired and limp. Later, her impeccable hair starts to frazzle, which indicates how severe her depletion has truly become.*

The link here between repressed anger and health is implied in the physical portrayal of Marge rather than in any explicit conversation. There's also a great example involving Homer in "Furious Yellow" when he becomes the model for Bart's comic "Angry Dad." After being told he is a "rageaholic" by Marge and Lisa, he tries to suppress his anger, but it manifests itself in hideous bumps all over his neck which enlarge with each stifled anger episode. Eventually, he turns into a version of the Incredible Hulk, but having released his anger, becomes normal again and proclaims, "Anger saved my life."

## 3. Anger Means You're a Weak, Emotionally Unstable Person

Nope. Let's stop and think for a minute—why is it generally seen as a sign of assertiveness and power when men express their anger, but when women do the same, the result is negative? Like the good feminist I am, I will suggest this is because it is in men's best interests to have us believe that. The male powers that be have a vested interest in keeping women timid and self-blaming for our strong emotions. What a perfect set-up! If I buy into the idea that I should feel bad about myself for being angry, well lo and behold, I might try not to act on my feelings of irritation and outrage. When I shut down, I am not a threat. A righteously angry woman is something to be reckoned with, as many know—and fear. So we are kept "in our places" by a series of insults. We are nags, bitches, feminazis or losing it…The truth is that anger is power, not weakness. Letting your anger guide your behavior in a constructive way makes you strong; holding it in and pretending that someone didn't make you angry will only come back to haunt you. Are Marge and Lisa stronger or weaker for their anger? Let's look:

> In "Two Cars in Every Garage and Three Eyes on Every Fish," both Lisa and Marge are angry at Mr. Burns for polluting their local water supply with mutating nuclear waste. The situation is intensified by Mr. Burns running for mayor (Lisa and Marge actively support the other candidate). When Homer agrees to have Mr. Burns in their home as a publicity stunt, and he asks Lisa and Marge to behave themselves, things reach the breaking point. At the table, Marge and Lisa initially try to suppress their irritation and disgust. During a break in the kitchen, Lisa protests to her mom, "We've become the tools of evil!" Marge replies, "We're learning many things tonight, and one of them is to give your mother the benefit of the doubt." Marge then puts into action a plan she created while fuming in bed some nights before, and serves up the three-eyed fish to Mr. Burns. In front of all the media, he must try to gag it down, but can't and his run for mayor is ruined.

*When Lisa becomes outraged at what comes out of her Malibu Stacy doll's mouth, she is moved to action. Tired of hearing lines like, "Thinking too much gives you wrinkles," "Let's bake some cookies for the boys" and "Don't ask me, I'm just a girl," she proclaims, "It's sexist! Something has to be done." In spite of her family's attempts to calm her down, she persists in her quest to change the situation. After an unsuccessful visit to the Malibu Stacy company's management, she seeks out the wealthy, reclusive, original creator of the doll and convinces her to make a new doll, Lisa Lionhart. The new doll is meant to empower girls, with great feminist lines like, "If I choose to marry, I'll keep my own name" and "Trust in yourself and you can do anything." While Lisa Lionhart is largely a commercial failure (but not totally), Lisa continues to feel good about herself (as well she should) for the actions she took because of her righteous anger.*

In these two situations and many others, anger is the motivator for changes both in personal relationships and in social issues. Most of the time it works for Marge and Lisa.

## 4. You Can Permanently Steer Clear of Anger

Wrong again. Try as you might, it's going to be there. We simply can't go through life without some degree of conflict with others that generates annoyance, and if nothing else, simply because we are individual people. You want to stay home and he wants to go out. Your sister calls you at just the wrong time. You have a slacker coworker who is assigned by your boss to work on a report with you. Your kid breaks your favorite vase. The list could go on forever. You can fake it and try to make others believe that pretty façade, but it will either leak out or manifest in your body (that repressed anger thing again).

What is this "leaking out," you ask? This is all our wonderful passive-aggressive behavior, as well as nonverbal cues that we are feeling something different than what we are saying. And believe me, no one believes your words for a second if your face, body and voice tone don't match. You can protest, "I'm not angry!" but if you're tapping your pencil on your desk a mile a minute and your face is red, guess what people cue on? Right. Passive-aggressive behavior is also popular. Somehow you forget to do one or two things for that colleague who pissed you off. Somehow it just gets too late at night and you're too tired for romance when your darling partner has irritated the hell out of you earlier in the day. So whether or not you are even conscious of it, you can't avoid anger. I once interviewed a woman who said she never got angry anymore and that she used to, but that she "didn't know *that other person* anymore." She was so dissociated from her emotions that it literally made the hair stand up on the back of my neck.

At any rate, when we look at the women in the *Simpsons*, Marge and Lisa actually don't often try to stay out of the way of their own anger or that of other people. Good for them! Occasionally, we see them try to repress it for a period of time, but it never lasts. In fact, in none of the nearly fifty episodes of *The Simpsons* in which Marge or Lisa's anger figures prominently, is the anger just shut down never to reappear. Truly they are role models for the rest of us!

## 5. Anger Makes You Stupid and Makes It Difficult to Think Rationally

As with the health issue, there is a grain of truth here, but only at the most extremes of rage when the body is so flooded with biochemicals that cognition becomes difficult. All other times emotion is more informative and helpful rather than hindering to thinking.

So, our anger isn't stupid and it doesn't make us stupid. In the majority of cases, anger actually gives you great ideas about what you need to do to solve problems in your life. You may have to craft your initial idea a bit to be realistic, but anger gives us great images from which to work. For example, I used to get really irritated when graduate students of mine didn't get going on their research projects in a timely way, and then expected me to review their work, when it finally came in, overnight. I had images of slapping them upside the head, shaking them by the shoulders and yelling at them. This would, of course, be highly unprofessional (and probably constitute assault). Turns out other faculty members had similar feelings. So we took that angry energy, and made a policy to more figuratively shake up students. Now, if students don't get their research done by a certain time, they are stopped from taking classes, and if they don't get done in a year, are kicked out of our program. Oh, and they are required to give us seven to ten days to review their work. So our collective annoyance pushed us to change the system. Hardly stupid!

But more than any other myth, the women in *The Simpsons* are portrayed as buying into the idea that anger makes for poor decisions. When Lisa and Marge get angry, they sometimes do make stupid choices:

*In "My Sister, My Sitter" Lisa makes Bart jealous when she starts to*

*make lots of money being an ultra-responsible and reliable babysitter.
She gets such great reports from family, friends and neighbors that her
parents are convinced that she can babysit Bart when they go out for
the evening. Once their parents are gone, the power struggle between
Lisa and Bart begins. Lisa bosses him around and insults him, for example: "You need a bib" and "Don't act like a baby." He retaliates by
calling all kinds of people to come to the house and make deliveries,
giving Maggie coffee ice-cubes and then taunting Lisa with her failure
to maintain order: "You're going to be in so much trouble when Mom
and Dad get home!" Lisa ends up screaming and twitching (essentially losing it) and shouting at Bart to go to bed. "Make me!" he replies.
At the outer edge of what she can bear, Lisa snaps and chases him; the
two of them get in a physical fight and Bart falls down the stairs unconscious.*

Here, Lisa's rage and ongoing frustration contribute to her difficulty
in making good choices about what to do with her emotions. Beating
someone up rarely solves the root of the problem, and it doesn't in this
episode either. But more often than not, feminine anger in *The Simpsons*
leads to good outcomes, positive change or right thinking. Here's a con-
trasting example to the episode above:

*Lisa initially becomes irritated in "Lisa the Skeptic" when she is rid-
ing in the car and notices that a mall is about to go up on a site known
for its potentially important fossils. She tries at first to get her family to help: "Pull over so we can complain! Who wants to complain
with me?" When no one does, Lisa takes the energy from her annoyance, hires an attorney and visits the site, where the mall developers
grant her and the kids at her school the right to dig for fossils. Success number one. However, the dig turns up nothing until at the last
minute Lisa discovers a strange skeleton. Onlookers decide it is an
angel and Homer seizes it and takes it home, eventually figuring out
he can charge 50¢ a visit for people to see it. Lisa is again infuriated
("You can't claim it's an angel!" and "Those morons make me so angry! How can grown adults believe that?") Eventually she gets to the
point where she is ready to dismantle it ("Time to put an end to this!")
but it has disappeared. By now, the townspeople of Springfield are convinced that the Apocalypse is upon them, and they all gather at the
church to await the end of the world. Lisa is still agitated, and continues to shout, "Nothing is going to happen!" Yet even she has a wa-*

*vering moment when the skeleton angel rises above the hilltop next to the church, and a booming voice is heard, "Prepare for the end!" But when it is followed by, "...the end of high prices!" Lisa rants, "Hope you all learned!" Still angry, she confronts the mall developers again: "You planted a phony. You exploited people's deepest beliefs to hawk your cheesy wares!"*

In this episode Lisa's anger keeps her mind sharp for critical thinking. Her anger gives her energy to confront social injustice and to try to set things right.

## Special Cases of Anger

There are some things that make us angry that are in a different category altogether—pain and drugs are both prime examples. These biological causes for anger affect both men and women and are portrayed regularly on *The Simpsons*. The episode "Strong Arms of the Ma" specifically addresses the issue of steroid rage:

*Marge, in an attempt to overcome a case of rapid-onset agoraphobia, works out in the basement. Her newfound strength leads her not only to a cure for her fear, but into the wacky world of women's bodybuilding. There, an old acquaintance, Ruth, convinces her to try steroids. After bulking up, finishing in second place in the local competition and hanging out while boasting about it at Moe's, Marge turns livid when she is accused of losing her femininity and goes wild, trashing the place in a steroid-induced fury. Ironically, only Homer's appeal to "the sweet girl I once knew" can get through to her and make her stop. In a flash of insight Marge realizes, "Steroids have turned me into everything I hate."*

While I don't condone the type of violent destruction portrayed in this episode, it would appear that both the other characters on the show and the viewing audience can easily attribute Marge's behavior to the drugs (rather than her having an innately mean personality). I have recently been on a rather large and sustained dose of steroids myself (all perfectly legal, medically necessary and otherwise on the up and up, I assure you!). I thought weird things I never thought before and was extremely cranky and had a hair-trigger for irritation. I wasn't "myself" and I would argue that perhaps Marge was not either in this case. A substantial body of medical literature has documented the side effects of prolonged steroid usage, including mood changes and aggression. However, it is also a shame that once more a woman's anger, steroid-induced or not, can be squelched by the fear of appearing unattractive to a man.

## A Qualitative Content Analysis

In my own research-prone, academic way, I went through and analyzed all the available storyboard descriptions of *The Simpsons* episodes I could in order to determine who got angry at whom, and what the outcomes of anger were (something positive, something negative or "mixed"). Here's what I found out: Marge rarely gets angry at Lisa or Maggie. Most often she gets mad at Homer, followed by Bart. Occasionally, she is angry about social issues or at a secondary character. Lisa, on the other hand, is most regularly outraged by social injustice, followed by her brother or sometimes her dad. She is rarely angry at her mother or other characters unless they are somehow connected to the issue at hand. Whether or not these patterns mimic real life is debatable. I expect many sisters have anger at each other, as do mothers and daughters. Yet these are rare themes in the Simpson family.

So that's the "who." In terms of the outcomes of anger, I present the data below:

|  | Positive Outcomes | Mixed Outcomes | Negative Outcomes |
|---|---|---|---|
| **MARGE** | | | |
| Relationships | 56% | 38% | 6% |
| Social Issues | 25% | 50% | 25% |
| **LISA** | | | |
| Relationships | 43% | 43% | 14% |
| Social Issues | 42% | 16% | 42% |

It is clear that Marge has at least some good come out of a whopping ninety-four percent of her interpersonal anger episodes. Lisa racks up an impressive eighty-six percent of interpersonal anger events with positive or mixed outcomes. Where social issues are concerned, success is less assured for both Lisa and Marge. Sometimes the bad guys win, or public opinion remains unmoved. Still, Lisa in particular is able to institute social change forty-two percent of the time—a rate that any civil rights attorney or left-wing lobbyist would envy.

## In Conclusion

Hopefully, my scrutiny of the emotions and actions of Marge and Lisa has helped to convince you that women's anger is often a good thing, both useful and empowering. Of course, like the rest of us, Lisa and Marge are imperfect. Sometimes it doesn't work. Both often resort to violence, an option no respectable psychologist (like myself) would promote, but it does make for good television ratings (and for good comedy). We can relate to the things that make Marge angry—the incompetence of her husband, the lack of help around the house from Bart or Homer, being humiliated in front of others, people who expose her kids to danger or indecency, and the inconsiderate houseguest. Likewise, many of us cheer for Lisa as she takes on corporate greed, pollution, cruelty to animals, the oppression of indigenous peoples and sexism. Or Bart.

I guess the thing to keep in mind are the wise words that Marge, attempting to reform her road rage in "Screaming Yellow Honkers," learned in her traffic school class:

*"Anger makes America great. But find an appropriate outlet"*

and

*"What would Curtis E. Bear do?"*

## References

Cox, Deborah, Bruckner, Karin H., and Stabb, Sally D. *The Anger Advantage: The Surprising Benefits of Anger and How It Can Change a Woman's Life*. New York: Broadway Books, 2003.

Cox, Deborah, Stabb, Sally D., and Bruckner, Karin H. *Women's Anger: Clinical and Developmental Perspectives*. Philadelphia: Taylor & Francis, 1999.

NOTE: These two books summarize over seven years of the authors' research, as well as hundreds of individual, professional journal articles and other relevant works. Detailed reference sections can be obtained in either one, or by request to Sally D. Stabb.

Sally D. Stabb, Ph.D., is an associate professor of counseling psychology at Texas Woman's University and a licensed psychologist. Her teaching and research interests include gender and emotion, sexuality, qualitative methods and other nerdy stuff. When not doing the professor thing, she enjoys travel, ethnic food/music/art/dance, reading, scuba diving, cooking, Scrabble and spending time with her sig-o (Martin) and her girlfriends. She is a serious amateur (twelve plus years) in the study of Middle Eastern dance.

# Self-Esteem in Springfield

## Self and Identity in the Land of D'oh

### Robert M. Arkin and Philip J. Mazzocco

*"These fumes aren't as fun as beer. Sure, I'm all dizzy and nauseous, but where's the inflated sense of self-esteem?"*
—B. GUMBLE

*"I pity the fool who derives his self-esteem from mocking other people's clothes."*
—MR. T (guest spot)

MANY FACETS OF PSYCHOLOGY are explored and lampooned mercilessly on *The Simpsons*. Psychiatrists and psychologists are often featured prominently and are shown delivering all kinds of help, some of it wanted, but much of it neither wanted nor useful. There is shock therapy ("There's No Disgrace Like Home"), spank therapy ("Hurricane Neddy"), in-depth psychoanalysis of Marge's childhood trauma ("Fear of Flying") and even the involvement of the entire family ("Family Therapy"). Characteristically, Homer is often only interested in himself ("Did you talk about me today?") and rails against therapy ("It breaks up families, turns wives against husbands, children against parents, neighbors against me."), even interrupting it to inquire about payment and a sliding scale ("Keep sliding.").

In addition to poking fun at the profession and therapy in particular, *The Simpsons* also uses psychology in a more subtle way to spotlight characters and their interpersonal relationships. Within any family, and between each family member and the outside world, psychological concepts arise continually. When the Simpson family members are the characters on this stage of everyday human social relations, bringing these concepts to life, our laughs are not only about the stories and situations, but also about seeing ourselves in the reflection. Usually, the psychological concepts are portrayed with insight, clarity and surprisingly great accuracy (or they wouldn't ring as true as they do or seem as funny as they are).

The topic of self-esteem falls under the discipline of social psychology. Social psychology is the study of how people think about, influence and relate to one another. Often, social psychologists examine the influence of the social environment on the average individual. For example, the mere presence of other people has been shown to alter the thoughts, feelings and behaviors of the average individual in fundamental ways. For instance, the mere presence of others leads to measurable increases in physiological arousal and excitement. *The Simpsons* invokes the dynamics of social psychology in its frequent mob scenes, where arousal leads to contagion and inflames what is usually pretty bad behavior. *The Simpsons* also frequently deals with other key social psychological concepts, such as helping behavior, hurting behavior, stereotypes and prejudice, persuasion and relationships.

One area of great interest to social psychologists is the self. Roughly speaking, the self can be thought of as people's ideas about who they are and what they are like. In one classic way to introduce and explore the self, people are asked to fill out the "Who am I?" inventory by completing twenty statements, each beginning with "I am _____." Common answers range from ascribed identities (age, race), roles (occupation, political affiliation) and interests (a painter) to personal characteristics (kind, shy), abstractions (human) and major senses of oneself (competent, determined). Importantly, most answers to these questions only have meaning with respect to the larger social context. For example, a given age is not noteworthy unless the range of human ages is considered. Similarly, competence in any given domain can only be measured against the relevant competencies of others. The fictional magazine *Self-Test Monthly* ("Kill the Alligator, and Run") permits Homer to learn what, as he says, "makes me tick." Bart guesses hunger and rage, but Homer wants to go a step further ("Yeah, but in what ratio?").

Beyond mere description, study of the self includes three broad phenomena (Baumeister, 1998), each based on a separate component of the self. First, the self refers to the sense of reflexive consciousness first noted by William James (1890). As in a reflection, people's conscious attention turns back toward its own source. Humans have the capacity to consider themselves, even to seek information about themselves. Our well-developed brain is responsible, both for the good this brings (e.g., taking stock of one's accomplishments) and the bad (e.g., ruminating about one's shortcomings). Second, the self is a tool for relating to others in the social world. The self is shaped through social relations (e.g., self-views are affected by how others treat you), and the self-presentation we make to others depends on our assessment of how it is received. Finally, the self has an executive function; it is a control unit that energizes and guides thoughts, feelings and behavior, enabling self-regulation (as in resisting another Duff or a doughnut) or not.

One may ask why the self is a topic of interest to *social* psychologists. Generally, social psychologists study the influences of the self on social behavior, and the influences of the social environment on the self. As the "Who am I?" inventory discussed above demonstrates, the self is seen as inherently social. Some animal research suggests that the absence of a social environment precludes the development of a self (Gallup, 1994). In these studies, chimpanzees were raised either in a normal social environment or alone (kept isolated from all other chimps). After a year, chimps from both groups were tested for the presence of a self. The researcher painted a red dot on their foreheads (while they were anesthetized) and then placed a mirror in their environment. On waking, chimps raised in isolation pawed at the mirror itself, captivated only by the dot of red seemingly on the glass. But chimps raised in groups felt their own foreheads to examine the dot, indicating awareness that the chimp in the mirror was its "self," at least a rudimentary self that recognizes the animal in the mirror as its own reflection. Of course, for ethical reasons these types of studies cannot be conducted with humans, but it seems a safe generalization that the development of a sense of self in humans is no less dependent on the opportunity to compare and contrast oneself with others. The self is social. The research on chimps is especially reminiscent of Homer, who was once described as either a below-average human being or a brilliant beast when scientists and journalists confused him with the ape-like Bigfoot ("The Call of the Simpsons").

## Self-Esteem

Self-esteem can be thought of as a person's liking for themselves (i.e., a self-evaluation). The topic of self-esteem is front and center in both the social psychological study of the self and the popular imagination. No "self-help" topic outsells it in your local bookstore. In the popular press, it is common to hear about primary schools' emphasis on creating positive self-esteem for students. Parents and educators in schools and recreational sports venues across the nation seem highly concerned with ensuring that children have self-esteem, the result being trophies for anything and everything, right down to showing up. Politicians, educators and others have even come to hope that self-esteem holds the key to solving many social problems. In California, in 1990, a statewide task force recommended steps to raise the self-esteem of citizens of the state. Of course, Springfield Elementary bucks this common trend. For example, in "The PTA Disbands," the teachers are on strike, and Edna and Skinner are arguing in the lunchroom:

> EDNA: Our demands are very reasonable. By ignoring them, you're selling out these children's future!
> SKINNER: Oh, come on, Edna: We both know these children *have* no future! [*All the children stop and look at him; he chuckles nervously.*] Prove me wrong, kids. Prove me wrong.

Generally, however, the Simpsons are right on target in their understanding of the importance of self-esteem and the dynamics involved in the interplay between the social world and positive self-regard. Below, we review some of the social psychological thought relating to self-esteem. Why do we have it? What determines our levels of self-esteem? And, of course, what do members of the Simpson family tell us about self-esteem?

Now we can turn to our next question: Why does self-esteem exist? There are three theories that address this question. According to the sociometer model (Leary, Tambor, Terdal, and Downs, 1995), self-esteem developed initially as an indicator (a meter, or gauge) of potential exclusion from important social groups. In other words, feedback suggesting that our standing in an important group is precarious, or that we might actually be excluded from a group, lowers our self-esteem. The associated negative feelings then motivate us to engage in actions that might preserve group membership. Given the survival and mating benefits that would have accrued to early peoples who had successfully integrated into bands or groups, it seems likely that evolution would have strongly selected for self-esteem. In some cases, when another person is seen as partially responsible for our exclusion from a group, the resulting low self-esteem can easily be converted to anger and vengeance. Hence, when Lisa meets a new gang of friends on a beach vacation and Bart is excluded from the group, it makes sense that Bart lashes out against Lisa in an attempt to protect or restore his injured self-esteem ("Summer of 4 Ft. 2").

The second theory of self-esteem, terror management theory (Solomon, Greenberg and Pyszczynski, 1991), centers around our unique human ability to contemplate our own mortality. According to TMT, a person's awareness of his or her mortality causes terror and positive self-esteem serves as a buffer against such terror. People seek meaning in their lives (e.g., writing a chapter about the self) to boost self-esteem, which holds their anxiety about mortality at bay. In TMT, the purpose of self-esteem is to help them overcome the fear associated with the knowledge that death is inevitable.

The third theory of self-esteem is provided by Immediate-Delayed Compensation Theory (Martin, 1999). ID Comp theory holds that self-esteem functions as an indicator of one's progress toward important goals. If you feel that you aren't making sufficient progress, this will be a blow to your self-esteem. According to ID Comp theory, awareness of one's own mortality influences self-esteem primarily by reminding us that there is a time limit for us to achieve our goals. The impact of mortality salience is clearly illustrated in the episode "One Fish, Two Fish, Blowfish, Blue Fish." Homer ingests a blowfish and learns later that the chef prepared it incorrectly. Dr. Hibbert gives Homer twenty-four hours to live. Homer makes a list of things to do before he dies, each focused on augmenting his self-esteem (e.g., spending time with his dad; making a farewell video for Maggie; listening to Bible tapes read by Larry King, etc.). Homer's efforts at redemption for even one day are targeted at allaying fears regarding death, or because he is suddenly aware that all of his life goals must be satisfied in twenty-four hours. In ID Comp theory, self-esteem supports our ability to accomplish our goals. Researchers backing ID Comp theory, terror management theory and the sociometer model have often butted heads, but the models are not mutually exclusive, and there is probably some truth to all three.

## Self-Discrepancy Theory

Regardless of its basis, it is clear that humans will go to great lengths to attain and preserve positive self-esteem. The mental gymnastics underlying changes in self-esteem are a longstanding research focus.

William James (1890) is responsible for psychologists' general assumption that there are multiple levels of the self. Self-discrepancy Theory (Higgins, 1989) relies on this multiple selves idea. According to SDT, there are three important self-images which we all recognize: the actual self, the ought self and the ideal self. The actual self is comprised of perceptions of one's own behaviors, habits, tendencies, traits, thoughts and feelings. The ought self, like a conscience, represents a personal guide to what we should or should not do, think or feel in any given situation. Finally, the ideal self represents what we would like to be or to achieve, ideally, in a world with no constraints. For example, a college student might ideally dream of being the valedictorian at commencement (ideal self). At the very least, though, the student feels the press to study for each test, work hard on each assignment and make those tuition payments matter (ought self). However, in reality, we all slip up, and this fictional student may sometimes skip class, fail to study and struggle to pass some classes (actual self). (We hope this example does not have a ring of familiarity.)

Discrepancies between the actual self and either the ideal or ought selves have implications for one's emotional life. Actual-ought discrepancies cause high arousal emotions such as guilt and anxiety (e.g., when you forget to call your mother on her birthday). Actual-ideal discrepancies may cause low arousal emotions such as sadness or wistfulness (e.g., realizing that you probably are not good enough to make varsity football).

For the Simpsons, self-discrepancies are commonplace, particularly in the first few seasons when the show was more focused on moral lessons. When Lisa purposely sabotages a schoolmate rival's diorama, the guilt drives her to hallucination ("Lisa's Rival"). Even Bart is wracked with guilt after cutting off the head of the statue of Jebediah Springfield ("The Telltale Head"). In both cases, Lisa and Bart do something that they know they *should not* have done. In contrast, when dreams are shattered, it is sadness rather than guilt that results. For instance, Lisa becomes severely depressed when she is told that her fingers are too stubby to play saxophone professionally ("Separate Vocations"). She writes in her daily log that: "This will be my last entry, for you were a journal of my hopes and dreams....And now, I have none." Frequently, the Simpsons have anthropomorphized the interplay between the various selves by using the time-tested gag where an angel and a devil (perched on one's shoulders) compete for influence. In other cases, Homer even argues with his own brain about a desired course of action, as in this scene from "Brother from the Same Planet":

ADMINISTRATOR: And what are your reasons for wanting a Little Brother?
HOMER'S BRAIN: Don't say revenge! Don't say revenge!
HOMER: Uh, revenge?
HOMER'S BRAIN: That's it, I'm gettin' outta here. [the sound of footsteps, and a door slam]

One offshoot of SDT is that the discrepancies will only be bothersome to the extent that we focus on them. Hence, people occasionally deal with painful discrepancies by intentionally reducing self-awareness, in some cases with drugs and alcohol. Homer recognizes this all too well, as reflected in his toast: "To alcohol! The cause of and solution to all of life's problems" ("Homer vs. the Eighteenth Amendment").

Aside from ignoring our discrepancies, probably the most common coping strategy is rationalization. Rationalization is an attempt to present oneself in a more positive, or at least less negative, light than may really be justified (Schlenker, Weigold and Hallam, 1990). In "Simpsoncalifragilisticexpiala-D'oh-cious," Barney attempts to rationalize his drinking behavior as high class, but fails:

BARNEY: Buy me brandy
A snifter of wine.
Who am I kidding?
I'll drink turpentine.

Rationalizations, or self-serving cognitions, can be intricate, complexly woven webs of half-truths and self-deceptions. For the Simpsons, however, they are usually far more simple. For example, Marge has convinced herself that Homer is not the dundering oaf that he appears to be:

MARGE: When I first met your father, he was loud, crude and piggish. But I worked hard on him, and now, he's a whole new person.
LISA: Mom. . . ?
MARGE: [curtly] He's a whole new person, Lisa.

## Self-Esteem and Performance

Personal performance, especially in important domains, accounts for a good deal of our feelings of self-esteem on a daily basis. Obviously, to the extent that we live up to our personal standards and expectations, our self-esteem will tend to improve. However, in many cases, people are unsure of their ability. In such situations, people have a number of different options to deal with this performance anxiety. *The Simpsons* is chock full of characters who personify these various options.

Bart is the classic underachiever. Convinced that his best effort might not be enough to succeed, he decides instead to withdraw effort. This distances Bart from the domain in question (academic performance, for example), and protects him from the implications of a stark, undeniable failure. Ironically, one technique people sometimes use to accomplish such feats is to purposely sabotage their own behavior. In "Bart Gets an F," Bart learns that his grades have been so poor that he is in danger of repeating the fourth grade. Homer and Marge are called to meet with Bart, Mrs. Krabappel and the district psychiatrist, Dr. J. Loren Pryor. Dr. Pryor suggests that Bart's underachievement is due to fear of failure. Bart bursts in to the conversation and proclaims, "Okay, okay! Why are we dancing around the obvious...I am dumb, okay? Dumb as a post! Think I'm happy about it?"

Fortunately, Bart is given one last chance to pass the class—a history test that he must not fail. Instead of studying, Bart wastes the majority of the time before the test. The night before the test he prays to God to cancel school, providing just one more day to study. Miraculously, there is a blizzard the next day (in the middle of June). When he hears that school is cancelled, Bart immediately suits up and prepares for a day of fun in the snow. Lisa, however, reminds him of his deal with God, and so Bart reluctantly heads down to the basement to get some studying done. While trying to imagine the signing of the Declaration of Independence, Bart's mind wanders again to the fun he could be having in the snow. The scene closes with Bart slapping himself in the face in an attempt to refocus on his studying.

Given the importance of the test, it may seem strange that Bart appears to be falling all over himself to avoid studying. However, Bart's behavior is consistent with a self-protective behavioral stratagem known as self-handicapping (Arkin and Oleson, 1998). Self-handicapping describes behaviors designed to sabotage one's own performance in order to provide an excuse for failure. If failure does occur, it can be attributed to the ready-made excuse (e.g., procrastinating, daydreaming, playing in the snow), and not to an enduring internal factor (being "dumb as a post"). Additionally, in the unlikely event of success following self-handicapping, the handicapper can feel exceptional for succeeding in spite of the handicap.

The perceived win-win nature of self-handicapping may account for the seductiveness of the technique. In fact, there are a number of drawbacks to self-handicapping. Most notably, failure is more likely. It is also not clear that others are fooled by self-handicapping-related excuses for failure (exemplified by Lisa's annoying reminder to Bart about the deal with God).

In "Bart Gets an F," Bart apparently worked hard enough to pass his test with a D minus. For many students, however, self-handicapping is a routine way of dealing with tests and other high-pressure assignments. Homer provides what is probably the most succinct depiction of the logos of underachievement in "Burns' Heir." After Bart and Lisa both fail in their attempts to become Burns' heir, Homer advises them, "Kids, you tried your best, and you failed miserably. The lesson is, never try."

Ironically, overachieving is yet another response to performance anxiety. Lisa, of course, exemplifies the overachiever. The root of underachievement and overachievement is the same: self-doubt and the anxiety about one's ability to succeed that it produces. Whereas the underachiever withdraws effort, the overachiever deals with the same anxiety by increasing effort, sometimes to unhealthy levels. Lisa is fond of listing her achievements (e.g., straight A's, perfect attendance, bathroom timer); and yet, she is actually quite insecure about her ability to maintain her high level of performance. At the extreme end of the high-effort continuum we find perfectionists. Ned Flanders personifies perfectionism as it applies to his religion. Perfectionists are so concerned about their performance in a particular domain that their entire lives become shaped around achieving success. Ned describes his manic obsession with good living while praying to God after his house is destroyed by a hurricane ("Hurricane Neddy"):

NED (TO GOD): Why me, Lord? Where have I gone wrong? I've always been nice to people. I don't drink or dance or swear. I've even kept kosher just to be on the safe side. I've done everything the Bible says, even the stuff that contradicts the other stuff.

Though perfectionists often seem to be "perfect," typically their extreme behaviors are indicative of an underlying anxiety relating to success.

Hence, the Simpsons demonstrate some of the main individual methods of dealing with self-esteem threatening performance anxiety. However, social psychologists are also concerned with how the social environment and performance interact to influence self-esteem.

## Self-Esteem and the Performance of Others

Although it is certainly true that our own performances have a great influence on self-esteem, we are also influenced by the performances of others. In many domains, in fact, our own performances can only be evaluated with respect to the performances of others. For example, an essay that receives eighty-two percent will have different implications for self-esteem if the eighty-two percent was the best score in the class, as opposed to the worst. Social comparison theory holds that performance comparisons yield the most accurate self-relevant information when made with others who are similar in a given domain or for a given trait (Festinger, 1954). For example, you would learn little about your tennis ability by playing either Pete Sampras or Maggie Simpson. More information is gained by comparing one's performance to people near one's own level.

However, people often intentionally seek out downward social comparisons that they know will augment their self-esteem (Wheeler and Kunitate, 1992). In fact, schoolyard bully Nelson Muntz's main role on *The Simpsons* is "enforcing" or permitting downward social comparisons. Nelson's life is a mess. He lives in poverty with a mom who could not care less about him. His clothing is ratty, his father ran away from home and his prospects in life are slim. Perhaps it is not surprising, then, that Nelson is always ready with a carefully timed "Ha Ha!" when someone else suffers a misfortune.

From a wider level of magnification, part of the joy of watching *The Simpsons* surely stems from the downward social comparisons allowed to the viewer. You can feel smarter than Homer and Ralph Wiggum, less anxiety-ridden than Marge, less insecure than Lisa, less nerdy than Professor Frink, less slimy than Moe, less drunk than Barney and so on. And, one hopes, your family life will be at least slightly more functional than that of the Simpsons.

Although in many cases we prefer to focus on others' failures, occasionally just the opposite happens. Sometimes, when the performance domain is one in which we personally do not compete, we prefer to focus on people's successes. For example, most college students are not on the football team, and so they are not threatened by superior performances on the gridiron each Saturday. In fact, Cialdini et al. (1976) found that college students were more likely to wear school colors and logos the Monday after a win, but less likely to identify with their college the Monday after a loss. The tendency to enjoy boosts to self-esteem based on the performances of others is referred to as basking in reflected glory. Homer exemplifies this principle, in typical Homer fashion, in the following bar scene ("Wild Barts Can't Be Broken"):

HOMER: What's the hub-bub? Did Moe finally blow his brains out?
LENNY: Quiet! We're watching the Isotopes.
HOMER: Shut it off, they're losers.
CARL: Where you been? The Isotopes are on fire!
MOE: Yeah, that sniper at the all-star game was a blessing in disguise.
LENNY: Now we're in the championship game!
HOMER: Championship? Hmm?
[*Homer ducks out of the bar, and reappears decked out in Isotopes gear.*]
HOMER:   Woo! 'Topes rule!
[*Local newsman Kent Brockman, shooting a piece on the Isotopes, notices Homer.*]
BROCKMAN: Well, here's a die-hard fan. Sir, your beloved Isotopes are about to make history. Any thoughts?
HOMER: Uh-huh, it's a great team, Kent. We never gave up hope...I wanna thank Jesus, and say hi to my special lady Marge. We did it, baby! Whoo! Hooooo!
BROCKMAN: The inspiring words of a fan who'll always root, root, root for the home team. Even if they lose this game. . . .
HOMER: They lost?! Those losers!
BROCKMAN: No, no, no, the game's not over.
HOMER: Whoo! Not over! Whoo!
BROCKMAN: There you have it...whoo.

Tesser's self-evaluation maintenance model (Tesser, 1988) integrates the various responses to the performances of others into one coherent framework. Generally, we will be happy when a close other succeeds (basking in reflected glory). However, if they succeed in a domain that is important to us, this may cause some anxiety and discomfort (the gap between our performance and their performance is a kind of self-discrepancy which can produce jealousy or envy). The SEM model suggests four ways of dealing with such discomfort. One way is to psychologically distance oneself from the other person. Another way is to psychologically distance ourselves from the domain of performance itself. Finally, we can attempt to close the performance gap by either working to improve our own performance, or by sabotaging the close other's performance. In the world of the Simpsons, it is perhaps not surprising that characters often eschew self-improvement in favor of the other three methods. For example, when Bart steals Lisa's spotlight in the world of broadcast news, Lisa responds by sending Bart off on a bogus interview at the dump that almost costs him his life at the hands of a vengeful Groundskeeper Willie ("Girly Edition"). Years later (in season fifteen), Lisa similarly attempts to sabotage Maggie when Maggie threatens Lisa's status as the smart one. When these attempts fail, Lisa does the next best thing. She runs away. She literally distances herself from Maggie and the family ("Smart and Smarter"). Finally, in "Lisa on Ice," where Bart and Lisa are hockey stars on opposing teams, the siblings are confronted with the choice of either forfeiting the championship pee-wee hockey match or severing their relationship as brother and sister. Because, perhaps, of the fact that the episode was coming to a close, they ended up choosing the former option.

## Conclusion

Though cartoon characters, the Simpsons experience the same psychological concepts, patterns and interactions as those that arise in any other family. It is the psychological truth of these characters, from Lisa to Barney and Homer to Bart, that allows us to laugh at the stories and situations, seeing ourselves in them and yet taking some solace from knowing that we are better off than whichever character is our personal favorite with which to identify (well, perhaps not if it's Lisa). Whether it's "Family Portrait," "Family Therapy," "The Mansion Family" or "Brawl in the Family," it's all about using family dynamics to portray human social behavior with stunning insight and clarity, in addition to a surprising fidelity to the theory and research in social psychology.

# References

Arkin, R. M., and Oleson, K. C. "Self-handicapping." In J. Darley & J. Cooper (Eds.), *Attribution and social interaction: The legacy of Edward E. Jones.* Washington, D.C.: American Psychological Association.

Baumeister, R. F. "The self." In D. T. Gilbert, S. T. Fiske, & G. Lindzey (Eds.), *The handbook of social psychology.* Fourth Edition. Vol 1. New York: Oxford University Press, 1998.

Cialdini, R. B., Borden, R. J., Thorne, A., Walker, M. R., Freeman, S., and Sloan, L. R. "Basking in reflected glory: Three football field studies." *Journal of Personality and Social Psychology, 34,* 1976: 366–375.

Festinger, L. "A theory of social comparison processes." *Human Relations, 7,* 1954: 117–140.

Gallup, G. G. "Monkeys, mirrors, and minds." *Behavioral and Brain Sciences, 17,* 1994: 572–573.

Higgins, E. T. " Self-discrepancy theory: What patterns of self-beliefs cause people to suffer?" In L. Berkowitz (Ed.), *Advances in experimental social psychology.* Vol. 22. New York: Academic Press, 1998.

James, W. *Principles of psychology.* (Vol. 1). New York: Holt, 1890.

Kolditz, T. A., and Arkin, R. M. "An impression management interpretation of the self-handicapping strategy." *Journal of Personality and Social Psychology, 43,* 1982: 492–502.

Leary, M. R., Tambor, E. S., Terdal, S. K., and Downs, D. L. "Self-esteem as an interpersonal monitor: The sociometer hypothesis." *Journal of Personality and Social Psychology, 68,* 1995: 518–530.

Martin, L. L. "I-D compensation theory: Some implications of trying to satisfy immediate-return needs in a delayed-return culture." *Psychological Inquiry, 10,* 1999: 195–208.

Schlenker, B. R., Weigold, M. F., and Hallam, J. R. "Self-serving attributions in social context: Effects of self-esteem and social pressure." *Journal of Personality and Social Psychology, 58,* 1990: 855–863.

Solomon, S., Greenberg, J., and Pyszczynski, T. "A terror management theory of social behavior: The psychological functions of self-esteem and cultural worldviews." In M. P. Zanna (Ed.), *Advances in experimental social psychology.* Vol. 24. San Diego, CA: Academic Press, 1991.

Tesser, A. "Toward a self-evaluation maintenance model of social behavior." In L. Berkowitz (Ed.), *Advances in experimental social psychology.* Vol 21. San Diego, CA: Academic Press, 1988.

Wheeler, L., and Kunitate, M. "Social comparison processes in everyday life." *Journal of Personality and Social Psychology, 62,* 1992: 760–773.

## Acknowledgments

Thanks are due Harris Cooper, Keith Payne, Gary Scanlon, and J. D. Arkin for helpful comments on an earlier version of this chapter and to Shawna Simmons for assistance researching *The Simpsons* episodes.

Robert M. Arkin is a professor in the social psychology program at Ohio State University. Arkin previously served as assistant and associate professor at the University of Missouri, Columbia, and was professor of psychology and held the Middlebush Chair in psychology at the University of Missouri, Columbia, when he moved to Ohio State as Undergraduate Dean. Arkin has served as associate editor of the *Personality and Social Psychology Bulletin* and the *Journal of Personality and Social Psychology: Personality Processes and Individual Differences*, and has also served on the editorial boards of the *Journal of Social and Clinical Psychology* and *Social Psychology Quarterly, Psychology and Marketing*. He is now the editor of the journal *Basic and Applied Social Psychology*. Arkin's research is centered on the self in social interaction, with special reference to attribution processes and general issues of motivation, achievement and social perception. His particular research interests recently include self-handicapping, overachievement and the core construct linking these (self-doubt), as well as issues of personal security in the post-9/11 era. Bart is his favorite *Simpsons* character.

Philip J. Mazzocco is currently a postdoctoral researcher at the Kirwan Institute for the Study of Race and Ethnicity at Ohio State University. He received his Ph.D. in social psychology recently (2005) at Ohio State. His research focuses on racial policy attitudes (e.g., affirmative action) and basic attitude change processes. He has consumed near-lethal doses of *The Simpsons*, but has lived to talk about it. His favorite character is Homer.

# Can Bart or Homer Learn?

## W. Robert Batsell, Jr.

*"When someone hurts you emotionally, you will hurt them physically, and gradually you will learn not to hurt each other at all."*
—DR. MARVIN MONROE

A S THE VARIETY OF CHAPTERS in this volume illustrate, a psychological analysis of *The Simpsons* can take many forms in which each specialist shines his or her expertise on a different facet of this enduring and humorous television show. These different approaches should enable us not only to appreciate the psychological themes and phenomena that occur in each episode, but they may also enlighten us about the factors that have made the show so popular.

A basic goal of experimental psychology is to understand the behavior of living organisms. Unlike Mr. Burns' hopes, the goal is not to predict the behavior of, or to control, an individual or society, but to have a broader understanding of the "laws of behavior." To accomplish this goal, experimental psychologists often conduct controlled experiments in a lab setting, but if the situation does not permit such an analysis, careful observation in a naturalistic setting will suffice. In regard to the most basic behaviors that can be systematically observed, the ability to learn has been extensively studied over the past 100 years. At its most basic level, the ability to learn or to adapt to a changing environment is the foundation on which all other behaviors exist. If an organism cannot learn, it is doomed to repeat the same mistakes over and over again. Even a casual fan of the program might conclude that the Simpsons, especially Bart and Homer, seem to make mistakes more than once. Are Bart and Homer's foibles caused by their inability to learn?

Because it's impossible to bring Bart and Homer into a lab for a controlled experiment, I adapted the technique of naturalistic observation to look for evidence of learning. Although the distinction is sometimes blurry, psychologists differentiate between the processes of memory and learning. Historically, memory research has been primarily conducted with humans and the testing materials have included written or spoken stimuli. As such, an episode like "Bart Gets an F" that focuses on Bart's inability to learn and recall factual information about American history is not relevant to the present analysis. Learning research, on the other hand, has focused on basic processes of acquiring behavior patterns that can be demonstrated in humans and other living organisms. Experimental psychologists have identified three major types of learning (observational learning, classical conditioning and instrumental conditioning), which can be distinguished by the environmental conditions required to produce learning (each are defined below). Two defining conditions were established to produce a more reliable analysis. First, the data sample was restricted to the first two seasons of *The Simpsons*. Second, extended analysis was only performed when one of the major types of learning was a crucial component of the plot. Four episodes met these conditions: "Bart the Daredevil," "One Fish, Two Fish, Blowfish, Blue Fish," "Bart's Dog Gets an F," and "There's No Disgrace Like Home."

## Evidence of Observational Learning

Albert Bandura (1963) popularized the study of Observational Learning. In some of his initial experiments, Bandura and colleagues showed nursery school children a five-minute film of two men, Rocky and Johnny (Bandura, Ross, & Ross, 1963). Johnny was playing with toys and would not let Rocky play. Rocky then hit Johnny with a rubber ball and a baton and took the toys away. Rocky said, "Hi ho, hi ho, it is off to play I go!" as the film ended, and, in one version of the film, the narrator declared Rocky the winner.

In the other version of the film, Johnny punished Rocky for his aggressive behavior. Shortly after viewing the Rocky and Johnny film, the children were allowed to play for twenty minutes with many of the toys displayed in the Rocky and Johnny movie. During this time, the experimenters observed the children through a one-way mirror. The children who saw Rocky's violent behavior go unpunished (positive consequences) displayed much of the aggressive behavior shown by Rocky. On the other hand, those children who saw Johnny punish Rocky (negative consequences) did not copy Rocky's behavior. Therefore, it is clear that the children had learned this behavior through observation.

Observational learning involves at least two individuals, a model and an observer. The model performs an action, and a consequence follows. If the consequence benefits the model, the observer is more likely to copy the model's behavior (for a review, see Baldwin & Baldwin, 1998). For example, if Barney strips off his clothes and streaks through the senior prom to the cheers of his classmates and the glares of Mr. Dondalinger ("The Way We Was"), one might predict that others would be scrambling to follow (birthday) suit and join him. In contrast, if Barney's naked dash is accompanied by disparaging comments about the state of his yellow behind and the shrinkage effects of cold weather, he will probably run alone.

Considering the numerous instances in which observational learning occurs in day-to-day human existence, one might expect there to be many examples of observational learning in *The Simpsons*. In fact, a prime example occurred near the beginning of the second season—"Bart the Daredevil." In this episode, the Simpsons go to the Springfield Speedway to see Truckosaurus—the car-eating monstertruck. The surprise main event that night is an appearance by the world's greatest daredevil, Captain Lance Murdock. Murdock successfully jumps over a water tank containing great white sharks, electric eels, piranhas, alligators, a lion and one drop of human blood! While Murdock is thanking the crowd from the edge of the ramp, he falls into the water, only to be bitten by a shark, stung by an eel and, ultimately, mauled by the lion. Most individuals would view this carnage and choose a sedate and safe life on the couch—but not Bart Simpson. The very next day, he is riding on his skateboard trying to jump over a car. Bart fails miserably, landing flat on his back on the concrete while his playmates scurry to avoid blame. Again, most individuals would learn that a life of daredevilry would lead to pain and broken bones, but Bart is undeterred. In this example, Captain Lance Murdock is the model and Bart is the observer. It is clear that Bart is capable of some rudimentary form of observational learning in that he copies the daredevil lifestyle espoused by Murdock, but Bart seems incapable of attending to the consequences of such a behavior choice. Even when Bart gets hurt and has to go to the hospital, he is immune to the consequences. In fact, Bart later attempts a surely fatal feat—jumping Springfield Gorge on his skateboard.

Interestingly, the very next episode, "Itchy & Scratchy & Marge," also included observational learning as a plot device. The three Simpson children are watching Itchy & Scratchy while Homer attempts to build a spice rack for Marge. After the typical aggression performed on Scratchy by Itchy, Bart and Lisa laugh uproariously, providing positive consequences for this type of behavior. Subsequently, Maggie cracks Homer in the head with a hammer. Obviously, this episode confirms that the youngest Simpson is capable of observing a model and copying the behaviors. These two episodes provide a striking contrast of Bart and Maggie both engaging in observational learning.

## Evidence of Classical Conditioning

Classical Conditioning, also termed Pavlovian Conditioning because of the early work of Ivan Pavlov, involves a situation in which the organism learns that a neutral stimulus predicts a biologically significant event. Food-aversion learning is a distinct form of classical conditioning in which an organism consumes a flavorful food or drink prior to an illness-inducing episode. The taste of the food is the neutral or conditioned stimulus, whereas the illness-inducing event is the unconditioned stimulus. Subsequently, when the organism re-encounters the taste of that food, they will avoid consuming it (for a review of food-aversion learning, see Barker, Best, & Domjan, 1977). This type of learning is highly adaptive because it helps the organism learn which foods are poisonous so that they can be completely avoided in the future. Although food aversions are commonly induced by illness, they can be produced by other unconditioned stimuli as well, including disgust (Rozin, 1986, Rozin & Fallon, 1987). Consider the following example derived from Rozin's work: A glass of clean water is placed in front of you. Would you drink it? Next, the experimenter dips a completely sterilized cockroach that is encased in a closed plastic wrapper into the water glass. Now would you drink it? Most people recoil at the thought of drinking from the glass, even though there is nothing wrong with the water itself. Nonetheless, most individuals conclude that once the roach has entered the glass, the glass and water have become contaminated, and it would be disgusting to drink it. Similarly, if an individual learns they have consumed a contaminated or disgusting substance, this can induce illness and nausea that is sufficient to produce a taste aversion (Rozin, 1986). Furthermore, the development of Lisa's eating habits represents an example of learning that has progressed across the series. The present-day Lisa Simpson, who is no older than the Lisa Simpson of the first season, is now a committed vegetarian. Technically, Lisa would be classified as a moral vegetarian because her food choice is shaped by her unwillingness to eat living organisms (Rozin, Markwith, & Stoess, 1997).

In the second-season episode "One Fish, Two Fish, Blowfish, Bluefish," the Simpsons decide to broaden their eating experiences after Lisa convinces them to try sushi at "The Happy Sumo." Although Homer initially displays neophobia (i.e., the fear of new foods), he quickly returns to his gluttonous ways and is ordering everything off the menu. Ultimately, he orders fugu. Fugu, or blowfish, is a delicacy because the ovaries of the blowfish can produce the poison tetrodotoxin (TTX). If the fish is prepared correctly, low levels of TTX provide a tingling sensation on the tongue. Yet, if the fish is prepared incorrectly (e.g., the liver or ovaries are not removed), consumption could be fatal. Of course, the main sushi chef is busy getting busy in the parking lot, so the sous sushi chef handles the task. Only after Homer has eaten every bite of fugu is he informed of the potential consequences. Dr. Hibbert informs Homer that he may only have twenty-four hours to live, and if he has consumed the poisonous parts of the fish, his heart will explode. Actually, this is wrong on two counts. TTX is a neurotoxin that shuts down the nervous system by rapidly producing paralysis and death.

It is at the point when Homer learns that he may have consumed a poisonous fish that his actions deviate from normal patterns of classical conditioning. As detailed above, a normal person should become violently ill because of fear and disgust. Later, they would reject the taste of fish for years to come because of this "near death experience." Yet, there is never any evidence that Homer's food choices change at all. Indeed, only three episodes later, Homer is seen buying a seafood burrito from the Kwik-E-Mart—which is wrong for so many reasons! Further evidence that Homer is deficient in food-aversion learning can be seen in various episodes that allude to his illness episodes following overconsumption of alcohol ("The War of the Simpsons"), which should produce at least a short-lived avoidance of alcohol. In sum, Homer appears to be missing an adaptive form of classical conditioning that has been demonstrated from cockroaches to cocktails.

## Evidence of Instrumental Conditioning

Instrumental Conditioning involves an organism voluntarily making a response to produce a specific outcome. For example, Bart frequently acts out in class to gain the approval of his classmates (and the ire of Mrs. Krabappel). The basic components of instrumental conditioning include the discriminative stimulus, the response, and the outcome. The discriminative stimulus can be any event, word or stimulus that signals the relations between the response and the outcome (the classroom). The response is any behavior the organism will voluntarily perform (boldly yelling "Eat my shorts!" at the top of his lungs). The outcome can be either an appetitive/desired event (the class laughing and Mrs. Krabappel fuming) or an aversive/feared event (going to detention or the wrath of Principal Skinner). The response-outcome relationship is crucial in determining whether the response will increase or decrease. There are basically four different response-outcome relationships that vary according to the contingency between the response and the outcome (positive or negative), and the nature of the outcome (appetitive or aversive). The effectiveness of learning each of these instrumental conditioning paradigms depends on the consistency of the response-outcome relationship and the quality or quantity of the outcome (for a review, see Domjan, 2005).

First, *positive reinforcement* involves a positive contingency with an appetitive outcome, and results in an increase in behavior. In other words, if the organism makes the response it will receive a desired reinforcer, and if it does not make the response, it will not receive the desired reinforcer. A good example of how positive reinforcement will not work occurred in the episode "Three Men and a Comic Book." The basic dilemma of this episode is that Bart wants the first edition of the Radioactive Man comic book, but Comic Book Guy is charging $100 for it. After Homer will not give him the money, Bart actually takes Marge's advice and decides to work (make an instrumental response) to earn the money (reinforcer). Bart tries to get bottle deposits, exchange foreign coins, and sell lemonade, but none of these produces a substantial reinforcer—even his attempt to sell Homer's Duff Beer is ineffective because the cops take the beer for free. Finally, Bart spends over two days doing onerous chores such as weeding and cleaning out the cat's litter box for his elderly neighbor Mrs. Glick. When it is time for payday, Mrs. Glick gives Bart a measly fifty cents. It is no wonder that Bart fails to learn in this situation because of the inadequacy of the reinforcer relative to how hard he worked. B. F. Skinner coined the term *abulia* (derived from the Greek *a-*, "without" + *boule*, "will") to describe the situation when the response requirement for the reinforcer was too demanding for the value of the reinforcer; as a result, the organism quits making the response. This same state of defeat settles over Bart after his interactions with Mrs. Glick. Here was a perfect scenario to develop Bart's work ethic, but every response he made produced a substandard reinforcement. Thus, at least in this instance, Bart's behavior was governed by the laws of learning.

The second response-outcome relationship, *positive punishment*, involves a positive contingency with an aversive outcome, and it produces a decrease in responding. In this scenario, if the organism makes the response it will receive an outcome it does not want. The episode "Principal Charming" contains an example of ineffective positive punishment. Bart uses sodium tetrasulfate to burn his name in the schoolyard. As punishment, Principal Skinner plans to make Bart re-seed the entire yard by hand. Up to this point, this could be an effective example of positive punishment. Yet, due to Seymour's infatuation with Patty Bouvier, he lets Bart off the hook, and Bart does not have to complete his punishment. Once again, a situation that could have produced effective learning to curb Bart's vandalism was wasted because the response-reinforcer relationship was violated.

Third, *negative reinforcement* involves a negative contingency with an aversive outcome, and it produces an increase in responding. Although negative reinforcement may seem counterintuitive, the organism will always respond at a high rate to avoid or escape from an aversive reinforcer. Bart and Lisa often employ a negative reinforcement scenario to manipulate Homer's behavior. In the episode "Brush With Greatness," for example, Bart and Lisa want to go to Mount Splashmore Water Park. So, they follow Homer around the house repeating, "Will you take us to Mount Splashmore?" ad nauseum. Eventually, Homer breaks down and asks if he takes them will the two of them shut up and quit bugging him? Of course, they agree. Thus, Homer makes the response and the aversive outcome is removed. Interestingly, this outcome represents positive reinforcement for Bart and Lisa as they learn that making the annoying response to Homer can produce reinforcement. In fact, a few episodes later in "Three Men and a Comic Book," Bart tries to use this same technique to get Homer to give him the $100 for the comic book, but Homer reverses the trick on Bart ("Are you going to stop bugging me? Are you? Are you?") and Bart stops trying. In these scenes, we can see effective use of negative reinforcement, but neither Bart nor Homer is aware of the contingencies to use them consistently to their advantage.

Fourth, *negative punishment* involves a negative contingency with a desired outcome, and it decreases behavior. A common example of negative punishment is the *time-out* procedure in which an unruly child is sent to his or her room as punishment for some indiscretion. The idea is that the child is removed from desired interactions and toys. Marge and Homer sometimes try to employ this technique, but rarely with any effectiveness. In "Bart vs. Thanksgiving," after Bart accidentally knocks Lisa's feminist heroes centerpiece into the fire, he is sent to his room. Not only does Bart have plenty of toys and entertainment in his room, he easily slips out the window and enjoys a day on the town. As a result, the punishment imposed by Marge and Homer is not effective. Luckily for them, Bart's desire to escape his own guilt (negative reinforcement) leads him to apologize to his sister...but this lesson will be quickly forgotten.

The previous paragraphs should provide evidence that there are numerous instrumental conditioning scenarios in *The Simpsons*, but there is not a single episode involving Bart or Homer in the first two seasons in which instrumental conditioning is the centerpiece of the plot. Ironically, the best example of instrumental conditioning in an early Simpsons episode features a different male member of the Simpson family—Santa's Little Helper in the episode "Bart's Dog Gets an F." It begins by showing all of Santa's Little Helper's misbehaviors: he demolishes the newspaper, he eats Homer's food, he digs up the backyard, and he swims in the neighbor's pool. Each time a Simpson family member tries to reprimand him, we see the interaction from the dog's perspective: a black-and-white screen with the babbling nonsense of "BLAH, BLAH, BLAH." Later in the episode, tensions escalate as Santa's Little Helper devours Homer's new Assassins' tennis shoes, and Santa's Little Helper is sent to Emily Winthrop's Canine College for obedience training. Although Bart is taking Santa's Little Helper to obedience classes, it seems to be doing little good as the dog still does not obey any commands and his mischief continues as he eats both the Bouvier family quilt and Homer's big cookie. At their wits' end, Homer and Marge are resigned to send the dog away. In the last few hours before Santa's Little Helper is shipped to a farm to pull a cart, Bart and Santa's Little Helper frolic in the backyard. Choking back tears, Bart says goodbye because Santa's Little Helper does not understand a single word that Bart says. At this point, the scene again shifts to Santa's Little Helper's perspective and we hear "BLAH, BLAH, SIT." Santa's Little Helper sits! Next, the dog hears "BLAH, BLAH, Lay Down," and Santa's Little Helper lies down! Then, Santa's Little Helper is able to respond to commands for "Shake Hands," "Stay," "Speak," and "Roll Over." As a result, Santa's Little Helper has demonstrated learning, passing his final exam, and graduating from Canine College.

In many respects, this episode is a great example of basic learning processes. At the beginning of the episode, Santa's Little Helper can make little sense of the verbal commands from the humans with whom he shares the house. The Simpsons have not consistently trained their dog, and as a result, every vocal utterance is processed as babbling nonsense. However, with repeated exposures to the key stimulus terms (e.g., sit, stay, lay down), the dog begins to discriminate the words. In this case, the words are discriminative stimuli that set the occasion for which response should be performed to earn reinforcement. At first, every command sounds the same, but through a process of trial-and-error learning, the differences between words become apparent, and the dog's evidence of learning is apparent. On the other hand, the evidence for Bart and Homer's instrumental conditioning was nebulous. At times it is clear that they have mastered various response-reinforcer relationships, but at other times, either by the ineptitude of others or their own deficiencies, learning has not occurred.

## Evidence from Classical and Instrumental Conditioning

At this point, the evidence suggests that Bart and Homer show little evidence of consistent learning. In fact, as early as the fourth episode— "There's No Disgrace Like Home"—there was evidence that all of the Simpsons have, at least, learning deficiencies. In this episode, due to a series of family mishaps, Homer takes the entire family to Dr. Marvin Monroe's Family Therapy Center. Eventually, each Simpson is seated in a chair, faced with a set of buttons, and attached with electrodes. Dr. Monroe instructs the family that the purpose of this aversion therapy is that when "someone hurts you emotionally, you will hurt them physically, and gradually you will learn not to hurt each other at all."

At this point, Dr. Monroe's aversion therapy technique is somewhat similar to other forms of aversion therapy, in that fear is harnessed to decrease problem behaviors. Technically, aversion therapy combines both classical conditioning and instrumental conditioning components in that the shock can act as both an aversive unconditioned stimulus and as an aversive reinforcer. A number of studies have confirmed the effectiveness of aversion therapy. For example, Marks and Gelder (1967) reported using shock aversion therapy to treat transvestism (although it should be noted that this type of treatment would now only be done with the patient's expressed commitment to change this behavior). In their study, Marks and Gelder reported that the male client identified those female garments (female panties, pajamas, skirt/blouse and slip) that caused him to experience sexual arousal. Then, the experimenters systematically paired panties with shock. Panty-shock! Panty-shock! Panty-shock! The patient no longer showed sexual arousal to panties, but continued to be aroused by pajamas, skirt/blouse, and slip. Subsequently, the experimenters systematically conducted pajama-shock trials, blouse/skirt-shock trials, and slip-shock trials. By the end of this treatment, the client was no longer sexually aroused by any of these female undergarments, although he continued to show sexual arousal to a nude photo of a female. Therefore, even though aversion therapy is not common, it can be an effective way to produce behavior change.

As we return to "There's No Disgrace Like Home," buttons are pushed and chaos ensues. We see each member of the Simpson family gleefully pushing the buttons in front of them to shock other family members, slowed only when they are incapacitated by shock. Eventually, the shock generator is overwhelmed, the lights flicker throughout Springfield, and Dr. Monroe worries that his practice may never recover from the public relations damage produced by the Simpsons. As a result, he bribes them with $500 to never speak of this moment again. At the end of the episode, the Simpsons are content with their reputation as Springfield's worst family, but we see no evidence that pairing negative thoughts of other family members with shock has decreased their treatment of one another. At least the Simpsons were not subjected to Dr. Monroe's twisted version of the Skinner Box—the Monroe Box, which is an isolation chamber in which the subject can pull levers to receive food and warmth, but the floor is electrified and showers of icy water randomly fall on the subject ("Old Money").

## Conclusions

We set out to determine whether Bart or Homer could learn according to established learning phenomena. Unfortunately for this analysis, the data are mixed. For example, there are instances where both Bart and Homer show the ability to use negative reinforcement to manipulate the other's behavior, as when they use annoying phrases to get their way. Yet, there are plenty more examples in which neither male Simpson shows the ability to learn. Moreover, it is clear that learning is possible within the city limits of Springfield, as evidence was obtained that Maggie could learn and so could Santa's Little Helper. So, what can one conclude from these inconsistencies?

One interpretation is that the inconsistent learning patterns of Bart and Homer are at the heart of *The Simpsons*' success. This conclusion is based on the above evidence and the following two observations: First, it is clear that Springfield is in a universe that shares principles of time and space with our own reality. For example, major tragedies such as the death of Maude Flanders and the divorce of Milhouse's parents have persisted since their occurrence. Clearly, these tragedies did not exist in isolation as everyone in the Simpsons' universe continues to acknowledge their impact long after the episode in which these events first occurred. Second, if Bart and Homer were completely incapable of learning, their adventures and mishaps would quickly become old hat. One need only consider other sitcom characters who have shown the inability to learn from their past mistakes (e.g., George Costanza of *Seinfeld*); ultimately, these individuals have little redeeming value. Instead, it appears that Bart and Homer have the ability to learn within a given episode, and this allows us to feel good about them and the lessons they learned at the end of the episode; but it is also clear that their learning definitely does not extend to future episodes. In other words, the foundation of the Simpsons' humor could be that they live in an Etch-A-Sketch world in which the lessons learned in a given episode are erased during the credits so they are free to make new mistakes in subsequent episodes. The take-home message is that if the Simpsons could *really* learn, we would not find them as funny.

# References

Baldwin, J. D., and J. I. Baldwin. *Behavior principles in everyday life*. Third Edition. Upper Saddle Hill, NJ: Prentice Hall, 1998.

Bandura, A., D. Ross, and S. Ross. "Vicarious reinforcement and imitative learning." *Journal of Abnormal and Social Psychology, 67*, 1963: 601–607.

Barker, L. M., M. R. Best, and M. Domjan. *Learning mechanisms in food selection*. Waco, TX: Baylor University Press, 1977.

Domjan, M. *The principles of learning and behavior*. Fifth Edition. Thomson-Wadsworth, 2005.

Marks, I. M., and M. G. Gelder. "Transvestism and fetishism: Clinical and psychological changes during faradic aversion." *British Journal of Psychiatry, 113*, 1967: 711–729.

Rozin, P. "One-trial acquired likes and dislikes in humans: Disgust as a US, food predominance, and negative learning predominance." *Learning and Motivation, 17*, 1986: 180–189.

Rozin, P., and A. E. Fallon. "A perspective on disgust." *Psychological Review, 94*, 1987: 23–41.

Rozin, P., M. Markwith, and C. Stoess. "Moralization and becoming a vegetarian: The transformation of preferences into values and the recruitment of disgust." *Psychological Science, 8*, 1997: 67–73.

W. Robert Batsell, Jr., is originally from Brownsville, TX. He earned bachelor's degrees in biology and psychology from SMU, and his Ph.D. in experimental psychology from TCU. Currently he is the Kurt D. Kaufman Associate Professor and Chair of Psychology at Kalamazoo College. He is a biopsychologist whose teaching interests include general psychology, experimental psychology, psychology of learning and biopsychology. His research focuses on the learning mechanisms that underlie food aversions in humans and nonhumans. He spends way too much of his time watching *The Simpsons* along with his eight-year-old son, Evan. He is indebted to his former students Aaron Blankenship, Karen Doyle, Dan Jacobson and Eric Zilli for their feedback on this essay.

# Sex and Gender in Springfield

## Male, Female and D'oh

### Linda Heath, Ph.D., and Kathryn Brown

SINCE 1990, the Simpsons have taken their place among the many other television families that have both shaped and reflected our ideas about American family life. As with *Ozzie and Harriet, I Love Lucy, Father Knows Best, The Donna Reed Show, Make Room for Daddy, The Jetsons, The Flintstones* and the prototypic *Leave It To Beaver*, the Simpsons live in a world where the father goes out to work, the mother stays home and the children are often precocious. There are differences, of course. The mother, Marge, has improbably tall blue hair; the father, Homer, works in a nuclear power plant; the son, Bart, has a bit more edge than other TV sons. *The Simpsons*, however, debuted at a time when many TV families had taken on many alternative forms (e.g., two divorced women, two single brothers, a single parent, two-career families, blended families), making it actually one of the more traditional television family structures on television over the past fifteen years (excluding reruns). Within this traditional framework, however, do the Simpsons present traditional gender stereotypes, or does the show use the traditional framework to challenge or poke fun at traditional gender roles and stereotypes?

## Definitions

To understand the Simpsons' place in the gender world, we must first define a few terms. Although the usage has evolved over the past several decades, currently *sex* (as in "what is your sex?" as opposed to "let's have sex") refers only to biological factors, such as chromosomes, hormones, genitalia and body fat distribution. This includes both the brain differences that are present at birth, such as the corpus callosum being more developed in females than in males, as well as the other biological differences that appear as the result of normal maturation, such as breast development and body fat distribution differences. *Gender*, on the other hand, currently usually refers only to social, rather than biological, factors, such as roles, stereotypes, expectations and schema relating to men and women. Although sex and gender can be separated conceptually, in application they generally overlap and are difficult to separate neatly. For example, contemporary American female gender roles and stereotypes point women toward being primary caregivers for children, but sex differences in regard to lactation and gestation also contribute to women's tendency to be primary caregivers. Similarly, contemporary American male gender roles and stereotypes point men toward being more aggressive and physically confrontational than women, but the hormone testosterone (which is in greater supply in men than in women) also predisposes people to higher levels of aggression. So most of the differences we observe between men and women contain elements of both gender differences and sex differences. For example, differences we observe in children's choice of toys clearly have a huge gender component, with girls being encouraged and rewarded for playing with dolls and boys often being actively discouraged from playing with dolls, but there could also be a sex difference (with a biological basis) lurking beneath this difference as well. Research with infants has shown that girls show more preference for looking at faces, whereas boys show a preference for looking at objects. In addition to all the social forces pointing girls toward dolls, there could also be an underlying biological basis for their preference for dolls over trains or trucks.

Once we understand that *gender* refers to social and cultural, rather than biological, factors, we can discuss *gender stereotype*, which is a set of beliefs about the behaviors, traits and characteristics typical of each gender. (Thirty years ago, researchers talked about "sex stereotypes," a term that no longer makes sense, as stereotypes are by definition social and cultural, and sex refers only to biological factors, in current usage.)

In the same way that people can have racial stereotypes, religious stereotypes, or social class stereotypes, they can also have stereotypes about gender. Stereotypes are learned, and they are culturally transmitted. In the same way that people can have a set of beliefs about behaviors, traits and characteristics typical of Quakers, or Muslims, or rich people, or Asian-Americans, they can also (and generally do) have a set of beliefs about behaviors, traits and characteristics typical of men or typical of women. In many (but not all) cases, the male and female versions of the stereotypes are opposites (e.g., men are strong/women are weak). *Gender roles*, on the other hand, refer to a set of beliefs about the activities and jobs that are appropriate for each gender. (Again, years ago we talked about sex roles, which makes less sense today with the current definitions.) The traditional male gender role in America, for example, includes leader, boss, plumber, president and soldier. The traditional female gender role in America includes caregiver, nurse, teacher, secretary and helper. Gender stereotypes and gender roles vary somewhat among different cultural, ethnic and socio-economic groups, and they change over time. Consequently, a gender stereotype or gender role description has to be placed within its social and temporal context.

## Doctrine of Two Spheres

Our current American gender ideas trace back to the Victorian era and the Industrial Revolution (10). Prior to that, most men and women lived collaborative lives on farms, often surrounded by large extended families. Consequently, women frequently worked in fields or pastures alongside men, watching flocks à la Bo Peep, milking cows, gathering eggs or tending crops. Children were frequently cared for by a grandmother or an older cousin, rather than by the mother. With industrialization and the advent of factories in the nineteenth century, men left the house to earn a living, while women stayed home to take care of children and tend to the house. From this pattern emerged the Doctrine of Two Spheres (2, 9), which holds that a woman's sphere is the home and a man's sphere is the world beyond the home. This underlying notion drives traditional gender stereotypes to this day.

Do the Simpsons reflect the Doctrine of Two Spheres? Marge generally stays at home with baby Maggie, unless she is shopping or schlepping. (There are a few notable exceptions, which we shall discuss later.) Lisa and Bart's teachers are both women (in line with the traditional gender role), and the school principal is male, also in keeping with traditional roles. Homer works outside the home, with a male boss (Mr. Burns). The store/bar owners (Apu, Moe), bus driver, and local criminals are male, consistent with traditional gender roles. Although many of the characters have personal characteristics that are at odds with the traditional stereotype (e.g., Lisa, Patty and Selma), the primary jobs and roles are in keeping with traditional gender roles. Another interesting gender pattern on *The Simpsons* is the vast over-representation of males among the recurring roles on the show. We count twenty-eight male recurring roles, and only ten female roles (excluding Maude, who died). So the world of the Simpsons (like most television comedy, drama, cartoons, news programs and even *Sesame Street*(7)) is disproportionately male, with almost seventy-four percent of the characters being male, in contrast to the real world where fifty-two percent of people are female. So the Simpsons, at least at the level of *roles*, reflect the Doctrine of Two Spheres, with the world outside the home being mostly occupied by men, and the women who do appear outside the home having traditional roles (e.g., schoolteacher).

## Gender Stereotypes in *The Simpsons*

When we move beyond a simple gender role analysis into a gender stereotype analysis, however, the situation changes. Gender stereotypes are much more fully formed than simply the belief that a woman's sphere is in the home and a man's sphere is the rest of the world. Both positive and negative characteristics are associated with both the female and male gender stereotype. For example, the female stereotype includes descriptors such as nurturing, warm, sensitive and caring, but it also includes traits such as passive, dependent, weak and timid. The male stereotype includes descriptors such as strong, leader, confident and capable, but it also includes aggressive, rude, uncaring and arrogant.

Beyond traits and personality descriptors, stereotypes also capture other aspects of gender, including gender roles. Beliefs about role behaviors (e.g., who cleans the house), occupations (e.g., who is the boss or store owner) and physical traits (e.g., who is taller, stronger, more athletic) must be added to traits (e.g., who is aggressive, who is nurturing) in order to gain a full appreciation of gender stereotypes (5). Again, these other aspects of gender stereotypes can have positive and negative aspects within each stereotype. Men are seen more often as political leaders but also more often as criminals. Women are seen more often as warm nurturers, but also as weak incompetents.

Despite *The Simpsons'* use of traditional roles, the series frequently diverges from the traditional gender stereotypes. In one episode, Lisa was elected student body president and received a make-over from the school administration (to distract her from the issues she wanted to address). When Marge saw her, she said, "Lisa, you look so successful— like you married a businessman!" (ouch).

Homer, who was doing dishes, said, "I wish I'd married a businessman. Then I'd have nice things." In this episode, *The Simpsons* displays overt, in-your-face stereotyping (in order to ridicule it) while at the same time subverting the stereotype. (Homer was doing the dishes, after all, and he seemed to be confused about his own role in the marital relationship.)

Probably the most direct attack on gender stereotypes in *The Simpsons* occurred during the episode "Stacy." Malibu Stacy is *The Simpsons'* version of our own wildly popular Barbie dolls. In this episode Lisa received a new, talking Malibu Stacy. She was horrified to discover that when she pulled the string, Malibu Stacy said things like "I wish they taught shopping in school," "Don't ask me. I'm just a girl," "Thinking too much gives you wrinkles," and "Let's bake cookies for the boys." (In art imitating life, there was an actual Teen Talk Barbie doll marketed by Mattel Toy Company in 1992 that said "Math class is tough." It was quickly pulled off the market.) Lisa was apoplectic and made a speech against the doll, calling it "sexist" (whereupon the other kids giggled and said, "Lisa said a dirty word!"). Marge tried to calm Lisa down, saying people aren't actually influenced by toys, so it won't really have an effect. Then Marge said, "Now let's forget our troubles with a big bowl of strawberry ice cream." Lisa pulled Malibu Stacy's string and she said, "Now let's forget our troubles with a big bowl of strawberry ice cream." Lisa pitched the idea for a new doll, which she said could have the common sense of Elizabeth Cady Stanton, the tenacity of Nina Totenberg, and the good looks of Eleanor Roosevelt. She got someone to produce her new doll, Lisa Lionhart, who said things like "Trust in yourself and you can achieve anything" and "When I get married I'm keeping my own name—that should be, IF I CHOOSE to get married." The media picked up Lisa's idea and the doll got lots of coverage, becoming the new must-have doll. But just as Lisa Lionhart hit the stores, a new form of Malibu Stacy came out, instantly displacing Lisa Lionhart as the new best thing.

Were Lisa (and *The Simpsons* writers) right to be worried about the effect of a toy on creating gender stereotypes? Toys aimed at young children clearly separate into three subgroups: those for girls (e.g., dolls, kitchen sets, make-up and dress-up kits); those for boys (e.g., trucks and construction equipment, tools and weapons); and those that are gender-neutral (e.g., puzzles, blocks and markers). Advertisers clearly pitch toys to boys or girls, to such an extent that ads for toys can be identified by six-year-olds as being for boys or girls by sight or sound alone, without the product even being identified (6). Ads for boys' toys are loud, bright and filled with action. Ads for girls' toys have soft melodic music, soft tones and hazy dissolves from scene to scene. Young children have been observed turning to a previously unwatched television after an ad for "their type of toy" begins (14).

So girls are clearly pointed toward stereotypically female roles and traits (e.g., cooking, fashion, childcare, concern with physical appearance) by advertisements and the toys they show. Similarly, boys are pointed toward stereotypically male roles and traits (e.g., being active, being tough, building things, being aggressive) by advertisements and the toys they show. But are advertisers and toy manufacturers creating the preference children show for "gender appropriate" toys, or are they merely filling a stereotypic demand that has been created elsewhere?

Before we lay the blame for gender stereotyping in toys at the feet of the advertisers and toy manufacturers, we must first examine the role of parents and even the children themselves in creating the patterns we see. Research has found that when parents chose toys for their children, they showed a preference for masculine toys for their sons and feminine or neutral toys for their daughters (13). Other research (3) shows that other adults showed even stronger stereotyping of toy preferences than did parents. So children are showered with and rewarded for playing with "gender appropriate" toys. Studies done recently show that these trends are a bit weaker in the twenty-first century than they were previously, but they are still clearly discernable. Cross-gender preferences in toys are especially discouraged among sons. Parents seem less concerned that their daughters are playing with building blocks or science kits than that their sons are playing with dolls or make-up. Adults not only reward children for playing with "gender-appropriate" toys, but they also can punish or show extreme disapproval for children playing with "gender-inappropriate" toys, leading to even stronger preferences on the part of children.

But what about a child left to his/her own choices about toys? Do boys naturally gravitate toward trucks and active play and girls toward dolls and social play? As much as we might like the answer to be a resounding "No," so we could charge toward gender equity in the home and in the workplace if we could just get those pesky toy manufacturers and advertisers under control, the answer appears to be "Maybe." A few threads of research lead to this possibility. First, boy humans as well as young males of most other animal species show more rough-and-tumble play than do females. Notable exceptions are girls who are exposed to extra androgen prenatally (4). Second, girls from very young ages prefer looking at faces, a social stimulus, rather than inanimate objects. The opposite pattern is found with young boys. These differences could lead to innate differences in toy choice in line with gender stereotypes.

Finally, the first author can offer her own experience as the feminist mother of a son and a daughter. My own children had the full array of toys from which to choose. My daughter Katie even received a truck from her eighteen-month-old brother Zack when he first saw her in the hospital. (Of course, he presented it by unceremoniously dropping it on her head.) So what happened in this single case study? I had the two poster-children for gender stereotypical toys. For example, my son received a Beauty and the Beast male doll for Christmas when he was three, and he promptly tied it onto the end of his backhoe and pretended it was a sewer pipe. He loved his backhoe, and carried it everywhere with him. And he wanted a weapon so much that when we refused to let him have toy guns, he fashioned what he called "the ultimate weapon" out of Duplo blocks and pretended the state of Florida from his jigsaw puzzle was a gun. My daughter never played with a truck after being conked on the head by one during her first day of life, but she lugged her favorite doll Sue-Babe with her everywhere, leading to many frantic dashes after zoo trains and back to McDonald's when Sue-Babe didn't come home with the rest of the family. Of course, my children were exposed to the normal socializing agents of television, friends and grandparents, so their behavior does not prove these preferences are innate. It does, however, prove that these patterns are not easily overcome by merely offering and encouraging a wide array of toy choices.

As children age, they are confronted with more sophisticated toys but the same gender stereotyping. Video games are clearly pitched to a male market. The most popular games contain lots of violence, lots of action and women who (if they appear at all) are buxom and scantily dressed. Increasingly, women who appear on the video screen are there as victims, with twenty-one percent of popular games including violence directed toward women (2).

The negative consequences of the male domination of the video game market extend beyond the violence level and women-as-victim message. Video games actually improve spatial abilities and mental rotation (12). Spatial abilities are related to math abilities, an area where males already enjoy an advantage. Girls who play video games show the same improvements as boys, but they are less likely to play them because of the male-oriented themes. So the male advantage in math might be growing larger, thanks to gender-typing of video game themes. As Teen Talk Barbie might now say, "Math class is tough, and about to get tougher!"

## Gender Roles in The Simpsons

In most episodes of The Simpsons, Marge stays well within the stereotypical female gender role. She is the wife and mother. She takes care of the house and children. She shops, cleans and carpools. But in the Springfield Pops episode, Marge clearly stepped outside the female gender role. In this episode, Marge captured a con artist by chasing him and hitting him with a trash-can lid.

Marge was so happy with her new, capable image that she decided to become a police officer. Marge succeeded in joining the police force, which was threatening to Homer. In the end, people running a counterfeit blue jean ring grabbed Homer. Marge freed Homer, but the designer jeans evidence mysteriously disappeared (as the other police all showed up in new designer jeans). Marge was so disillusioned by the corruption that she resigned from the police force.

Throughout this episode, Marge was departing from the traditional role of wife and mother. First, by pursuing the criminal and subduing him physically, she was showing herself to be competent and assertive, not weak and helpless. This assertiveness carried through as she went through police training and joined the force, in spite of Homer feeling threatened. Here she again took the assertive path instead of the nurturing path. But by the end of the episode, Marge returned to the female stereotype, being the principled one, the one who cannot tolerate dishonesty among her coworkers. And she retreated back into the female domain, the home.

Daughter Lisa is probably the least gender-stereotypical character on The Simpsons, and she clearly stepped in and out of the traditional female role in the episode "The President Wore Plaid." In this episode, Lisa was elected school president and immediately set out an agenda for her presidency. This alarmed the school administration. As the school principal said, "She is very popular and thinks for herself" and added, "like a female Eleanor Roosevelt." A female teacher pointed out that vanity is women's weak spot, so the school administration offered Lisa a makeover, ostensibly so she would look more successful. When Marge saw Lisa after the makeover, she enthused, "You're like Geraldine Ferraro, except you won and she failed miserably." Lisa became quite full of herself, with her new look and her access to the teacher's lounge, eventually being tricked into signing a form that eliminated art, music and gym from the school curriculum. Lisa was horrified at how she had been used, so she resigned as president and led a student protest that brought back the programs that had been cut.

This episode bounces back and forth between endorsing and challenging gender roles. Lisa, who is usually strong and capable, won the leadership position, which was a traditional male role. But she was sidetracked by vanity into becoming incompetent as a leader, putting her in the female gender-stereotypical pattern. Then she realized the error of her ways and returned to being competent and principled, but only by resigning from the traditional male role of president. So this episode bounces the viewer back and forth between traditional and non-traditional roles for Lisa like a wild roller-coaster ride.

## Masculinity and Femininity

Underlying gender stereotypes and gender roles is the concept of masculinity/femininity. Psychologists have struggled with defining and measuring masculinity and femininity since the 1936 work of Lewis Terman and Catherine Cox Miles (2). Their Attitude Interest Analysis Survey (AIAS) contained a masculinity/femininity (MF) scale, which conceptualized masculinity and femininity as endpoints of one continuum. On this scale, as one became more masculine, he or she of necessity became less feminine. The scale, unfortunately for Terman and Miles, was a flop. It didn't work to separate out men from women, much less high masculine men from less masculine men. Some researchers suggest that the AIAS MF scale measured idealized concepts of Victorian masculinity and femininity, rather than actual masculinity and femininity as it appears in real people (8).

The next big attempt to measure masculinity/femininity appeared in 1940, as the Mf scale of the Minnesota Multiphasic Personality Inventory (MMPI). The main purpose of the MMPI was to measure psychological disorders, not normal personality traits. The Mf scale was included in this instrument as a means to identify homosexual tendencies, so the scale was validated by comparing thirteen homosexual men with fifty-four heterosexual men. "Femininity" was thus defined by the responses of thirteen homosexual men (9)! This scale was also unable to separate out real men (as in, living, breathing, not as in "Real Men") from real women (again, living, breathing). It also confused the concepts of masculinity and homosexuality for years.

After decades of trying unsuccessfully to create or use one-dimensional scales that worked to separate masculinity from femininity, researchers finally realized that masculinity and femininity were not two ends of one continuum but two separate continua. Harkening back to the work on gender stereotypes, some researchers equate the masculine dimension with Competence (or Instrumentality) and the feminine dimension with Warmth (or Nurturance). Brannon (2) uses these two dimensions to identify the four possible subgroupings. She suggests we feel admiration for people who are high on both Competence and Warmth (Lisa?), envy for people high on Competence but low on Warmth (Mr. Burns?), pity for people low on Competence and high on Warmth (Homer?), and contempt for people low on both Competence and Warmth (Groundskeeper Willie?). Into which of the four classifications would you put the characters from *The Simpsons*? Will this become a new brainteaser?

Sandra Bem (1) produced a measure based on the two-dimensional idea of masculinity and femininity. The Bem Sex Role Inventory (BSRI) includes twenty characteristics representing the cultural stereotype of femininity (e.g., warm, childlike, understanding), twenty characteristics representing masculinity (e.g., ambitious, independent, aggressive), and twenty filler items that were judged equally true of males and females. The respondent then rates each characteristic as "always or almost always true" to "never or almost never true" on a seven-point scale. People are then categorized as high or low on masculinity and high or low on femininity. The resulting four groups correspond roughly to the four cells created by the crossing of Competence and Warmth, but the people who are High Masculine, Low Feminine are termed "masculine-typed" (regardless of whether they are male or female), those who score High Feminine, Low Masculine are termed "feminine-typed," those who score low on both are termed "undifferentiated," and those who score high on both masculinity and femininity are termed "androgynous." About one-third of people who take this test are "sex-typed" (meaning masculine males or feminine females), about one-third are androgynous (high on both), and only about ten percent are "cross-sex typed," meaning masculine females or feminine males (11).

Going back to our categorizations of the characters on *The Simpsons*, into which group would you place Krusty? Patty and Selma? Moe? Ned Flanders? Are Bart and Mr. Burns Masculine-typed? Is Marge Feminine-typed? Is Homer Undifferentiated? Is Lisa the only Androgynous one on the show?

## Conclusion: Sex and Gender in Springfield

As is true of most television programming, the male/female representation in Springfield is freakishly skewed toward men. The main characters all occupy traditional gender roles, with men working outside the home (the male domain) and Marge and the children occupying the home (the female domain). Masculine, testosterone-charged activity fills the episodes, with the kind, gentle, sweet notes being provided by Marge, Lisa, Maggie and sometimes Apu and Ned Flanders.

But males can certainly be incompetent (Homer, Bart, Sideshow Bob), so the male characters don't cleanly occupy the masculine stereotype. And some female characters (Selma and Patty) veer from the female stereotype with a harsh edge. In sum, Springfield is a town filled with traditional gender roles filled by characters that refuse to be caricatures of traditional gender stereotypes. And characters often move in and out of gender-stereotypic roles and actions, even within an episode, to great effect. So, in sum, the people who live on *The Simpsons* show are just like the real people who live in Springfield, Illinois. Or Massachusetts. Or Missouri. Or...D'oh!

## References

1. Bem, S. "The Measurement of Psychological Androgyny." *Journal of Consulting and Clinical Psychology*, 42, 1974: 155–162.
2. Brannon, L. *Gender: Psychological Perspectives*. Fourth Edition. New York: Pearson, Allyn & Bacon, 2005.
3. Campenni, C. E. "Gender Stereotyping of Children's Toys: A Comparison of Parents and Non-parents." *Sex Roles*, 40, 1999: 121–138.
4. Collaer, M. L. and M. Hines. "Human Behavioral Sex Differences: A Role for Gonadal Hormones during Early Development?" *Psychological Bulletin*, 118.1, 1995: 55–107.
5. Deux, K. and L. Lewis. "The Structure of Gender Stereotypes: Interrelationships Among Components and Gender Label." *Journal of Personality and Social Psychology*, 46, 1984: 991–1004.
6. Huston, A. C., D. Greer, J. C. Wright, R. Welch, and R. Ross. "Children's

Comprehension of Televised Formal Features with Masculine and Feminine Connotations." *Developmental Psychology*, 20, 1984: 707–716.

7. Jones, R.W., D. M. Abelli, and R. B. Abelli. "Ratio of Female: Male Characters and Stereotyping in Educational Programming." Paper presented at the annual meeting of the American Psychological Association, Los Angeles, CA, Aug. 1994.

8. Lewin, M. "'Rather Worse than Folly?' Psychology Measures Femininity and Masculinity: 1. from Terman and Miles to the Guilfords." *In the Shadow of the Past: Psychology Portrays the Sexes.* Ed. Miriam Lewin. New York: Columbia University Press, 1984a.

9. Lewin, M. "Psychology Measures Femininity and Masculinity: 2. From '13 Gay Men' to the Instrumental-expressive Distinction." *In the Shadow of the Past: Psychology Portrays the Sexes.* Ed. Miriam Lewin. New York: Columbia University Press, 1984b.

10. Lewin, M. "The Victorians, the Psychologists, and Psychic Birth Control." *In the Shadow of the Past: Psychology Portrays the Sexes.* Ed. Miriam Lewin. New York: Columbia University Press, 1984c.

11. Lips, H. *Sex and Gender: Fifth Edition.* New York: McGraw Hill, 2005.

12. Okagaki, L. & P. Frensch. "Effects of Video Game Playing on Measures of Spatial Performance: Gender Effects in Late Adolescence." *Journal of Applied Developmental Psychology*, 15, 1994: 33–58.

13. Wood, E., S. Desmarais, and S. Gugula. "The Impact of Parenting Experience on Gender Stereotyped Toy Play of Children." *Sex Roles*, 47, 2002: 39–49.

14. Yoder, J. *Women and Gender: Transforming Psychology.* Upper Saddle River, N.J.: Prentice Hall, 1999.

Linda Heath, Ph.D., is a professor of psychology at Loyola University Chicago, where her teaching and research interests focus on gender issues, media effects and psychology and law. She received her Ph.D. from Northwestern University and her B.A. from Ohio State University. She is a wife, mother and member of the Mixed Nuts Improv Troupe.

Kathryn Brown has been an ardent *Simpsons* fan for the past decade (since she was three years old). She peppers most conversations with her family with anecdotes from *Simpsons* episodes, which she watches at least daily. When she is not watching *The Simpsons*, she plays electric guitar, text-messages her friends and attends junior high school. Actually, sometimes she does several of these things concurrently!

# Hope Springs Parental

## The Simpsons and Hopefulness

### Karin H. Bruckner, M.A., L.P.C.

**I**F YOU HAVE HOVERED on the brink of despair for any amount of time, you most likely have come to appreciate the importance of hope. In desperate circumstances it embodies the power to bring us through to the other side, a means of enduring and then of persevering past all endurance. However, as crucial as it is, hope is not always accessible, as those who have actually tumbled over the edge of the abyss and had to climb their way up out of hopelessness can testify. How delightful, then, to find hope, whole and unblemished, dancing merrily through *The Simpsons*, a television world more typically associated with sarcasm and satire.

I must admit, the idea that hopefulness is somehow related to *The Simpsons* seems, at first blush, more than a bit of a stretch. My early conception of the series imagined it too crass, too critical and cynical, with characters that—on the surface—are just too dumb to find hope in the value-starved, cliché, sensationalistic world of TV suburban life. And besides, what successful television sitcom writers would be caught dead including something as un-hip, unsophisticated and sappy as hopefulness in their scripts? But whether or not they intended for it to be a vital

159

and evident component of the world they created, hope is as noticeably present in the Simpsons' lives as the humor it is known for. As I watch the characters maneuver through the cultural crises and familial conflicts that have resonated so clearly with viewers over the years, I can't help but notice the somewhat twisted, but nevertheless genuinely hopeful happy endings and make-the-right-choice resolutions found in most episodes.

Most people think of hope in terms of happiness—hopes fulfilled bring joy, and when we hope, we have something good to look forward to, something to be happy about. But psychological research tells us hope is more than just a feeling; it is a valuable psychological state, an essential part of a healthy and constructive approach to life. C. R. Snyder, an award-winning researcher and professor who has spent decades investigating hope in a variety of contexts, conceptualizes hope in terms of goals and the deliberate energy, or agency, employed to reach them: "I define hope as a thinking process in which the person clearly conceptualizes goals, but also perceives that s/he can produce the pathways to these goals and can initiate and sustain movement along those selected pathways" (1). This perspective goes beyond our emotional experience of hope to include factors that impact how we perceive, or see, our own capabilities as well as our environment, how we create a way forward for ourselves, and how we become and stay motivated during our life journey.

Hope researchers Karin Default and Benita Martocchio call hope "… multidimensional dynamic life force characterized by a confident, yet uncertain expectation of achieving a future good which, to the hoping person, is realistically possible and personally significant" (2). This view takes hopefulness beyond wishful thinking to a paradigm that says "life is good" and connects that goodness to one's own experience and future.

There is solid evidence for the impact of hope in our lives, as shown in research from multiple disciplines. Scientific study links hope with better physical health, the prevention of illness, improved recovery from cancer and other conditions, and greater pain tolerance (3, 4, 5, 6, 7, 8, 9). In addition, hope has been related to the enhancement of life satisfaction, coping skills, psychological well-being, stress tolerance, academic success, workplace efficiency and psycho-therapeutic outcome (10, 11, 12, 13, 14, 15).

A central paradox of hopefulness is described by people who should know, the ICIS Center for a Science of Hope. Dedicated to study the dynamics and the nature of hope, the Center was formed in 1984 as part of the International Center for Integrative Studies, and has contributed significantly to the current body of knowledge on the subject. In a formative seminar, they pointed out "...the tremendous vitality of hope in the midst of a civilization and a habitat that appeared to thoughtful people to be irrevocably condemned" (16). If we can be allowed to suspend reality just enough to characterize the typical *Simpsons* viewer as thoughtful (yeah, I know, it's a *cartoon*), then this description works well for Springfield and the universe in which it exists. The Simpsons' world is meant, among other things, to hold up a mirror to our own, supplying enough laughter to inspire the courage required for identifying and acknowledging the scary bits. The fact that the stories which unfold there contain abundant hopefulness is cause for celebration.

This is especially true when one considers the alternative, which is not merely a neutral, hope-free state, but hopelessness. Life without hope is, by definition, a life of despair—a human condition that comes with a set of serious psychological and medical sequelae. The loss of hope can lead to a number of unhealthy tendencies or states, ranging from depression and apathy to substance abuse and self-destruction. I know this not only because of what the research says, but because for four years in the late nineties, I worked as a crisis counselor for a large school district in the suburbs of a major metropolitan area. It was a front-line assignment, one in which drugs, violence, suicidal tendencies and abuse were daily fare. I witnessed a variety of self-destructive behaviors in children that that were intense and real, motivated in part by the futility they experienced in trying to deal with problems at home and at school. This desperation was not limited to children whose families were in dire economic straits or ravaged by traumatic misfortune. It extended across socio-economic levels and cultural backgrounds, and appeared in all types of family configurations, from the classic intact two-parent model to extended, mended and blended families.

What carried across all differences in context was the fact that these children had given up trying to escape the pain they experienced and instead, turned to face and pursue it with a vengeance. They found ample support in a popular culture that promotes alcohol and drug use as valid means for dealing with life problems, indulges fascination with violence and promiscuity, worships youth out of all meaningful proportion to its value and fixates on materialistic consumption. Along with encouraging addictive tendencies, this orientation offers no lasting relief for personal pain, and encourages short-term, symptom-alleviating quasi-solutions to these children's problems rather than effective resolution.

The Simpsons live in this society—our society—and pursue similar false remedies when seeking relief from the overwhelming stresses of modern life in the Western world. However, contrary to real life, they are not allowed to maintain delusions about their true state of being. At the writers' insistence, characters face their own mortality and humanity, even within the context of an animated world. In real life, each of us is allowed a choice between grappling with and growing from the tougher issues in life, or burying our heads a little deeper in the sand. With *The Simpsons*, however, the act of facing down and owning up to a little piece of human folly is a standard part of the action as well as the fun. Even Homer's constant and deeply rooted drive to maintain his favorite psychological state—total denial—can't save him from gaining some insight. In "Homer's Odyssey" he is snatched back from the brink of a suicidal act to become a leader in the movement for public safety and successfully navigates his way through the pitfalls of becoming a cult hero to retain his true identity. "I'm more and more interested in how to handle being aware of your own impending death, how to act with meaning in life," said Matt Groening in a 1999 *Mother Jones Magazine* interview. "...How do you handle your own freedom? [I'm] trying to see if I can get some of the ideas which keep me lying awake at night into an entertaining TV show full of way too many commercials" (17).

How to act with meaning in life and do so successfully is the key to happiness sought by Positive Psychology, a relatively new but important and growing segment of the discipline. Founded by Martin Seligman and colleagues, this innovative approach focuses on exploring critical factors in psychological health as opposed to concentrating on dysfunction and disease the way traditional psychology has. Those practicing Positive Psychology seek to discover and incorporate into their work characteristics that help us live fulfilling lives, achieve our goals and enjoy the journey. By studying experiences, traits and institutions that are wholly positive in nature, they hope to provide a road map for individuals and society to follow in the search for life satisfaction (18).

Although it was barely known only a decade ago, Positive Psychology has developed quite a high-profile reputation in recent years, with considerable attention paid by both the field of psychology and the popular press. Recent media coverage ranges from *Reader's Digest* to *The New York Times*, from Australia to Norway—it seems people are interested in learning more about finding happiness and its correlates. In addition, the Positive Psychology movement boasts sponsorship of fourteen initiatives, three centers, two task forces, twenty-nine research pods, four yearly international conferences, twenty-three educational grants and an annual summer institute (19).

Within this academia, Seligman's seminal work has succeeded in iden-tifying the specific experiences and individual traits that contribute to happiness, health and satisfaction. In collaboration with his colleagues, he has identified twenty-four strengths that make up five critical traits. Hope is one of these crucial five characteristics, along with zest, curios-ity, gratitude and love (10). Other recent studies by Positive Psychology researchers focus on hope within diverse contexts. Hope merits its own chapter in the *Handbook of Positive Psychology* (20), and has been iden-tified as the sole predictor of life satisfaction for young adults in a long-term study of Harvard graduates (21), featured prominently in work examining emancipation and social change (22), and recognized as ". . . an essential and distinctive feature of human agency," in an analysis of effective ways of hoping (23). In addition, there is the essential inqui-ry into the nature of the objects of our hope—the things for which we hope say as much about us as the act of hoping itself.

In his recent book *Learned Optimism*, Seligman reports on research examining the kind of life choices that produce rewards beyond the temporal and material. The study attempts to tease out those human qualities that contribute to achieving an authentic happiness, as op-posed to what he calls "taking a shortcut." Shortcuts to happiness most-ly involve things—pursuing those things we need and want in an effort to buy or obtain happiness. When we choose this path to fulfillment, we often become a slave to our appetites, attempting to feed them with-out constraint under the misconception that satiation equals happiness. Shortcuts also keep us looking outside ourselves for the source of hap-piness as a quick and easy fix, rather than doing the work necessary to finding fulfillment within.

Herein lies the irony of our Western hope, based as it is on the accu-mulation of material goods and the status they bring. In reality, they are not able to provide us with lasting happiness and in fact, are often tox-ic to our own sense of self. "The belief that we can rely on shortcuts to happiness, joy, rapture, comfort and ecstasy, rather than be entitled to these feeling by the exercise of personal strengths and virtues, leads to legions of people who in the middle of great wealth, are starving spiri-tually," says Seligman (10).

In our Western culture, we often place our hope in personal achieve-ment, and the magical combination of money, fame and power that has come to define the good life. While celebrating hope, *The Simpsons* is always on the lookout for our tendency to find shortcuts that bring temporary relief but no permanent happiness. The show skewers these shortcuts with bull's-eye accuracy, debunking the myths that other television families swallow whole every night of the week. Whether it is navigating a healthy work/life balance (Marge in "Mommie Beerest"), or challenging designer-toy mania ("Lisa vs. Malibu Stacy"), the family sets viewers straight time after time about the folly of taking too seriously the hopes and dreams Americans seem to relentlessly pursue through our longest-work-week, fewest-vacation-days-a-year lifestyle. Groening explains in his *Mother Jones* interview, "...what I'm trying to do in the guise of light entertainment, if this is possible—is nudge people, jostle them a little, wake them up to some of the ways in which we're being manipulated and exploited. And in my amusing little way I try to hit on some of the unspoken rules of our culture" (24). This refusal to accept the status quo, and the concomitant search for a path more worthy is one noticeable and compelling way that hopefulness stands out in *Simpsons* episodes.

For example, in the episode "Moaning Lisa," 8-year old Lisa has the blues. Because she is who she is, her average, everyday schoolgirl problems are experienced with existential angst—enough to fuel some impressively dark and brooding saxophone riffs, among other things. On the way to school one day, Marge decides to take a more active role in helping Lisa overcome her depression. She tells her daughter,

> I want you to smile today...it doesn't matter how you feel inside, you know, it's what shows up on the surface that counts. That's what my mother taught me, take all your bad feelings and push them all the way down, down past your knees so you're almost walking on them. And then you'll fit in, and you'll be invited to parties, and boys will like you and happiness will follow.

But as Lisa puts her mother's advice into action, Marge gets a good view of the fallout. When Lisa fakes her smiles, agrees with whatever others ask of her, and tolerates whatever they do to her without protest, Marge can't stomach seeing her daughter's real self disappear. Popularity and status, the attentions of the opposite sex, all are deemed unworthy of the sacrifice Lisa is making to become the perfect little girl through faking her happiness. " I take it all back!" Marge cries, "Always be yourself! If you feel sad, you go ahead and feel sad, we'll ride it out with you. From now on I'll do the smiling for both of us." Lisa's smile brightens considerably—and this time she really does feel like smiling! In this vignette we see Lisa and Marge demonstrate the importance of staying true to self and living genuinely. Here the writers touch on a theme that is foundational in the relatively new field of Positive Psychology.

In his book *Hope and History, An Explanation*, Professor Morton Smith puts forth a similar view of the importance we place on wealth as key to making our dreams come true. He states that focusing our hopes on the accumulation of wealth leads to "intense competition and perpetual disappointment" so that "one consequence of the general hope for wealth seems to have been a great extension of psychological poverty" (25). In the episode described above, Lisa is seeking a shortcut to happiness when she lies about her inner experience in order to accommodate others and win their approval. The fact that she is released from this fallacy and set on a straighter path offers us all hope of release for ourselves, hope of rescue from other lies, just as pernicious, buried in the messages popular culture sends on how to live the good life.

Defining the good life as it relates to a pleasant life and ultimately to a meaningful life is the focus of additional research by Seligman. He writes that a meaningful life has to do with rising to the occasion, and relates to connecting with something bigger than and beyond the self. For many, religious faith is the vehicle through which hope is found. The confident expectation of good described in Carter, Mische and Schwarz's definition of hope at the beginning of this chapter is "yet uncertain" without faith. But hope within a life of faith accepts the reality of an ultimate Goodness. Because there is God, perfect and uncorrupted by human imperfection, hope is possible in a world that is otherwise hopelessly flawed. Faith, then, is the means by which we experience and demonstrate our belief; our connection with the goodness we hope for. Researcher Jim Keen states that "...[hope] appears to have much to do with another human activity called faith. It particularly involves those dimensions of faith related to how one constructs one's sense of one's world in relationship to ultimacy, to the transcendent, to what is beyond one's grasp...from the developmental perspective, mature hope can most usefully be related to issues of faith and issues of commitment"(2).

As unlikely as it sounds, *The Simpsons* does not shy away from this connection between hope and faith, but in fact, treats the topic of religion with regularity (published reports claim 70% of episodes mention religion, while 10% focus on religious issues as the central plot (26)) and a surprisingly traditional flavor that includes regular church attendance and saying grace at mealtimes.

In fact, much has been written on *The Simpsons'* portrayal of faith and religiosity, in both popular and academic contexts (26, 27, 28, 29). Faith, religion, belief and hypocrisy are featured themes, all examined from a Christian perspective. The relationship between faith and hopefulness is perhaps best captured in the character of Ned Flanders, the Simpsons' born-again neighbor. Ned is genuine in his faith, goofy and clichéd at times, but always true to himself and his God. While the writers humorously portray the many faults and flaws that grow from his religious ideology and practice, they do not flinch from representing his faith in a positive light, as an important and constructive factor in Ned's life. When his wife dies, Ned is shown working through his grief and his anger at God, with his faith surviving intact in the end. His overzealous tendencies are exposed and thwarted (his attempts to force the Simpson kids into baptism are not allowed to succeed), but at the same time, he wins the grudging respect of characters and producers alike: the show's executive producers comment that, "Ned is everything Homer would love to be, although he'll never admit it" (30).

At the other end of the spectrum, Rev. Lovejoy, minister of the Simpson's church, exemplifies false faith in a delightfully humorous portrayal of the profane amongst the sacred. He plays out the hypocrisy characteristic of much of modern-day organized religion, providing a ready and abundant source of cynicism and pretense. In this area, however, the writers will only go so far in making fun of religious ideas and experiences. They focus on the false, the hypocritical, the ridiculous, but the show never degenerates into a blasphemous treatment of the holy. "*The Simpsons* is consistently irreverent toward organized religion's failings and excesses—as it is with most other aspects of modern life. However, God is not mocked. When *The Simpsons* characters are faced with crises, they turn to God" (31).

But more than anything, it is the way redemption is offered over and over again throughout the series that brings into focus the power of faith to bring hope to life. The Simpsons as a family seem to drive straight through each social issue or family problem and come right out the other side usually no better, but always no worse, than when the episode started. No matter how badly someone screws up, after we all have had a good laugh, there is forgiveness and a remedy of sorts in the end. In "Simpsons Roasting on an Open Fire," Homer bets the last of his Christmas funds on a loser dog at the track and dejectedly goes home to admit his failure as a provider. Instead of enduring a miserable reception at home, he's celebrated with cheers all round because he brought the pup home with him and thus delivered "the best present of all"—a family pet.

Perhaps the most pointedly redemptive story is told in "Bart the Daredevil," where Bart gains notoriety for his skateboarding prowess and, in an attempt to mimic a stunt car idol, promotes his own death-defying feat, announcing he will jump a local gorge on Saturday. Although he promises his parents he won't go through with it, he cannot face the shame of reneging, and so sneaks off to the gorge in a do-or-die attempt to maintain his reputation. Homer arrives on the scene at the last minute and declares he will jump instead. He is willing to take Bart's place not only to save his son, but to teach him the value of life itself as Bart experiences the pain of losing a loved one. This puts peer pressure in perspective for Bart, and offers him a more worthy paradigm for the concept of performing a heroic gesture. In the end, neither is compelled to risk life and limb crossing the gorge, and thus redemption is complete.

This episode also offers a primary illustration of a unique and interesting facet of *The Simpsons'* portrayal of hope. That is the fact that, contrary to expectations, Homer and Marge are consistently more hopeful, and hope in a much more naïve and childlike way, than their children, who entertain a cynically colored worldview. As parents, they come across as jaded and more simplistic in their belief in the goodness of life, love and family than Bart, who can't apologize to his sister without taking on the guilt of all creation ("Bart vs. Thanksgiving"), and Lisa, whose existential awareness takes her places her parents will never know. For instance, consider the scene where a coworker at the nuclear power plant tries to bring Homer face-to-face with reality. "Homer," he says, "It's time you learned a sad truth." Homer groans. "Ohhhh, can I learn it in a happy place?" The answer, of course, is yes, and a local amusement park becomes the setting for Homer's continuing education. Or consider the ultimate resolution of family conflict in "No Disgrace Like Home," where Marge and Homer come to the realization that their family is troubled in some serious ways. A brief discussion ensues:

HOMER: "We've got to do better as a family…sometimes I think we are the worst family in town!"
MARGE: "Maybe we should move to a larger community."

In spite of a course of family therapy that features aggression as a key intervention tool, Marge and Homer lead the way in expressing positive sentiments to each other, confirming their belief in the inherent good in each other and the world, and demonstrating their love in ways that ultimately outweigh the family's more negative dynamics. The children remain skeptical and sarcastic, but not immune to the hopefulness endowed to them by their parents.

These family roles are perhaps the opposite of the sort of arrangement we would expect to see in a family. In his book *Origins of Optimism*, Seligman explains that most kids hope persistently: "On the whole, prepubescent children are extremely optimistic, with a capacity for hope and immunity to hopelessness they will never again possess after puberty, when they lose much of their optimism"(32). Hardly an apt description of Bart and Lisa, but Marge, with her determined activism, and Homer, in his unabashed embrace of the easy way out, seem a good fit. With their childlike naiveté and purity, they are able to sustain hope more successfully than can their worldly children.

Herein lies the Simpsons' secret, I believe, and the key to the difference between this animated television family and the real-life families with whom I worked in my school system job. Where I found pint-sized runaways, twelve-year-olds who cut on themselves with abandon, and high-school juniors flirting with heroin, I also found, among many other things, parents without a clue about how to instill hope in their offspring. We may have forgotten how to pass on hope to our kids, but the Simpsons have not. While they retain that certain purity of heart and persistent optimism, we have let the world rob of us ours. We have allowed the hypocritical and unbelieving religion of Rev. Lovejoy to replace a true faith like Ned Flanders', one that is capable of nourishing hope through any kind of difficulty. Our dreams of happiness have been corrupted through materialism and a superficial value system.

Homer and Marge know a better way. Their love for each other and their children, while flawed and at times alarmingly misguided, is intact and unfailing. They teach us how, when our dreams are crushed either through our own folly or the cruel ways of the world around us, it is the power of love that makes it all right again, that love can restore our hope.

So, when a publicity-stunt dinner at the Simpson household turns into a disaster, Mr. Burns, the head of the nuclear power plant where Homer works, screams out that he will make sure Homer never realizes his most cherished dreams. Homer responds, "My dreams will go unfulfilled? Oh no, I don't like the sound of that one bit! That means I have nothing to hope for! Marge, please make it better! Can't you make it better?" Wise and loving Marge advises, "Homer, when a man's biggest dreams include seconds on dessert, occasional snuggling and sleeping 'til noon on weekends, no one man can destroy them." Homer pauses, considers... then cries, "Hey, you did it!" They kiss; the end (from "Two Cars and Three Eyes").

This kind of love as a source for enduring hope, set within the show's overall context of irreverence and rebellion, is perhaps best explained by Matt Groening in a 2002 BBC interview. At one point in the show, a listener asked, "Most people think *The Simpsons* decries family values, but I think the opposite is true, it promotes very conservative values, women staying home, families going to church. What do you think?" Groening answered this way:

> ...there isn't any single message, other than my own personal gut feeling that the authorities are not your side, no matter what they say. So we make fun of authority on the show. I think it's more fun to show a family that drives each other crazy and you try to figure out how to try to love anyway. I think that's been my experience in watching all my friends. You are driven crazy by the people who love you the most and that's part of what families are, and what the Simpsons deal with as well (33).

In the end, it is the show's confirmation in the power of this love to carry the day that gives *The Simpsons* its essence of hope.

# References

1. Snyder, C. R., *Hope Research Web Page*, 18 August 1999 (15 September 2005). <www.psych.ku.edu/faculty/rsnyder/hoperesearch.htm>.
2. Carter, L., Mische, A., and Schwarz, D., eds., *Aspects of Hope: The Proceedings of a Seminar on Hope* (New York: ICIS Center for a Science of Hope, 1993), 101.
3. Salovey, Peter, Rothman, Alexander J., Detweiler, Jerusha B., and Steward, Wayne T., "Emotional States and Physical Health," *American Psychologist*, 55, no. 1 (2000): 110–121.
4. Scioli, Anthony, Chamberlin, Christine, Samor, Cindi M., LaPointe, Anne B., Campbell, Tamara L., MacLeod, Alex R., and McLenon, Jennifer, "A Prospective Study of Hope, Optimism, and Health," *Psychological Reports*, 81 (1997): 723–733.
5. Richman, Laura S., Kubzansky, Laura, Maselko, Joanna, Kawachi, Ichiro, Choo, Peter, and Bauer, Mark, "Positive Emotion and Health: Going Beyond the Negative," *Health Psychology*, 24, no. 4, (2005): 422–429.

6. Jenkins, C. David, "...While There's Hope, There's Life," *Psychosomatic Medicine, 58,* no. 2 (1996): 122–124.

7. Grossarth-Maticek, R., Eysenck, H., Boyle, Gregory, Heeb, J., Costa, S., and Diel, I., "Interaction of Psychosocial and Physical Risk Factors in the Causation of Mammary Cancer, and its Prevention Through Psychological Methods of Treatment," *Journal of Clinical Psychology, 56,* no. 1 (2000): 33–50.

8. Barnum, David, Snyder, C., Rapoff, Michael, Mani, M., Thompson, Rosie, "Hope and Social Support in the Psychological Adjustment of Children Who Have Survived Burn Injuries and their Matched Controls," *Children's Health Care, 27,* no. 1 (1998): 15–30.

9. Snyder, C. R., Berg, Carla, Woodward, Julia, Gum, Amber, Rand, Kevin, Wrobleski, Kristin, Brown, Jill, Hackman, Ashley, "Hope Against the Cold: Individual Differences in Trait Hope and Acute Pain Tolerance on the Cold Pressor Task," *Journal of Personality, 73,* no. 2 (2005): 287–312.

10. Peterson, Christopher, and Seligman, Martin E., *Character Strengths and Virtues : A Handbook and Classification,* New York: Oxford University Press, 2004.

11. Snyder, C. R., *Handbook of Hope.* San Diego: Academic Press, 2000.

12. Snyder, C. R., Cheavans, Jennifer, and Sympson, Susie C., "Hope: An Individual Motive for Social Commerce," *Group Dynamics: Theory, Research, and Practice, 1,* no. 2 (1997): 7–18.

13. Curry, Lewis A., Snyder, C. R., Cook, David L., Ruby, Brent C., and Rehm, Michael, "The Role of Hope in Academic and Sport Achievement," *Journal of Personality and Social Psychology, 73,* no. 6 (1997): 1257–1267.

14. Adams, V., Snyder, C. R., Rand, K., King, E., Sigmon, D., and Pulvers, K., "Hope in the Workplace," in *Workplace Spirituality and Organizational Performance.* New York: Sharp, 2000.

15. Onwuegbuzie, Anthony J., and Snyder, C. R., "Relations Between Hope and Graduate Students' Coping Strategies for Studying and Examination Taking," *Psychological Reports, 86,* no. 3 (2000): 803–806.

16. Carter, Mische, and Schwartz, p. 3.

17. Doherty, Brian, "Matt Groening Interview," *Mother Jones Magazine,* March/April 1999, <www.motherjones.com/arts/qa/1999/03/groening.html.>

18. Seligman, Martin E., "Positive Psychology Executive Summary," *Positive Psychology Center,* 7 November 2005, (27 June 2005). <http://www.positivepsychology.org/executivesummary.htm>.

19. Seligman, Martin E., "Positive Psychology Network Progress Report," *Positive Psychology Center,* 26 January 2005, (27 June 2005). <http://www.positivepsychology.org/progressreport2004.pdf>.

20. Snyder, C. R., and Lopez, Shane J., eds, *The Handbook of Positive Psychology.* New York: Oxford University Press, 2002.

21. Isaacowitz, Derek M., Valiant, George E., and Seligman, Martin E., "Strengths and Satisfaction Across the Adult Lifespan," *International Journal of Aging & Human Development, 57,* no. 2 (2003): 181–201.

22. Braithwaite, John, "Emancipation and Hope," *Annals of the A emy of Political and Social Science, 592* (2004): 79–98.

23. McGreer, Victoria, "The Art of Good Hope," *Annals of the A emy of Political and Social Science, 592* (2004): 100–127.

24. Doherty, <http://www.motherjones.com/arts/qa/1999/03/groening.html>.

25. Hession, C., review of *Hope and History, An Explanation*, by M. Smith, *Aspects of Hope: The Proceedings of a Seminar on Hope*, ed. L. Carter, A. Mische, and D. Schwarz (New York: ICIS Center for a Science of Hope, 1993), 121.

26. Lewis, Todd, "Religious Rhetoric and the Comic Frame in *The Simpsons*," *Journal of Media and Religions, 1* (2002): 153–165.

27. Cantor, Paul A. "The Simpsons: Atomistic Politics and the Nuclear Family," *Political Theory, 27,* (1999): 734–749.

28. Herren, J., "The Simpsons and Religion," paper presented at the Society for Scientific Study of Religion conference, Houston, TX (October, 2000).

29. Lobdell, William, "D'oh God! *The Simpsons* and Spirituality," *Los Angeles Times*, September 1, 2001, sec. B.

30. Lewis, Todd, "Religious Rhetoric and the Comic Frame in *The Simpsons*," *Journal of Media and Religions, 1* (2002), 157.

31. Pinsky, M., "Dear God, This is Marge—Irreverent *Simpsons'* Look to Heaven," *The Seattle Times*, September 18, 1999, sec. D, quoted in T. Lewis, "Religious Rhetoric and the Comic Frame in *The Simpsons*," *Journal of Media and Religions, 1* (2002): 153–165.

32. Seligman, Martin E., *Authentic Happiness* (New York: Free Press, 2002), 125.

33. Greenaway, Richard, and Angwin, Richard, "Matt Groening Answers Your Questions," *Bristol Features*, The British Broadcasting Company, 2002. <http://www.bbc.co.uk/bristol/content/features/2002/animated_encounters/groening/groening_answers4.shtml>.

Karin H. Bruckner, M.A., L.P.C., is a writer, researcher and licensed therapist with a master's degree in psychology from Texas Woman's University. Her interests center on gender, spirituality, and the development of healthy paradigms for experiencing anger on a personal as well as a global level. She is the mother of three children and, along with her kiwi husband, currently enjoys a bi-continental lifestyle in the U.S. and New Zealand.

# Looking for Mr. Smarty Pants

## Intelligence and Expertise in *The Simpsons*

Frank C. Keil,
Kristi L. Lockhart, Derek C. Keil,
Dylan R. Keil and Martin F. Keil

THERE IS VIRTUALLY no culture, either real or fictional, that does not have experts in different areas of endeavor. In traditional cultures, artisans and craftspeople develop bodies of knowledge that are deeper and better articulated than in the minds of non-experts. In advanced societies such as our own, knowledge specialization has developed to the point that tens of thousands of experts exist in all manner of specialties. In this manner, the divisions of labor lead to corresponding divisions of cognitive labor. What we do for a living doesn't just define how we spend our time; it also characterizes a very substantial part of our mental lives and capacities.

These divisions of cognitive labor, or areas of expertise, raise a number of interesting questions about both intelligence and expertise. These include:

- What does it mean to be intelligent?
- Does the possession of high intelligence provide one with very general cognitive powers, or more circumscribed ones?
- How does intelligence relate to expertise?

- How is expertise best understood and how is it typically understood?
- If someone is especially talented in one area of performance, in what other areas is he or she likely to be talented?
- When should experts be consulted for advice?

Many of these questions have only recently been the subject of research and theory in cognitive science; but we are blessed with a large set of "thought experiments" in *The Simpsons*. In the course of writing episodes that cover topics ranging from nuclear reactor design to evolution to the stock market, we see views of expertise, the divisions of cognitive labor and how children and adults might differ. We also clearly see views about natural abilities and how they might be bounded. The writers of *The Simpsons* don't usually have particular cognitive scientific theories in mind, but they do, as keen observers of human behavior, often capture realistic patterns and sometimes, by caricaturing them, make it easier to see fundamental processes that we all share in real life. In other cases, they seem to deliberately take on common-sense conceptions of expertise and authority as a way of making fun of, or debunking, what many of us take for granted. In this chapter, we consider several case studies across episodes as examples of different aspects of the cognitive science of expertise and intelligence.

## Intelligence Versus Expertise

In psychological discourse, there has been considerable debate over whether there is a general intelligence factor, or "g" (e.g., Spearman, 1904; Thurstone, 1938). People with "high g" are thought to be able to excel at virtually anything mental, and therefore quickly become experts in any area where they devote a little attention and effort. The alternative view is that there is no such "g" and instead that, whatever intrinsic abilities people have, those abilities are more compartmentalized, such that one person might be able to become an expert in mathematics, a different person an expert in biology and still another an expert in language structure. In the research literature the consensus has tended to shift away from "g" views toward views of more specific intelligences (e.g., Gardner, 1983; Thurstone, 1938, 47; Sternberg, 1985); but, in the broader public's conceptions, the "g" view may persist.

In *The Simpsons*, the "g" view is dominant. Lisa, for example, seems to be the Renaissance girl, someone who is able to quickly master everything from the arts to the sciences to the humanities. She shows, for example, an extraordinary ability to have the best science fair project in fair after fair. She discovers that nerds give off special pheromones that attract geeks, thereby explaining their special persecution. She conducts a covert set of studies for another science fair to determine whether Bart or a hamster is more intelligent. In both cases, it is assumed that she is doing the science correctly. She doesn't always win the science fairs; but when she doesn't, it is made blatantly clear that she was one of the most deserving candidates. In one fair, Ralph wins the event when Principal Skinner is impressed by his diorama of Star Wars action figures (still in their plastic packages); but there is little doubt that Lisa and a rival girl have far better exhibits. In most cases, Lisa's intellectual prowess and creativity are the reasons for her outstanding performance, and they are recognized by others.

Lisa's "g" is thought to extend to musical ability, as she is repeatedly portrayed as having extraordinary musical talent, playing on a par with the professional saxophonist Bleeding Gums Murphy. There are interesting nuances here concerning the parts of "g" that contribute to musical talent and those that do not. Thus, Lisa's "g" talent is carefully kept distinct from her motor skills when she is told that her gene for stubby fingers will prevent her from ever achieving greatness as a musician despite the intellectual gifts that make her so musically sophisticated.

The notion of "g" as a kind of biological essence is further reinforced in an episode in which Lisa fears that she has a stupid Simpson "gene" that will emerge as she matures, much like Huntington's Chorea. Lisa develops this fear when she can't solve a brainteaser and then, shortly thereafter, experiences some other failures. As a result, based on a "g"-like assumption, she infers that she must be stupid in general. Grandpa Simpson's mention of a defective Simpson gene helps amplify her fears. Even the resolution of the "g" deficit problem reinforces the idea of a biological essence. Lisa learns that all the female members of the Simpson family are in fact brilliant achievers in diverse areas across the sciences and the professions. Thus, a "g" factor that is apparently genetic and sex-linked affords easy access to expertise in almost any area. Rather than there being a stupid low "g" gene for the Simpsons in general, it appears that there is a low "g" version of the gene for the men and a high "g" version for the women.

Lisa's possession of a high "g" factor is further reinforced in an episode in which she despairs of the general level of intellectual incompetence of the Springfield populace, a despair that is proximally triggered by a particularly low-brow "gross out" contest. To address the problem, Lisa joins Mensa, where her admission to the "high intelligence" organization is based on the obvious intelligence displayed in a letter that she writes to Mensa. Yet, here *The Simpsons* writers clearly recognize the limit of high "g" when Mensa takes over the administration of Springfield and tries to develop a paradise. At first, things indeed do improve dramatically, and Springfield is rapidly on its way to becoming a utopia. Later, however, instead of a paradise, the Mensa folks show a lack of social savvy as town affairs soon descend into chaos. High academic smarts don't seem to translate into good government. At the same time, the crisis is resolved by Stephen Hawking, perhaps suggesting that what is needed is not an alternative form of practical intelligence but simply a higher level of "g." Alternatively, by bringing in a theoretical physicist to solve problems in city administration, *The Simpsons* writers may have been poking fun at the idea that a high enough "g" is adequate to solve any problem.

Lisa's expertise clearly does not extend to all domains of ability, and the intuitive sense of the limits of her skills reflects a model of the reach of "g." It does not extend, for example, to athletic ability. In one story, Lisa decides that she wants to become a great dancer and takes lessons from a former actress. She soon learns, however, that she is hopeless as a dancer and has no chance of ever achieving at a high level of proficiency in that arena. Even the help of another expert, Professor Frink, via a pair of special dancing shoes cannot rescue Lisa. (Lisa does, in one episode, gain great skill as a hockey player, but we learn that her skill in blocking pucks does not arise from any sort of native talent but rather from years of practice attained in blocking personal attacks from Bart).

Lisa's limits are further revealed when Maggie is discovered, through a nonverbal intelligence test, to apparently have a higher IQ than Lisa. This result initially devastates Lisa, who then considers whether she should try to be something other than the smart child. She goes on to try to excel at stand-up comedy, posturing as a moody goth figure, a cheerleader, a rapper, a soccer player and a cowgirl. In all cases, she is quite incompetent. Here we see that high intelligence does not predict the social insight of a good comic, the ability to take on a social persona, physical competence or, more generally, how to be "cool."

Lisa's incompetence in social intelligence is also suggested in several cases where Bart shows far superior social skills. Moreover, in those few cases where Bart is nice to Lisa, it is often through facilitating her social life and enhancing her practical intelligence. For example, in one episode, after going to college for a while, Lisa alienates her normal friends and is only able to win them back when Bart shows her how to ruin a cake honoring Principal Skinner. Lisa, however, appears clueless as to why such an act will help her regain her old friends.

Although Lisa may be the dominant vehicle for modeling notions of an intellectual "g," the same message is conveyed by other characters. One of the most dramatic examples involves Homer. It is discovered that Homer has had a crayon embedded in his brain ever since childhood. Upon its removal, Homer becomes brilliant. The realm of the acquired brilliance again conveys a theory of the general intelligence factor. Homer immediately becomes aware of technical issues at the nuclear power plant that lead to safety concerns. He also ends up proving that God doesn't exist. Yet he starts alienating all those around him (except Lisa), and can no longer relate to many of his old friends. Indeed, the social strains are so high that he has the crayon reinserted so he can once again be slow witted. It is not clear here whether Homer's alienation while intelligent is because his intelligence in itself is off-putting, or whether it is the failure to have a corresponding accelerated social intelligence that is causing the problem; but, as in the case of Lisa, it is clear that high intelligence does not translate into improved social skills or happiness. In fact, a recurring theme of *The Simpsons* is the negative correlation between intellect and social skills and happiness.

In short, *The Simpsons* explores in considerable detail a "g" model of intelligence and seems to support a middle-of-the-road view in which "g" is seen as enhancing virtually all aspects of traditional academic performance, but not other forms of intelligences such as emotional, social and practical intelligence. This is a common view (Sternberg, 1985; Neisser et. al., 1996). *The Simpsons'* version may underestimate the extent to which differing academic skills also pattern differently across individuals, such as mathematical versus verbal skills, but it does resonate with a considerable literature. It also seems to embrace a largely innate view of intelligence, although it is worth noting that Lisa works very hard, as well. When Homer becomes intelligent after crayon removal, however, he becomes smarter without any additional effort. A natural intelligence is simply released.

The children themselves in *The Simpsons* also seem to endorse the idea of intelligence and other abilities as natural rather than learned talents. This conception has also recently received attention in research. Even quite young children are well aware of the notion of natural talent and how it differs from acquired talent. Children often think that one's natural abilities, whether good or bad, as well as more traditional personality traits, will "leak out" over time, sometimes despite overwhelming efforts to behave differently (Lockhart and Aw, 2005). The similar patterning of intelligence and other personality traits reflects ways in which intelligence is often seen as part of one's intrinsic personality. In this way, *The Simpsons* may capture children's biases toward "the natural" kind of person. Related research issues concern the extent to which children are essentialists, believing that people have inner essences, often biological, that determine who they really are (Gelman, 2003).

## Domains of Expertise

Above and beyond notions of a general intelligence factor in *The Simpsons*, there is also considerable attention paid to relevant domains of expertise. In psychological research, we know that people use a variety of ways to understand how knowledge might be clustered in other minds, and that they rely on their intuitions of such clusters to know how to access relevant forms of expertise (Danovitch and Keil, 2004; Keil, 2003). We can think of people who know everything about a particular kind of thing, such as a trivia expert on all facts associated with a narrow topic. Thus, Ned Flanders' Beatles collection suggests expertise on everything associated with Beatles, including Beatles dolls, Beatles lunchboxes and mugs, posters signed by the Beatles, suits worn by the Beatles on *The Ed Sullivan Show*, books such as *Learn Carpentry With the Beatles* and special Beatles beverages (e.g., John Lemon). Comic Book Guy seems to know everything and anything having to do with comic books, including (as shown on his comic book displays) having a comic book series known as "Mr. Smarty Pants."

We can also think about people who know a great deal about everything that helps them support a goal. Thus, if a person has the goal of selling shoes, we might attribute to that person any knowledge that supports that goal, such as knowledge of the latest fashions, of podiatry and healthy shoes, of the economics of offshore manufacturing, of the ways shoe sizes change over the course of a day and so on. This way of understanding expertise is an important part of real people's mental lives and is especially salient to young children (Danovitch and Keil, 2004). There seem to be fewer such cases in *The Simpsons*. The closest example might be with Mr. Burns, who seems to have extraordinary expertise in anything that has to do with making money, a kind of goal-based knowledge organized around financial gain.

Finally, there are clusters of knowledge in ways that are common in the sciences. Here, *The Simpsons* tends to spend more time making fun of the expertise of scientists than accurately depicting what they are likely to know. Consider, for example, Professor John Frink. It is never clear that Frink even has a legitimate area of expertise. Instead, he is portrayed as a mad, and often misguided, inventor, even though he also wins the Nobel Prize in a Halloween special. He helps find the Loch Ness monster, provides Lisa with magical tap-dancing shoes, invents a time machine, builds a battling robot, uses astrology and computers to predict the future, builds a missile to stop a comet (though the missile is flawed and destroys the only bridge out of town), develops a matter transporter and creates a shrinking ray device. Frink's expertise is loosely associated with all science and technology, or perhaps with popular media depictions of scientists in movies such as *Back to the Future* and the mad scientist films of the 1950s and '60s. It is a curious blend of different areas of science, engineering and clear pseudoscience (e.g., astrology).

Does this view accurately depict the public conception of scientists and would such a breadth of expertise actually strike many people as plausible? Are *The Simpsons* writers therefore accurately portraying public conceptions of science? Scientists are also frequently portrayed as having baser motives than the pure pursuit of knowledge. For example, a character bearing striking resemblance to Jane Goodall is first portrayed as studying gorillas in the wild in the best traditions of science. Later, however, it turns out that she is crassly using the gorillas to mine diamonds. Given the decline of the public understanding of science and the rising embrace of alternative non-scientific approaches such as "intelligent design," *The Simpsons* writers may in fact, in a humorous way, be anticipating a real-world shift in public attitudes.

Other sorts of academic specialists don't fare much better. We encounter a Swigmore University, with bartending professors, and Clown College, which teaches the art of clowning. In an adult education curriculum, we see Lenny teaching people how to spit and an obviously clueless Homer teaching people about successful marriages. In the episode in which Stephen Jay Gould is presented as an expert on fossils and is consulted on a DNA test, there is a more plausible domain of expertise; but, in the end, Gould admits to never performing the test. The theoretical physicist Stephen Hawking explains why Ray the mysterious roofer was never noticed by anyone else but Homer, suggesting that he has a broad capacity to explain any mystery ranging from black holes to missing persons. As noted earlier, Hawking also rescues Springfield from a mob riot in reaction to Mensa members' attempts to create a paradise. Why should Hawking be so good at such a range of abilities?

It is fascinating that, with the repeated mention of nerds over several episodes and with many descriptions of Lisa's aspirations to scholarly greatness, sometimes as a scientist, no plausible content domains of the sciences are presented. As noted earlier, this omission may be because the writers feel that the public poorly understands what the sciences really are and how expertise in that area is organized. But, at the same time, there is also recent experimental work suggesting that even quite young children understand knowledge clusters roughly corresponding to biology, mechanics and mathematics, and how one might be knowledgeable in one of these domains but not the others (Keil, 2003). For example, if one tells an elementary school child that a particular person knows a great deal about why basketballs bounce better on the sidewalk than on the grass (a case of mechanics), they will judge that the same person is more likely to know why a big boat takes a really long time to stop (mechanics) than why ice cream cones cost more in the summer than in the winter (economics). Perhaps, in the end, *The Simpsons* underestimates the sophistication of some of the tacit knowledge we all do have about areas of scientific inquiry, while more accurately representing the limits of our explicit knowledge. Alternatively, perhaps *The Simpsons* is relying on our understanding of fields of expertise in trusting that we will get the joke of Hawking also being an expert in applied psychology.

## Who Should Provide Advice?

We can also look for notions of expertise in the dynamics of advice and deference. Under what circumstances do characters seek out advice? Whom do they consult, and under what conditions do they accept the advice? *The Simpsons* is full of characters seeking and receiving advice, and often following it. In most cases, however, the advice is not sought from conventional experts. The one exception may be religious figures who are sought out for advice on religious matters and for solutions to personal problems. Yet, even in those cases, the figures are often represented as incompetent, such as the Reverend Lovejoy, who gives dreadful advice on personal affairs. More commonly, we see characters seeking advice from people with unclear expertise or from people with a very specific job skill. We see Krusty asking the Simpson family for advice on his routine, Bart asking Kent Brockman for advice on how to be a news reporter, Homer seeking advice from other food critics on how to give reviews, Apu and Manjula getting advice from Homer on how to conceive a child, Krusty getting parenting advice from Homer to guide him with his newfound daughter, Bart and Homer getting advice from Grandpa Simpson on grifting and Mr. Burns seeking advice from Homer on romance (as does Ned Flanders, when he asks Homer about dating). Even a janitor provides advice outside of his assumed expertise, telling the Simpsons how to reroute air traffic.

Homer listens to Lisa's advice on several occasions and things usually turn out disastrously, such as when he takes Christmas presents away from everyone in Springfield because he believes such an action follows the Buddhist principles he learned from Lisa. Moreover, when Lisa suggests reasonable explanations for a phenomenon, such as how the Coriolis force predicts that toilets flush in different directions in the northern and southern hemispheres, she is doubted. (Bart calls Australia to check). Although Lisa is incorrectly turning an urban myth into science here, Bart doubts her not because of his own scientific prowess, but simply because he doubts the claims of science.

There is no sense here of seeking advice from appropriate authorities, or of knowing when to take advice with a grain of salt. Instead, residents of Springfield seem to seek advice from just about anyone and often follow it for no good reason, and very often to disastrous results, such as when the town follows the advice of a self-help lecturer to find their "inner child" and then descend into mayhem as they act as they please. When there is some rationale for an expert, it is in the form of one who practices the activity rather than one who studies it. Thus, when Chief Wiggum is seeking expert advice on the criminal mind, he seeks out an expert criminal, Sideshow Bob, not an expert in criminology. The question arises as to whether the *Simpsons* characters are showing a pattern that mirrors human behavior. People do sometimes seek out advice from quite unqualified sources who often seem very eager to provide it (Williams and Ceci, 1998); but equally often, people and even preschool children do have some reasonable sense of who plausible experts are and when they are speaking with authority (Lutz and Keil, 2002).

## Expertise and Development

A different way of thinking about expertise and authority is the assumption that adults generally know more than children and are more qualified to offer advice and evaluate explanations. Yet in *The Simpsons*, adults are often terribly misguided, while there may be considerable wisdom in children's remarks. Not only does Lisa often outshine adults, but so also does Bart and, sometimes, even Maggie. In one episode, Lisa, who has been reading a book on heart surgery, provides critical advice to the surgeon Nick Rivera when he is operating on Homer. Outside the Simpson family, the precocious and annoying Martin Prince also often outshines the adults around him. The show takes considerable pleasure in pointing out the follies of adults and the good sense sometimes shown by children. Even when children are shown in the classroom, there are relatively few cases of an adult imparting valuable knowledge to a child or even of adults being wiser than children. (One clear case of an ignorant child is Ralph; but his streams of non sequiturs only serve to showcase the relative intelligence of all the other children around him). The children's teachers are often shown in unfavorable terms as compared to their students. In one episode, Bart steals all the teachers' guides (ancillaries to the class textbooks), and the teachers begin to panic without the guides on which to rely. Their "expertise" is portrayed as being completely external.

Across all the episodes, it is very unclear whether there is any plausible trajectory from being a child novice to an adult expert. This commonplace aspect of development in all cultures is left out perhaps just because it is far more humorous to lampoon the ignorance of adults by making them no wiser than the children around them.

There is, however, an interesting line of work on islands of expertise where children can far outstrip adults. This has been experimentally demonstrated with young children who are chess or dinosaur fanatics, where they not only know many more facts in these arenas, but also show more sophisticated patterns of thought even as they seem very childlike in other domains (Chi, 1978; Chi and Koeske, 1983; Chi et. al., 1989). Little chess wizards who can only remember a string of three numbers in their head can nonetheless also remember massive chessboard configurations that easily overwhelm adult novices in chess. *The Simpsons* may well be picking up on these local expertise effects and using them as a basis for making plausible claims about children as more knowledgeable than adults.

A different pattern in recent research concerns children's views of the depth of knowledge of those older than them. There is reason to think that they are very optimistic about how much more one is likely to know when one matures. This inference follows from work showing that children are more generally highly optimistic about their futures, thinking that even the slowest, shortest and most uncoordinated child is quite likely to end up being one of the fastest, tallest and most athletic adults (Lockhart et. al., 2002). We see evidence in *The Simpsons* of at least some children having grandiose expectations about their futures. Lisa is the most notable example, with her frequently boundless optimism about future careers, as well as about admission to elite universities. Milhouse also envisions a wonderful future. For example, in one episode he predicts that he will grow up to be a major league slugger. This prediction seems wildly optimistic given that, shortly after making it, Milhouse whiffs in his first attempt to hit a ball on a T-ball stand and then, after finally hitting the ball a short distance, trips over the stand. In contrast, Bart's future aspirations are often less lofty, as in the episode when he hopes to become so fat someday that he qualifies for workman's compensation. Bart may be a vehicle for showing a more realistic, if not even pessimistic, view of the future so as to contrast with the views of other children.

The great expectations of most Simpsons' children differ from the much more humdrum way in which most adult lives are portrayed, again supporting the thesis of youthful optimism. This high optimism about future abilities seems likely to extend to knowledge and expertise as well. Here, however, the Simpsons' children have yet to show wildly optimistic expectations about their future knowledge states as adults.

## Conclusions

*The Simpsons* provides an interesting mix of insight into notions of expertise, ability and intelligence as well as portraying popular misconceptions and distortions. The show's depictions of intelligence and its limitations are often quite sophisticated. There is a good representation of the "g" theory of intelligence both in terms of its appeals and in terms of its limitations. With regard to areas of expertise, the show tends to focus on trivia and goal-based skills, not on bodies of knowledge that we associate with domains of scholarly expertise. The one recurring professor is brilliant, crazy and not represented as having any coherent body of expertise. Other areas of academic expertise are trivialized by showing courses on spitting, clowning and successful marriages. A few genuine scholars do appear in some episodes, such as Stephen Hawking and Stephen Jay Gould; but even their expertise is either vague or plays no important role in the story. The sciences are probably given the most attention in discussions of elementary school science projects; but again, they are often used for comical effect, such as an exhibit of farts in a jar. It is in this respect that the show may depart from somewhat more sophisticated views of experts by the laypeople. At the same time, a rising tide of skepticism about science in the public and an increasing embrace of bogus alternatives to science may be depicted somewhat appropriately, albeit usually as caricatures, by The Simpsons characters.

The show, however, is skeptical of the value of advice. There are a great many cases when bad advice is given by people unqualified to give advice, and the advice is nonetheless blindly followed. Moreover, the show's general irreverence makes it difficult to ever represent adults as having much more sophistication than the children around them. In many ways this may be one of the best intentions of the series: to deflate pomposity and intellectual confidence in self-pronounced experts around us. In doing so, it may distort some of what we really do know about expertise and how people use experts, but it may also provide a more valuable lesson in humility.

# References

Chi, M. T. H. "Knowledge structure and memory development." In R. Siegler (Ed.), Children's Thinking: What Develops? Hillsdale, NJ: Erlbaum, 1978.

Chi, M. T. H., J. E. Hutchinson, A. F. Robin. "How inferences about novel domain-related concepts can be constrained by structured knowledge." Merrill-Palmer Quarterly, 35, 1989: 27–62.

Chi, M. T. H. and R. Koeske. "Network representation of a child's dinosaur knowledge." Developmental Psychology, 19, 1983: 29–39.

Danovitch, J. H., and F. C. Keil. "Should You Ask a Fisherman or a Biologist? Developmental Shifts in Ways of Clustering Knowledge." Child Development, 5, 2004: 918–931.

Gardner, H. Frames of mind: The theory of multiple intelligences. New York: Basic Books, 1983.

Gelman, S. A. The Essential Child: Origins of Essentialism in Everyday Thought. Oxford: Oxford University Press, 2003.

Gould, S. J. The mismeasure of man. New York: Norton, 1981.

Jensen, A. R. The g factor. Westport, CT: Praeger, 1998.

Keil, F. C. "Categorization, Causation and the Limits of Understanding." Language and Cognitive Processes, 18, 2003: 663–692.

Lockhart, K. L., B. Chang, and T. Story. "Young children's beliefs about the stability of traits: Protective optimism?" Child Development, 73, 2002: 1408–1430.

Lockhart, K. L. and J. Aw. "A Natural Bias? Children's Beliefs About Natural and Acquired Traits." Poster presented at the 2005 meeting of the Society for Research in Child Development, Atlanta.

Lutz, D. R., and F. C. Keil. "Early Understanding of the Division of Cognitive Labor." *Child Development*, 73, 2002: 1073–1084.

Neisser, U., G. Boodoo, T. J. Bouchard, Jr., A. W. Boykin, N. Brody, S. J. Ceci, D. F. Halpern, J. C. Loehlin, R. Perloff, R. J. Sternberg, and S. Urbina. "Intelligence: Knowns and unknowns." *American Psychologist*, 51, 1996: 77–101.

Spearman, C. "'General intelligence' objectively determined and measured." *American Journal of Psychology*, 15, 1904: 201–293.

Spearman, C. *The nature of "intelligence" and the principles of cognition.* New York: Arno Press, 1973/1923.

Sternberg, R. J. *Beyond IQ: A triarchic theory of human intelligence.* New York: Cambridge University Press, 1985.

Thurstone, L. L. "Primary mental abilities." *Psychometric Monographs*, 1, 1938.

Thurstone, L. L. *Multiple factor analysis: A development and expansion of the vectors of the mind.* Chicago: University of Chicago Press, 1947.

Williams, W. M. and S. J. Ceci. *Escaping the Advice Trap.* Kansas City: Andrews McMeel, 1998.

NOTE: Some of the research described in this paper was supported by NIH grant R-37-HD023922 awarded to Frank C. Keil.

Frank C. Keil received a B.S. in biology from M.I.T. in 1973, a M.A. in psychology from Stanford University in 1975, and a Ph.D. in psychology from the University of Pennsylvania in 1977. He was a faculty member in the psychology department at Cornell University from 1977 to 1998. Since 1998 he has been professor of psychology and linguistics at Yale University where he is also Master of Morse College. He has been a Guggenheim Fellow, a Fellow at the Center for Advanced Study in the Behavioral Sciences, and has received national awards from the American Psychological Association and NIH for his work in cognition and cognitive development.

Kristi L. Lockhart received a B.A. from Pomona College in 1975, an M.A. from Stanford University in 1975, and a Ph.D. in psychology from the University of Pennsylvania in 1980. She was a faculty member in the psychology department at Cornell University from 1980 to 1998. At Cornell she received two of Cornell's highest awards for teaching of undergraduates. Since 1998 she has been lecturer in psychology at Yale

University where she is also an Associate Master of Morse College. In 2004, she received the Elm-Ivy Award from the City of New Haven and Yale University for important work fostering relations between the city and the university.

# The Personalities of The Simpsons

## Simpsons' Big Five

### David A. Kenny and Deirdre T. Kenny

*"'cause you got personality!"*
—Lloyd Price song from the 50s

PEOPLE ARE CLEARLY DIFFERENT from one another. Unmistakably they differ in their looks; they also differ in their personalities.

Psychologists have investigated these differences for over a century. Among some of the most examined aspects of personality are self-esteem, intelligence, depression, sensation seeking, optimism-pessimism and internal-external control. However, in the last decade or so, research in personality has focused on the Big Five. Although there are several different versions of the Big Five, we refer to the most researched version, that by Costa and McCrae (1997). The Big Five factors, with several indicators, are as follows:

**Extroversion**: outgoing, energetic, humorous
**Agreeableness**: warm, accepting, trusting
**Conscientiousness**: conventional, careful, organized
**Neuroticism**: stable, well adjusted, calm (indicators of low neuroticism)
**Openness**: independent, creative, adventurous

One way to remember the Big Five is the acronym OCEAN. There is a debate among personality psychologists whether there is a Big Five or a Big Six or even a Big Seven. Moreover, there is even some evidence that the Big Five factors are different in different cultures (Yang & Bond, 1990). Whether the personality pie is sliced into five or seven pieces, the Big Five provides a convenient framework for summarizing personality differences.

How does the field of psychology measure these differences in people's personality, using the Big Five? Historically, the standard approach to the measurement of a person's personality is for a person to take a personality test. The person is asked a series of questions, and based on his or her answers, a measurement is made as to whether the person has the Big Five factor. These tests are used in a wide variety of settings, among which are: employment, vocational counseling, diagnosis of psychopathology and mate selection. Several books and websites offer personality tests; while some personality tests are subtle, most are very transparent. That is, the test taker can quite easily figure out what personality dimension is being assessed by the question. For instance, if you were asked, "Do you like to go to parties?" it would not surprise you that by choosing "yes" you indicate that you are extroverted. "No" would indicate that you are introverted.

Because of the transparency of self-report personality inventories, many psychologists have questioned their validity. That is, there are concerns that a personality test may not accurately measure what it purportedly claims to measure. What are the bases of these concerns? One concern is social desirability. People may be unwilling to describe negative features about themselves, especially in certain situations. For instance, if you were filling out a personality questionnaire for a job application, you may not be willing to admit that you cheated on tests and used illegal substances. Another concern is self-presentation. People have a self-image of who they are, and that self-image may have little or nothing to do with what they are really like. For example, you may fancy yourself as quite the athlete and competitor, despite the fact that you never played sports in high school and you are seventy-five pounds overweight.

Psychologists are aware that personality tests are biased, in part. However, it is not correct to say that personality tests are totally invalid. Any measure, even a very good one, has sources of error. No measure is perfect. Even physical measurement has errors. If you are five feet six, you are likely not *exactly* five feet six. Also, your height will vary by time of day, posture and measuring instrument. It should then come as no surprise that psychological measurement has error and bias. The current view is that personality tests do provide information about a person, but they do have biases.

You might wonder how we would ever know whether a personality test was valid or not. Psychologists have asked themselves this question too. Most accept that some measures of personality are more valid than others. In particular, the best way to determine whether a personality measure is valid is to see whether it predicts a person's behavior. Thus, although we can never ascertain with 100 percent certainty what someone's personality is, we can pretty closely approximate it.

## Peer Assessment

In the last twenty or so years, an alternative approach to the assessment of personality has been developing. Instead of asking people about their own personality, others who know the person are asked about that person's personality. The personality psychologist who pioneered this effort is David Funder, author of the *Personality Puzzle* (Funder, 2004), who is currently at the University of California at Riverside. The rationale for this method is that others are, presumably, less biased than the persons themselves. This is not to say that peers are unbiased, but rather biases are not as strong in the ratings of others as they are in self-ratings. Recall that all measurement contains some error, and even good measures have sources of bias and error.

How well do informant ratings work? Actually quite well. There is some evidence that they are more valid than self-reports. For instance, in a study conducted by Kolar, Funder & Colvin (1996), people were placed in a group and interacted with each other. After the interaction, each person was asked to rate him or herself on several traits, e.g. dominance, and the person was also rated on these traits by others. Kolar et al. concluded that the ratings of others were better, that is more accurate (i.e., related more strongly to behavior), than the self-ratings.

An additional advantage of observer ratings is aggregation. When we add up the judgments of several informants, some of their biases will be cancelled out. Therefore, by getting several judges to rate a person, we can obtain more reliable and valid ratings than from a self-rating.

A final advantage, and one particularly useful for the research that we later describe, is that knowledgeable informants can be used when a self-report is not a possibility. For example, Gosling, Kwan and John (2003) were interested in the personalities of dogs. Obviously, they could not ask the dogs to complete self-ratings of personality, so they used people to judge the dogs' personalities.

How well do informants need to know the person they are rating? Ideally, they would be knowledgeable informants. We would seek to ask the person's close friends, their romantic partner or family members. However, a very surprising finding is that virtual strangers are surprisingly accurate at knowing other people's personality. They are not as accurate as knowledgeable informants, but they are remarkably close. Albright, Malloy and Kenny (1988) developed the zero acquaintance paradigm. They had groups of strangers judge one another on the Big Five. These might be students who simply view each other on the first day of class. Surprisingly, many studies have found astonishing validity in these first-impression judgments. Total strangers can quite accurately read your personality.

Ambady and colleagues in several studies have shown that thin slices or little bits of behavior can also lead to valid judgments. For instance, Ambady and Rosenthal (1993) showed students a thirty-second clip of a professor giving a lecture. Surprisingly, the observers of this thin behavioral slice agreed very closely in their assessment of the professor's teaching ability with students who completed a semester-long course with the professor.

Finally, Gosling and colleagues (Gosling, Ko, Mannarelli & Morris, 2002); Vazire & Gosling, 2004) have shown that you do not even need to observe a person to know that person's personality. Just by viewing the person's bedroom, office or website, you can fairly accurately know the person's personality.

In sum, judgments by others are a good way to assess a person's personality. Ideally, these others should know the person well, but even strangers are surprisingly accurate.

## The Study

How do *The Simpsons* shake out when it comes to the Big Five? Of course, we cannot ask Marge and Homer to complete a Big Five questionnaire. However, we can ask viewers to evaluate the personalities of the cast. We recruited thirteen "Simpsonites," people who are heavy viewers of the show. While thirteen might seem like a small number of judges, we shall see that they provided sufficiently reliable data for the type of conclusions that we wish to draw. The sample consisted of eight men and five women; the age range was from twenty to fifty-four years old. They were heavy viewers of *The Simpsons*, and had watched the program, on average, for twelve years.

We presented the judges with a standard measure of a shortened Big Five (Gosling, Rentfrow, & Swann, 2003) called the Ten-Item Personality Inventory or TIPI, and we asked them to rate twenty characters from *The Simpsons* on ten traits on a seven-point scale. We did not include the baby Maggie, because she does not talk (although she did once say "Homer"), nor did we include Marge's twin sisters Selma and Patty, because they are a pair, and thus, may not have two distinct personalities. Our list of twenty characters are Homer, Marge, Bart, Lisa, Ned Flanders, Milhouse, Nelson, Barney, Moe, Groundskeeper Willie, Principal Skinner, Edna Krabappel, Otto Mann, Krusty, Apu, Abe Simpson, Ralph Wiggum, Reverend Lovejoy, Smithers and Mr. Burns. Because of time limitations, we limited the questionnaire to these twenty characters, and thus did not obtain judgments of some minor regular characters (e.g., Lenny and Chief Wiggum).

Our focus was on agreement in the perception of personality. Would our judges agree in their perception of the personalities of these characters; would they agree as much as others tend to agree in the judgments of real people? We might think that there would be more agreement on fictional characters. The very term "cartoon character" would seem to imply that the character is distinct and facets of their personality would be sharply drawn. Alternatively, it might be thought that cartoon characters can be made to do just about anything, and they are not necessarily consistent with any personality. For instance, in one episode Homer is a cheating college student and in another he is a charismatic prophet predicting the end of the world. If cartoon characters are inconsistent, then people will judge them quite differently. Thus, we are unlikely to find more-or-less agreement in the judgment of *Simpsons* characters.

Our volunteers stated they knew the characters very well, the mean on a 1 (do not know well) to 7 (know well) scale being 6.03. Homer is the best-known character (Mean equal to 6.77) and Reverend Lovejoy was least well known (5.54). We also measured how much they disagreed on each character (i.e., the standard deviation), and this measure did not correlate across the Big Five factors, the average correlation being essentially zero. This tells us that the judges either agreed or disagreed with each other equally in judging the characters. Thus, the judges know the characters equally well, even the characters that were not featured regularly, like Lovejoy and Groundskeeper Willie.

We performed detailed statistical analyses of the data, which can be found on http://davidakenny.net/doc/simpsons.htm. We present here the key results from those analyses (without including the statistical details.) The website also contains the questionnaire that we used, and you can compare your answers to those of our thirteen judges.

## Results

In Table 1, we have the ratings of the characters on the Big Five averaged across the thirteen judges. You can look for your favorite character and see how it is judged. For instance, we see that Abe Simpson is pretty low on all of the measures, except Neuroticism.

The central question of this research is whether judges agree with one another in their assessment of the characters' personalities. For example, do they agree that Homer is extroverted and open to experience? We used a measure of consensus (Kenny, 1994), which is equal to zero if agreement was only at chance level, and would be one if there was perfect agreement between all the perceivers. Based on past research (Kenny, 1994), we, and others, have found that the level of consensus using this measure is .275.

What did we find for the characters that we studied? As shown in Table 2, judgments of the characters' personality are quite reliable. Normally, with judgment data, we would hope for a minimum reliability of .7, and anything above .8 is quite good. Using these standards, we see that the judgments of the characters are very good, and that thirteen judges are sufficient, the average reliability being an impressive .924. When we look at the consensus results, we see three particularly interesting features.

First, we find much more agreement in the judgment of the characters than we do for real people. Judges agreed to an exceptional extent about the personalities of the characters. Perhaps the characters "behave" much more consistently than do real people because the writers of the show have clear conceptions of their characters' personalities.

Second, we find the weakest level of agreement for extroversion, which is surprising, because it is the one Big Five factor for which we usually find the greatest level of agreement. We think the reason for this is that virtually all the *Simpsons* characters are extroverted, and thus, they do not vary a great deal in their extroversion. Note that the mean on extroversion is 4.59 on a scale that ranges from 1 (not extroverted) to 7 (extroverted), which is the largest mean of the Big Five factors. In

| Character | Extroversion | Agreeableness | Conscientiousness | Neuroticism | Openness |
|---|---|---|---|---|---|
| Abe Simpson | 3.73 | 2.96 | 3.12 | 5.46 | 2.58 |
| Apu | 5.31 | 4.85 | 6.12 | 3.27 | 4.19 |
| Barney | 5.19 | 5.08 | 1.35 | 4.35 | 3.92 |
| Bart | 6.73 | 2.73 | 2.54 | 3.31 | 5.54 |
| Edna Krabappel | 4.00 | 2.81 | 4.58 | 4.77 | 3.23 |
| Homer | 6.15 | 3.54 | 1.69 | 5.19 | 5.35 |
| Krusty | 6.19 | 2.77 | 2.38 | 5.42 | 5.12 |
| Lisa | 4.27 | 4.62 | 6.69 | 4.08 | 5.35 |
| Marge | 3.81 | 5.46 | 6.54 | 3.92 | 4.04 |
| Milhouse | 2.96 | 4.42 | 4.08 | 5.92 | 3.12 |
| Moe | 3.15 | 2.96 | 3.62 | 5.15 | 3.08 |
| Mr. Burns | 4.50 | 1.35 | 4.85 | 3.92 | 3.35 |
| Ned Flanders | 5.15 | 6.27 | 6.42 | 3.12 | 2.38 |
| Nelson | 5.46 | 1.85 | 2.15 | 4.96 | 3.96 |
| Otto Mann | 5.27 | 5.27 | 1.96 | 3.08 | 5.19 |
| Principal Skinner | 3.69 | 3.27 | 5.69 | 4.81 | 2.15 |
| Ralph Wiggum | 4.58 | 4.92 | 2.23 | 4.62 | 3.65 |
| Rev. Lovejoy | 4.00 | 4.04 | 5.54 | 2.65 | 2.27 |
| Smithers | 2.92 | 5.15 | 5.92 | 4.27 | 3.42 |
| Groundskeeper Willie | 4.73 | 2.50 | 4.31 | 5.73 | 3.54 |

**TABLE 1**
Big Five Ratings Made by 13 Judges of 20 *Simpsons* Characters

*Scores can range from 1 to 7.

contrast, the thirteen judges saw themselves as scoring lowest on extroversion, relative to the other Big Five factors. Cartoon characters cannot be too introverted or they would not be very interesting. Jung (1999) obtained a similar finding when he studied celebrities (e.g., Jerry Seinfeld and Madonna), the least agreement for Extroversion. Again, celebrities are all generally extroverted and so the differences between them on Extroversion are weaker.

Third, and what we find most interesting, is that the level of agreement for conscientiousness is incredibly large, a value of .773. This val-

| TABLE 2 | | |
| --- | --- | --- |
| Consensus or Agreement in the Judgment of 20 *Simpsons* Characters on the Big Five | | |
| Big Five Factor | Reliability | Consensus* |
| Extroversion | .887 | .354 |
| Agreeableness | .952 | .574 |
| Conscientiousness | .980 | .773 |
| Neuroticism | .892 | .389 |
| Openness | .910 | .419 |

*Prior research normally finds consensus at about .275.

ue is almost three times larger than what we typically find. We suspect that much of what makes *The Simpsons* a very interesting television program is about the contrast in the conscientiousness of the different characters. The most conscientious characters are Lisa, Marge, Ned Flanders and Apu—the least conscientious are Barney, Homer, Otto and Nelson. Perhaps surprisingly, Bart is only the seventh least conscientious character of the twenty we measured. We do note, perhaps unsurprisingly, that our thirteen judges, all serious *Simpsons* fans, viewed themselves higher on Conscientious than on any of the other Big Five.

How are the different characters seen on the Big Five? In Table 3, we list the two characters who are the highest and lowest for each of the Big Five using the results from Table 1. For instance, Milhouse and Groundskeeper Willie are seen as the most Neurotic, and Otto Mann and Ned Flanders as the least. It is clear that the characters are seen differently on the Big Five. Note that fourteen of the twenty characters are either among the two highest or the two lowest. Thus, the cartoon characters are not seen as entirely good or bad and have, in fact, complex and multidimensional personalities.

| TABLE 3 | | |
| --- | --- | --- |
| Characters with the Most and Least of the Big Five Factors | | |
| Big Five Factor | Most | Least |
| Extroversion | Bart, Krusty | Smithers, Milhouse |
| Agreeableness | Ned, Marge | Mr. Burns, Nelson |
| Conscientiousness | Lisa, Marge | Barney, Homer |
| Neuroticism | Milhouse, Groundskeeper Willie | Otto Mann, Ned |
| Openness | Bart, Homer | Skinner, Ned |

In Figure 1, we present the ratings, averaged across the thirteen judges, of the four major characters—Bart, Homer, Marge and Lisa—on the Big Five. Looking first at extroversion, Bart and Homer are seen as very extroverted, whereas Marge and Lisa are seen as average. The pattern is just the opposite for the next two factors, but most clearly for conscientiousness. It is the two females who are conscientious and agreeable and the two males who score low on both these factors. The characters are about average in neuroticism, but Homer scores higher than the other three. Interestingly, Bart is the least neurotic. Finally, the characters are all scored relatively high on openness, but Marge scored least. In fact, Marge is the most "normal" family member in that her scores are closer to the scale midpoint of 4 than they are for any other character. It is interesting to note the one gender difference we find in our studies of college students is in conscientiousness, with women being perceived as more conscientious than men. At least in this case, the Simpson family mirrors real life.

Do we find agreement for liking? That is, do judges tend to particularly like some characters and dislike others? It may surprise you to learn that, in general, people agree less about whom they like than about that person's personality (Kenny, 1994). What do we find about the *Simpsons*

## FIGURE 1
### Ratings of the Four Major Characters on the Big Five

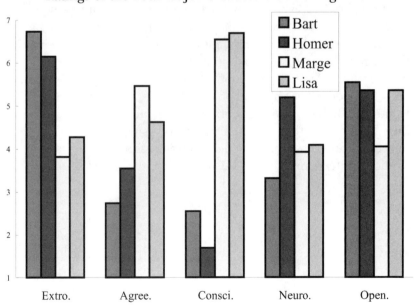

characters? The level of consensus in liking is .200, a value comparable to the .16 value that Kenny (1994) found for people who were well-acquainted with each other. Homer and Bart are the most liked, whereas Lovejoy and Skinner were the least liked.

Does liking correlate with the Big Five? Normally with real people, liking is most highly related to agreeableness, but instead, in this study we find that liking is most strongly related to openness to experience, r = .721. (A correlation of .5 is considered strong, and a .7 correlation is very strong.) To see the relationship between liking and openness, we have presented the results in a diagram, called a scatterplot, that is presented in Figure 2. The X axis has the measure of how much the character is viewed as being open to experience, and the Y axis is how much the character is liked by the perceivers. A data point in the scatterplot is denoted by the first three letters of the character's name. We see in the upper right of the figure that Homer is very open to experience and liked a lot. Whereas, in the bottom right, we see that Skinner and Lovejoy are disliked and seen not as open to experience. The graph clearly shows a relationship such that increased openness is very strongly correlated to liking.

The relationship of liking to agreeableness is complex, but very interesting. Unlike past studies, there is little or no relationship between how agreeable a *Simpsons* character is overall with how much that character is liked. However, we can relate agreeableness with liking for each character and that correlation is .263, the largest of any of the Big Five. For instance, for Ned Flanders, judges who see him as more agreeable like him more. There is an additional complication. This positive relationship holds for the least popular characters (e.g., Lovejoy and Skinner), but it does not hold for some of the most popular characters (e.g., Homer and Bart), and in fact, for these characters the more disagreeable they are the more they are liked. The results suggest that we are willing to accept and even appreciate disagreeableness among those we like. It would be interesting to see if this pattern holds for real people.

## Summary

Perhaps, some readers know more about Homer Simpson than they know about some of their friends. Moreover, they may spend more time observing Homer than they do observing their less close friends. Possibly, at least in part, Homer and the other *Simpsons* characters are as real to some people as are their real-life friends.

## FIGURE 2
### Scatterplot of Openness with Like

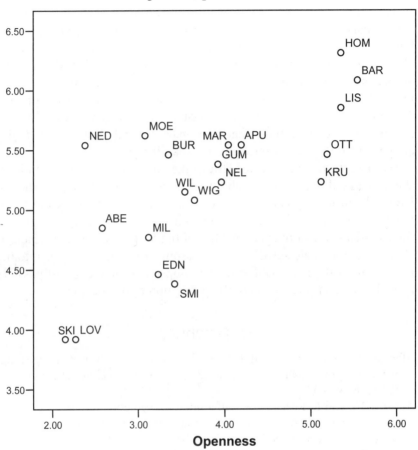

In general, the cartoon characters' personalities are much more extreme, and consistent, than those of real people.

Another result that differs for the *Simpsons* versus real people is that openness relates much more strongly to liking for the cartoon characters than it does for real people. However, agreeableness correlates with liking much more in studies of real people. Although it may be fun and entertaining to view cartoon characters trying out new things and entering unusual circumstances (i.e., being open), these same characteristics may not be as amusing or entertaining in a family member, close friend, or coworker. Similarly, agreeableness is a very important trait in real-life interactions with people, but viewing Homer being disagreeable to Flanders may be quite entertaining.

There are, however, several results of the *Simpsons'* study that are very consistent with judgments of real people. The judgments of the Simpsons characters were complex, as are those of real people. That is, characters were not perceived as entirely good or entirely bad, but rather, as possessing a mixture of good and bad traits. Both in this study and in those of real people, we also find limited consensus in judgments. There is indeed "no accounting for taste." Interestingly, both studies of real people and of cartoon characters have tended to show that males are perceived to be less conscientious than females.

We need to realize that our study, like any research, has limitations. We only asked ten questions about each character's personality, and we have only thirteen perceivers. We chose to look at twenty of the most well known, rather than all of the possible characters. We have also ignored the fact that some of the personalities of the *Simpsons* may have changed over time. Nonetheless, we have gained some interesting insights into the perception of the personalities of the Simpsons characters, and possibly gained some comprehension of the perception of real people.

# References

Albright, L., D. A. Kenny and T. E. Malloy. "Consensus in personality judgments at zero acquaintance." *Journal of Personality and Social Psychology,* 55, 1988: 387–395.

Ambady, N., and R. Rosenthal. "Half a minute: Predicting teacher evaluations from thin slices of nonverbal behavior and physical attractiveness." *Journal of Personality and Social Psychology, 64,* 1993: 431–441.

Funder, D. C. *The personality puzzle.* Third Edition. New York: W.W. Norton, 2004.

Gosling, S. D., S. J. Ko, T. Mannarelli and M.E. Morris. "A room with a cue: Judgments of personality based on offices and bedrooms." *Journal of Personality and Social Psychology, 82,* 2002: 379–398.

Gosling, S. D., V. S. Y. Kwan and O. P. John. "A dog's got personality: A cross-species comparative approach to evaluating personality judgments." *Journal of Personality and Social Psychology, 85,* 2003: 1161–1169.

Gosling, S. D., P. J. Rentfrow and W. B. Swann, Jr. "A very brief measure of the Big Five personality domains." *Journal of Research in Personality, 37,* 2003: 504–528.

Jung, T. *A new look at moderator variables of agreement: The role of target standing.* University of Connecticut, 1999.

Kenny, D. A. *Interpersonal perception: A social relations analysis*. New Guilford, 1994.

Kolar, D. W., D. C. Funder and C. R. Colvin. "Comparing the accuracy of personality judgments by the self and knowledgeable others." *Journal of Personality*, 64, 1996: 311–337.

McCrae, R. R. and P. T. Costa, Jr. "Personality trait structure as a human universal." *American Psychologist*, 52, 1997: 509–516.

Vazire, S. and S. D. Gosling. "e-perceptions: Personality impressions based on personal websites." *Journal of Personality and Social Psychology*, 87, 2004: 123–132.

Yang, K. S. and M. H. Bond. "Exploring implicit personality theories with indigenous or imported constructs: The Chinese case." *Journal of Personality and Social Psychology*, 58, 1990: 1087–1095.

# Acknowledgments

We would like to thank Marina Julian, who provided many valuable comments on a prior draft of this chapter. Additionally, we thank our thirteen judges, without whom we would not have a chapter.

David A. Kenny is a Distinguished Board of Trustees professor at the University of Connecticut, where he has taught since 1978. He has also taught at Arizona State University and Northwestern University. He is the author of six books, the most recent being *Dyadic Data Analysis*, and over 100 journal articles and book chapters. Besides his work in person perception, he is known for his contributions in the area of methodology. He is the proud father of three children, one of whom co-authored this chapter.

Deirdre T. Kenny is a graduate of the University of Connecticut, and she is currently a center coordinator for Planned Parenthood of Connecticut. She has been a *Simpsons* enthusiast since 1989 and is responsible for her father's interest in *The Simpsons*. In some ways, Deirdre is the Lisa of her family, as she has a strong social conscience and is a vegetarian. She even views her father as Homer, but she is quick to state that, unlike Homer, he is not that much of an irresponsible, insensitive, fun-loving drunk.

# Lyle Lanley, You're My Hero!

## The Social Psychology of Group Membership and Influence

Chris Logan

*"Ah, it's not for you. It's more of a Shelbyville idea."*

HI. I'M CHRIS LOGAN. You may remember me from such pages as the cover and the title page. The chapter you will read today is about social influence, or how to get other people to do your bidding.

If you want to get people to do something you want them to do, and they may not necessarily want to, you have two powerful sources of influence: the power of groups and the power of interpersonal influence tactics. The power of numbers lies in the fact that we are a social species and take some of our identities from the groups to which we belong. We have a strong desire to feel connected to our groups and the effective influence tactician can take advantage of this. We also attach ourselves so closely to our groups that we feel good when our groups look good and we distance ourselves from our groups that are underperforming. Just look at sales of shirts and hats for sports teams that are doing well versus those that are doing poorly.

The interpersonal tactics work a little differently. These are the psychological tools you can use in one-on-one situations to get people to do what you want them to do. These tactics do not necessarily require the presence of group pressures to work, but often rely on norms or appeals to larger numbers of people, even if those numbers are not physically present. By taking advantage of well-researched principles in social psychology, you can become adept at influencing others to do what you want them to.

## Power of Numbers

Why do we join groups? The most basic answer is that we have a fundamental need to belong. We have a strong need to feel connected to others, particularly but not exclusively close others like spouses and friends. These connections can even affect physical and psychological health. Some social psychologists argue that the need to belong is one of our most fundamental needs and is right up there with food, water and shelter.

Frequently, we join groups to boost our self-esteem. We take some of our identity from the groups to which we belong[1] and for us to feel good or better about ourselves we need to view those groups in the best possible light. We can do that either by boosting how we perceive our own group or by denigrating other groups. One of the most basic consequences of group membership is an ingroup bias. The ingroup is any group to which we belong. The outgroup is any group of which we are not a member. Once we form groups the biases start. We don't even have to have a strong personal connection to the group for the biases to occur; participants even experience these effects in psychology labs when assigned at random to groups. We will do things to benefit other members of our own group. We view members of the outgroup negatively. You can look at the rivalry between Springfield and Shelbyville as an example. Mayor Quimby's response to the Lyle Lanley quote I used to open this section was: "Wait just a minute! We're twice as smart as the people of Shelbyville. Just tell us your idea and we'll vote for it." By making salient the group memberships, Lyle Lanley activates the strong defense of the ingroup. There are plenty of other examples of this rivalry as well.

We make ourselves feel good by attaching to successful groups and people and avoiding the losers. When we link ourselves to the success of others, we are basking in reflected glory, or BIRG-ing. When we distance ourselves from the failures of others, we are cutting off reflected failure,

---

[1] This is part of social identity theory.

or CORF-ing. BIRGing and CORFing are not diseases treatable by Dr. Nick, but are tools of self-esteem maintenance. In many situations, we attach ourselves to group members who are accomplishing great things. "We" won the first game, but "they" lost the next week. When Homer thinks the Isotopes baseball team is going to have a terrible season, he stops watching and distances himself from that bunch of losers. Later in the season he shows up at Moe's and finds the team in a pennant race. He quickly steps outside and returns in full fan garb, including shirt, hat and oversized foam hand. He switches from CORFing to BIRGing at the drop of a hat, but both serve the same purpose—making Homer feel good about being Homer (and selling a lot of merchandise).

Anyone can be a fan, but exclusive groups, like the Stonecutters or No Homers or the country club, are valued largely because of their exclusivity. Membership is not offered to just anyone. Homer learned as a child about being excluded from clubs ("Homer the Great"). He wanted to get into the No Homers Club but was denied access ("It says no Homers. We're allowed to have one."). When he is older, he runs into the same problem with the Stonecutters. He has no idea what the club is or does, but knows that he wants in simply because he can't get in. Having someone tell us "no" activates psychological reactance, which is a motive to re-establish a sense of self-control. Every parent knows that if you tell a child not to do something and then leave the room, the first thing the child will do is exactly what he or she was told not to. We like to feel in control of our lives, and the rules of others diminish that control (Bart to Lisa: "Water doesn't obey your rules!"). You can actually get children to happily go to bed earlier than their regular bedtime by giving them the control to choose when to go to bed. If the regular bedtime is 9:00, at 8:15 you ask the child if she wants to go to bed in fifteen minutes or thirty minutes. She will likely choose thirty minutes and be in bed fifteen minutes before she was supposed to be. If you tell her to go to bed, she will say, "I don't want to" but if she has the control, she is more likely to go quietly. This doesn't always work, but the illusion of control can be a powerful ally. Challenges to our self-control are met with attempts to re-establish that control one way or another.

## Excellent!

We may want customers to purchase items at the Leftorium or have a town purchase our monorail left over from the World's Fair of 1964. We may want to find new members for our cult, country club or grass-roots movement. Many of the influence tactics we use or fall victim to are based on our affiliations with groups.

Group influence refers to how individuals are influenced by the behaviors of groups and usually leads to conformity (changing our public behavior to match that of a group). Normative influence and informational influence are two ways individuals are led to conform. Normative influence is the real or implied pressures individuals feel to go along with the group simply to get along with the group. In scenes from the class struggle in Springfield, the Simpson family has a chance to gain entry to the exclusive country club and Marge wants everyone in the family to be on their best behavior to be accepted. She is looking to how members of Springfield's social elite behave to guide the behavior of her and her family in order to be accepted and fit in. When all of Springfield prepares to celebrate their founder Jebediah Springfield, Lisa succumbs to normative influence when she decides to hide the negative information she finds out about Jebediah. She knew that he was less than reputable, but decided to say he was great to not disrupt the illusions of the town folk. With informational influence, individuals go along with a group because they are unsure of what the correct decision or behavior is and look to the group for information about a situation. Both of these types of influence result in conformity, but for different reasons and through different mechanisms. When Marge tries to get Itchy & Scratchy cancelled, she carries a banner that reads, "I'm protesting because Itchy & Scratchy are indirectly responsible for my husband being hit on the head with a mallet." Her attempt at getting other Springfieldians to go along with her is not based on trying to make them feel "cool" or accepted, but on providing information about the dangers of watching cartoon violence.

## The Power of, Well, Power

With interpersonal influence, we are investigating how one person can get another individual to act in a desired manner. You can either figure out sources of leverage to almost force others to do what you want them to do, or use the more subtle tactics of influence to get them to more freely choose your intended behaviors. Let's take a little walk through the manipulative abilities of some of Springfield's residents:

"Oh look! Some careless person has left thousands and thousands of dollars just lying here on my coffee table. Smithers, why don't we leave the room and hopefully when we return, the pile of money will be gone?" Mr. Burns is effective at using power to get others to do his bidding. The preceding quote is a nice attempt at bribery.

While there are almost unlimited sources of power, there are a few ways that social psychologists and conflict resolution theorists have categorized these sources. Social psychologists have traditionally categorized power into one of six sources: Expert, Referent, Informational, Legitimate, Reward and Coercive.[2] Conflict and negotiation researchers typically refer to the same sources of power as types of leverage. Expertise as power is similar to the influence tactic of authority which will be addressed in a later section. It is based on knowledge, skills or abilities that are valued by others. Referent power is based on an association with something positive, like a religious leader highlighting associations between church and God. Referent power can also come from individuals' abilities to draw others to them, commonly through charisma and personal warmth. Informational power is the power of arguments. The source of power in information lies in a speaker's ability to convince an audience of the merits of a specific position. Legitimate power is power that is freely given to someone. For example, when voters elected Homer Simpson as Director of Sanitation, they granted him certain powers over decisions and behaviors that affected their daily lives. Clearly legitimate power is not always used legitimately, but the source of the power lies in the position. Reward power is the carrot and coercive power is the stick. We can attempt to get people to do things we want them to do by offering something valued or threatening something unwanted. Mr. Burns has a tremendous amount of money and attempts to get a nuclear regulatory agent to overlook a problem or two at the Springfield Nuclear Power Plant in return for a hefty bribe. The ability to offer money, or any other tangible reward, can be very effective. "Mary Bailey won't fire me if I don't vote for her." When Monty runs for governor against Mary Bailey, he instills the fear of punishment in Homer.

Conflict and negotiation theorists usually discuss leverage, rather than power. The sources of leverage are essentially the same as the sources of power, but the connotations are not quite as negative. With leverage, you figure out what tools you have to try to sway the behaviors of others. In a negotiation you will figure out what your opponent desires and offer that (like a reward) in exchange for something you desire. You dangle that reward to get him or her to offer something in re-

---

[2] These categories are based on French and Raven (1959) and Raven (1965). These have been slightly updated more recently but still are based on the six categories.

turn. Leverage is usually about resource control, charisma, or personal connections.

*Influence.* Social psychologists are more likely to discuss influence than power or leverage. Robert Cialdini is the leading authority on influence.[3] He has developed a list of six types of social influence. Influence takes advantage of what are almost programmed responses. Cialdini refers to this process as "Click, Whirr." When there is a trigger, like an announcement of a limited-time offer, we have programmed responses, like buying a special Krusty rib sandwich. These responses can be so strong that we feel almost powerless to stop them.

*Reciprocity.* We are all somewhat guided by norms. Norms frequently tell us how we should behave in any given situation. What do most people do when in our situation or what should people do when in our situation? One of the stronger norms in western cultures is the norm of reciprocity. It is the social rule that you must return favors. If someone does something for you or gives you a gift or concession, you are expected to reciprocate. If you don't, you feel guilty unless of course you are Homer Simpson. Social psychologists would expect that Ned Flanders would be able to get Homer to do just about anything by pointing out how many times he has "loaned" items to Homer, but they would be wrong. Homer is not particularly subject to the norm of reciprocity but the rest of us are to varying degrees. When a researcher or non-profit sends you a questionnaire in the mail and includes a dollar or a shiny bauble or some free address labels, they are hoping to capitalize on the norm of reciprocity. By receiving this "gift" they can actually increase response rates. We don't all respond to this by filling out the questionnaire, though. If a "gift" is not viewed as such, but an intentional attempt at compliance, we are released from the norm. We are not obligated to return favors that are not really favors but attempts at exploitation. To effectively use this tactic you need to find a way to present something as a gift and then sit back and reap the benefits.

*Social Validation.*

LISA: Everyone likes Whacking Day, but I hate it. Is there something wrong with me?
HOMER: Yes, honey.

---

[3] For an excellent book on using and avoiding being a victim of social influence, check out Robert Cialdini's *Influence: Science and Practice.*

Social validation is the category of influence tactics that uses the behavior of others to influence our behavior. "Sorry, Mom, the mob has spoken!" This is the closest example of group influence of the interpersonal tactics. Social validation, or social proof, relies on having individuals seek interpretations of ambiguous situations from the responses of others. We decide how funny something is by how hard others laugh. We decide how to vote by looking at opinion polls to see how others are going to vote. We decide how to act in a new situation by looking at what everyone else is doing. Homer succumbs to social validation regularly.

When on vacation in Japan, Homer emerges from a bathroom in the hotel and sees the other members of his family having seizures while watching a cartoon. He doesn't call an ambulance or attempt to help them, but starts writhing on the floor with them. At first he has not seen the seizure-inducing cartoon the others have, but just joins in. To get this tactic to work, all that someone needs to do is stage a behavior to model appropriate behavior, or comment that "everyone is doing it." Take a look at an infomercial or a home shopping channel and see if there is a counter indicating how many people have already bought a specific item. How could so many people be wrong?

*Commitment and Consistency.* No one likes to look like a flake. We don't like to appear to be hypocrites, even if we are on occasion. How many times have you seen a baseball umpire change a call from a strike to a ball after announcing his ruling when the batter complains? It doesn't happen because the behavior is done publicly. When we publicly commit to a decision or course of action, we feel pretty strong pressures to stay the course. We can vacillate in private all we want, but once we publicly commit to a course of behavior we are unlikely to change. Diamond Joe Quimby is not particularly concerned with this tactic, but the rest of us non-corrupt-politicians are. He doesn't mind changing with the wind, but we do. Skilled politicians master the art of avoiding public commitments to anything in order to be able to change with changing public sentiment.

MAYOR QUIMBY: In other news, the chick in *The Crying Game* is really a man.
CROWD: Boo!
MAYOR QUIMBY: I mean, man is that a good movie.
CROWD: Yeah!

If you can get your target of influence to make even a mild public statement of support for a behavior or cause, you dramatically increase your chances of getting them to follow through with that behavior.

*Friendship or Liking.* Lyle Lanley is probably the best character at taking advantage of the liking influence tactic. He is the person who sells the town on the idea of building a monorail. He is essentially the prototypical snake oil salesman. He constantly grins from ear to ear. He has a friendly response to every question raised. He is very complimentary ("*Miss* Hoover? That is hard to believe!"). When challenged by someone intelligent seeking actual information, he has the ability to defuse the situation without wavering and can even make the skeptic a supporter.

> LYLE LANLEY: Hello, little girl. Wondering if your dolly can ride the monorail for free?
>
> LISA: Hardly. I'd like you to explain why we should build a mass transit system in a small town with a centralized population.
>
> LYLE LANLEY: Ha ha! Young lady, that's the most intelligent question I've ever been asked.
>
> LISA: Really?
>
> LYLE LANLEY: Oh, I could give you an answer, but the only ones who'd understand it would be you and me. And that includes your teacher.

After this transaction, Lisa turns from skeptic with a valid question to a smiling, giggling yes-girl. There was no effort to actually answer the question. There was no fear alleviated. But with a smile and a personal connection with a charismatic figure, he is able to get Lisa, or anyone, to go along with him. Likeability is an essential tool in the toolbox of the scam artist, sales person, or influence tactician.

*Scarcity.* The influential effects of scarcity are based on the reactance mentioned previously. Membership in the Springfield Country Club is about as exclusive as life gets in Springfield. Outsiders see rich and pretty people playing golf and dining at a fancy buffet. Membership is normally out of the range of possibilities for the Simpson family but they were once given the chance to gain entry. Marge is the only member of the family who truly falls prey to scarcity in the episode. Marge seems to dislike everyone she meets in the club, yet goes to extreme lengths to get in. She wants in because she can't get in. Take another look at the home shopping channels. Many of them have counters that count down instead of up. The ones that count down, indicating the number of units remaining, try to take advantage of scarcity rather than social validation. By telling you there are only a few units left, they are hoping that scarcity will activate your reactance and make you reach for the phone and credit card.

*Authority.* Authority as a tactic of influence usually works through obedience. About the only time viewers see Mr. Burns at the mercy of others is in "Homer the Great." He is a member of the Stonecutters, which is a hierarchical organization. Members' rank in the organization is based on the order in which they join. Lenny and Carl rank far below Mr. Burns at the Springfield Nuclear Power Plant, but at Stonecutters' meetings, he has to do whatever they ask. Homer ends up ruling the club because of a birthmark implicating him as the chosen one. With some encouragement from Lisa, Homer decides to take the group in a new direction. He tells the group to do good charitable works like painting a community center sky blue. The members do not want to do any of this, but obey because he is the authority figure (as disturbing as that may sound). They do whatever he says until they decide to resign from the club, removing Homer's authority. We can't always be the authority, but we can frequently get an authority to act on our behalf.

So far I have kept the tactics separate but to truly be effective, try combining tactics. There are several episodes of *The Simpsons* that show how you can effectively put several of these tactics together to get a greater return on your investment of effort.

## Examples of Applying Influence Tactics

*"Marge vs. Singles, Seniors, Childless Couples and Teens and Gays."* Politics are a breeding ground for influence tactics. In this episode, following the aftermath of a Roofi concert, some of Springfield's childless residents move to make the town less dominated by child-friendly policies and ordinances (Lindsay Naegle: "Let's kill every child-[pause]friendly thing in town!"). Marge responds by organizing PPASSCCATAG (Proud Parents Against SSCCATAG). Predictably, once the two sides form, group polarization occurs. When people join issue-oriented groups, there is a tendency for members to shift their opinions further in the direction in which they were initially leaning. That means that people who start off slightly against the child-dominant policies will shift to having a more negative view of those policies. The parents will become more activist-minded as a result of associating with other like-minded parents. Group polarization hap-

pens in part because of exposure to new ideas and arguments from the other members. It also happens because group discussion gives us a chance to figure out where we stand in the group. There can be an almost competition to be the philosophical leader of the group and few groups are led by the least extreme members.

In the SSCCATAG episode, we see a conflict that started largely because of scarcity. When Roofi was trying to sell tickets to a Woodstock-like festival for Springfield's babies, he pointed out that tickets would sell fast. "Hello, Springfield! Roofi is coming to your town. One show only! Tickets will go fast. Very fast! So your parents should be getting in line." That activated a very powerful influence tactic. When consumers feel they may not be able to get something desired, like Roofi tickets, they feel a strong desire to assert self-control. Marge rushed out to get tickets, and other parents even "disgraced" themselves to get them. Limited-time offers make us feel nervous that we may miss out on something. It turns out that it doesn't really matter if we even wanted that item in the first place. If someone tells us we can't have something, we respond with a quick "I'll show them!" and we go out and get it. This is that psychological reactance discussed previously that drives us to re-establish self-control which is implicated with scarcity.

Marge also tries to take advantage of likeability. She has Bart and Maggie hide while presenting Lisa to Miss Naegle as the perfect exemplar of wonderful children. She wants Miss Naegle to give up the fight against children out of affection for a very likable child. This almost works ("I would be proud if one of the eggs I sold turned out like you.") until Bart emerges with Maggie and a "soiled" purse. It is difficult to do harm to someone you like, and we feel drawn to those we do like.

Mr. Burns is actually a force of good in this episode (assuming supporting the Families Come First Initiative is a good thing). Carl and Lenny witness Mr. Burns signing Marge's petition for the initiative and succumb to social validation.

LENNY: Hey! If Burns is signing that petition, maybe we should too.
CARL: Yeah. Rich guys always want what's best for everyone.

Homer joins the social validation club to support his beloved Marge. Homer's TV commercial includes the following statement: "Families Come First is supported by lifelong Springfieldians you know and trust like me, Milhouse's dad, Bumble Bee Man, Surly Duff and that jerk that goes yeeeeessssss." By referring to members of the local community,

Homer is attempting to influence the audience to support the Families Come First Initiative. Influence affects various behaviors in political groups, but what about more extreme ones?

*Joy of Sect.* Cults seem to apply psychology very effectively for recruitment and maintenance of membership. The Movementarians are no exception. Why would anyone consider joining a cult? People don't usually join cults; they strengthen ties to friends and search for meaning and value and eventually find that they are deeply committed. There is no section in the yellow pages under Cults. That is a label people outside of the organization apply to exclusive groups with charismatic leaders, rituals of devotion, and isolation from the surrounding "evil" or "morally bankrupt" culture.

For the Movementarians, that charismatic leader is the Leader. Cult leaders tend to be very charismatic, which takes advantage of the likeability tactic. They establish authority through a connection to a higher power. In most cults, that is commonly a religious or spiritual entity, or some sort of alien being. For the Leader, that connection is based on his ability to apparently communicate with the aliens on Blisstonia. That connection makes the Leader an authority figure. He has knowledge or abilities that others do not, but want. The Leader is the one who builds the spaceship to take the members to a planet of pure happiness. The Leader is good. The Leader is great. We surrender our will as of this date.

A typical course of indoctrination for a cult begins with a request for a simple behavior, like passing out flyers. If a friend asked you to hand out a few flyers, you probably would. The cult isn't going to jump right in to assuming ownership of all your possessions. If they can get you to agree to a small request, like passing out some flyers in the airport, they can then actually increase your level of commitment to the group. Once we publicly agree to do something, we have a lot of trouble saying no to further requests. So, a cult member may approach you while you are walking down the hallway at the airport and offer you something for free, like a free weekend at a resort and a new and better life.

Once you are on their turf, the games begin. You are completely free to leave. This is key. The influence tactics don't really work if we don't feel that we are freely choosing our behaviors. In the Movementarian complex the soon-to-be members watch a nice little six-hour film, during which several of them get up to leave. When they do, they are reminded by a voice over a loudspeaker that they are, of course, free to leave. With a spotlight on them, they are asked why they want to leave, and they all just sit back down. They have now chosen to watch the rest of the film. They have chosen to stay at the Movementarian Agricultural Compound, and thereby the cult. That spotlight is subtle pressure compared to the razor wire, landmines, angry dogs, crocodiles and evil mystery bubble Marge confronts to escape, while being reminded again that she is certainly free to leave.

Once people are there and committed, the pressures to continue are strong. We like to think of ourselves as fairly intelligent people, and intelligent people would never join a group that was not worthy of them. Cognitive dissonance kicks in when there is a discrepancy between action (behaviors like signing the deed of the Evergreen Terrace house over to the Leader) and thought (intelligent people would not join a cult). In situations like this, we have to make a change to our thinking to maintain consistency (the group must be worthwhile because I am doing so many things to support it). That is the normal process, but we are talking about Homer Simpson. Homer does not really seem to experience any sort of cognitive dissonance, but most people would in that situation. When presented with a discrepancy like this, most people would feel anxiety and a desire to remove the unpleasant arousal. A sense of calm would follow the reduction of dissonance.

Kent Brockman's initial report of the activities of the Movementarians is pretty hard on the group, but he very quickly changes his tune when he finds out the station has been bought by the leader. His commentary changes not through dissonance, but through obedience to authority. This is a "if you can't beat them, take them over" kind of event. He is willing to give up his own views to ingratiate himself to his new boss.

The psychology of decision-making is discussed more fully in another chapter in this book, but Homer is becoming a full-blown member of the Movementarians not by a rational choice ("Would you rather have beer, or complete and utter contentment?"), but through the process of escalating behavioral commitments. We don't get to see Bart's process of indoctrination, but we do know that it is a result of a Li'l Bastard Brainwashing Kit.

## Conclusion

We are all occasional victims of social influence, whether it comes from normative influence driving our desire to belong, or scarcity activating reactance. The Stonecutters, PPASSCCATAG and SSCCATAGAPP are groups based on shared interests, whether it is getting drunk and playing ping-pong or community political change. The formation of groups based on shared interests heightens the feeling of belonging. The Movementarians is a group based on obedience to authority and a shared view of hope for a better life. The kinds of influence tactics that are used in those episodes demonstrate the six categories of influence identified by Cialdini.

By learning about the social psychology research on groups and influence, you too can become an effective manipulator of people (or avoid being a victim of manipulation). The ethics of using this information are definitely open for debate, but anyone can put together a fairly effective campaign to increase membership, avoid having your nuclear plant shut down, or sell a monorail. Not all tactics work the same way for or on all people, but the toolbox of influence is large enough to find either single tactics or combinations of tactics to work.

The presentation of these tactics in episodes of *The Simpsons* serves as a useful and humorous portrayal of what actually is used effectively in industries like toy and car sales, exclusive club membership drives and grass-roots political movements. We can all learn from Homer's resistance to influence attempts to feel a little more self-control in our lives. He may be weak as a kitten against social validation and authority, but he puts up a good fight against the other tactics simply by being a self-involved cognitive miser. Wait, is that really a good lesson? What do you think? I really need to know!

Chris Logan is a lecturer in the psychology department at Southern Methodist University. His area of expertise is the social psychology of conflict resolution. He has forced references to *The Simpsons* on friends, family members, innocent bystanders and countless psychology students at three universities over the last ten years. He has a B.A. in psychology from SMU and a Ph.D. in experimental psychology from Texas Tech. He lives in Dallas, Texas, where he teaches and consults.

# Springfield— How Not to Buy a Monorail

## Decision-Making (Mostly Bad) in *The Simpsons*

David A. Rettinger and James Rettinger

THERE ARE COUNTLESS decisions that have been made by the Simpsons and the other denizens of Springfield that have resulted in over 350 hilarious adventures. Who can forget the time that Homer purposely gains weight to get on disability ("King-sized Homer") or drives the monorail ("Marge vs. the Monorail"); when Marge decides to try and ban Itchy & Scratchy ("Itchy & Scratchy & Marge") or takes a job in the nuclear plant ("Marge gets a Job"); when Bart decides to get Krusty's autograph on a check ("Bart the Fink") or Lisa decides to become a vegetarian ("Lisa the Vegetarian"); or even when Maggie decides to disrupt the Ayn Rand School for Tots in an homage to "The Great Escape" ("A Streetcar Named Marge")? Well, this chapter will not deal with any of these antics. We will not be concentrating on the wacky end results that come from these odd decisions, but instead, looking at the thought processes we believe that all people use and pointing out how they manifest themselves in *The Simpsons*. As we all know, people are constantly making decisions that we find perplexing. By taking this behavior to its end result, *The Simpsons* shows some of the common things that people do when making decisions, in addition to providing brilliant satire.

There are two schools of thought when it comes to understanding how people make decisions. The first comes from economics and takes as its basis the idea that people do what they think is in their best interests. So, given a choice between making more money or less money, if all other things are equal, people will choose more money. This view has entered psychology as a family of theories that have *utility, value and/or rationality* as their basis. The goal of these theories is to explain decisions by evaluating the options people choose from based on the utility or value of each option.

For example, when Homer decides to stop at Moe's for a drink after work, the value of that experience is weighed against the negative value of the chance of getting a ticket or crashing on the way home. This is often referred to as the *algorithmic* view of decision-making. An algorithm is a step-by-step process that uses a formula in an unvarying way to reach a solution. Algorithms usually take a lot of work, but if executed correctly always lead to the best or correct answer to a particular question.

Consider this arithmetic problem: 1 x 2 x 3 x 4 x 5 x 6 x 7. To solve it using an algorithm, you do the multiplication: "One times two is two. Two times three is six" and so on. If an exact answer is needed, there is no real substitute for the algorithm. We can see algorithmic thinking in action when Homer meets Ray Mangini in Knockers ("Don't Fear the Roofer"). When Ray asks him to help finish a pitcher of beer, Homer's thought is depicted as a pitcher plus driving equals his car wrapped around the tree. Of course, in Homer's world this does not compute and he must recalculate so that a pitcher plus driving equals Homer as president! As we see, Homer is not very good at applying algorithms.

The other way of thinking about decisions is called the *heuristics and biases* approach, named for a book by Daniel Kahneman, Paul Slovic and Amos Tversky (1982). In contrast to an algorithm, which is always applied the same way each time, heuristics are "shortcuts" used to come up with rough and ready solutions to problems easily. There is no guarantee that a heuristic will lead to a correct decision, but depending on the situation, it's possible for heuristically made decisions to be quite accurate and extremely efficient. Experts often use heuristics to integrate lots of information to arrive at a conclusion (i.e., a doctor making a diagnosis); the complexity and ambiguity of the information may make the algorithmic approach impossible for the expert to undertake in the time allowed, especially as the expert may not even be aware of all the factors he is integrating into the heuristic conclusion.

But since a heuristic involves shortcuts it is always subject to error. Consider the multiplication problem above. If a quick estimate were needed, you could eyeball it and come up with something quickly and easily but not necessarily accurately. The really interesting part comes when you consider the problem 7 x 6 x 5 x 4 x 3 x 2 x 1. Let's hope you're more Lisa than Bart and so realize that the answer to the two problems is the same number (5,040, by the way). If you ask people to estimate (which is a heuristic method to make this judgment), you get much bigger estimates than if they estimate the same problem in reverse order. What's going on? The heuristic we use depends heavily on the first few numbers we look at, so when those numbers are larger, our estimates are larger. This creates a *bias*, and helps explain the pitfalls of the heuristic method.

Another important difference between the algorithmic and heuristic viewpoints is the matter of right answers. Historically, algorithms are linked to the idea that there's a right answer to every decision. You might call this *Marge or Lisa-based thinking*. When a decision-maker does something that violates certain rules of good decision-making, it's called "irrationality." A major element of algorithmic decision research is designed to point out irrationality. Within the heuristics and biases school, more emphasis is placed on our own thought processes and saving mental energy, and less on the rules for good decisions. You might think of this as *Homer or Bart-based*. After all, who uses less mental energy than Homer? We simplify our lives by using general purpose mental structures like our memories to aid in making choices and judgments, sometimes with bad consequences.

Homer himself describes the difference between the heuristic and algorithmic methods of decision-making in "Lost Our Lisa." As he says to Lisa, "Stupid risks are what make life worth living. Now your mother, she's the steady type and that's fine in small doses, but me, I'm a risk-taker. That's why I have so many adventures!" Homer relies on his past experiences of taking massive, death-defying risks and winding up okay to justify forging ahead in the most extreme circumstances, while acknowledging Marge's insistence (which she has passed on to Lisa) on using algorithms to find the right thing to do in every circumstance, regardless of how long it takes or whether it results in doing what you want to do.

In this chapter, we'll examine some particular ways of explaining decisions that can be categorized as either Marge/Lisa-based (algorithmic) or Homer/Bart-based (heuristic). We'll examine two types of algorithmic decision-making, utility theory and prospect theory, and three types of heuristic decision-making, availability, representativeness and anchoring/adjustment. We'll also look at biases in heuristic decision-making, such as overconfidence (a Bart specialty) and hindsight (à la Homer).

## Algorithmic (Marge/Lisa-Type) Decision-Making

All algorithms are based on numbers. Because they are formulas applied to situations, the only way for them to function is if the situations can be described numerically. If you were to build the simplest possible algorithmic theory of decision-making, what would it be? It would probably contain the idea that people would choose the thing that they like best from among their options. We're now left with the task of describing what people like best. In order to apply this simple rule, we must have a way of ordering people's desires from most to least. Putting a number to those desires is at the core of algorithmic decision-making. The most popular number for describing the value people place on things is *utility*. Daniel Bernoulli (1738/1954) proposed that while things or situations have certain intrinsic values, people perceive those values differently, and their perception of the value of something is a number that he called utility. Most importantly, he illustrated that increasing monetary value leads to "diminishing returns" of utility. As Hastie and Dawes (2001) point out, you would value $1 million a great deal and $2 million more, but not twice as much.

Once the notion of utility was established, it was possible to build psychological/economic theories to relate people's choices to their preferences. Those most associated with these first efforts were von Neumann, Morgenstern and Savage. The result of their work is a theory called *subjective expected utility theory*. The main principle here is that people, whether they realize it or not, are striving to be rational decision-makers. This means that we can calculate utilities and understand people's decisions because they will choose the thing with the greatest utility to them. Let's discuss the theory now, and later we can see how well it describes what people really do.

We rarely know exactly what the future will bring. We may have a good sense that if we order a Duff Beer at Moe's, it's likely that we'll get a Duff Beer, a sneer from Moe and, finally, a demand for some money (and possibly have a shotgun pointed at us). We won't know how good that beer will taste, or exactly how angry Moe might be. This all means that any choice we make will have some amount of uncertainty to it. We call utility for an uncertain event *expected utility*. We make choices based on our expectations about an uncertain future. Discussing that $1 million again, we can imagine a situation in which we are lucky enough to get the choice of that amount guaranteed (a hundred percent chance) or a fifty percent chance of getting $2 million with a fifty percent chance of getting nothing. The expected utilities in these cases represent the weighted average of the possible outcomes. In the first case, that's $1 million, because there's only one possibility. In the second case, it's also $1 million, but for a different reason. Now it's because there's a fifty percent chance of $2 million (.5 x 2 million = 1 million) and a fifty percent chance of nothing (.5 x 0 = 0). Adding those up gives an expected utility of $1 million.

This now gives us a simple formula for finding the utility of events and predicting people's decisions, but only if certain rules of rationality are followed. Just what rules must hold for this all to work? The first rule is *comparability*. This means that when forced to make a choice, people can, even when they seem indifferent. The next rule is *transitivity*. This means that if you prefer apples to bananas and bananas to cherries, you must therefore prefer apples to cherries. If this were not true, we could take serious advantage of you. Let's say Bart and Milhouse are at lunch. Milhouse's mom sends him to school with a banana, while Bart has stolen an apple on the way to school. Milhouse would gladly trade his banana for an apple, and would be willing to pay for the privilege. Now suppose Lisa comes by with some cherries. If Milhouse were not rational and preferred cherries to apples, he would trade his apple for Lisa's cherries, paying yet more money. Now he's faced with Bart again, and would pay Bart again to trade his cherries for the same banana, and so on forever. Since this behavior is patently nonsensical, for someone to be rational, they must show transitivity. The third and final rule of rationality we will discuss here (there are others, but they're not as psychologically important) is *independence*. This means that if you prefer one thing to another, you should prefer the same thing when they are put in an uncertain situation. For example, if you prefer a trip to an amusement park to a spa vacation, you should prefer a contest with a 1/100 chance of winning a trip to Itchy & Scratchy Land (and 99/100 chance of winning nothing) to the same contest with a 1/100 chance of winning a trip to Rancho Relaxo.

Summarizing subjective expected utility theory, people's decisions can be explained by their choosing the situation that gives them the most expected utility. Expected utility is calculated by finding the numerical personal value that people place on each outcome and multiplying it by their estimate of the likelihood of that outcome. This system works as long as people are rational, meaning that they follow the rules outlined above (among others).

So, how well does the theory work? The answer depends on your perspective. If you are a traditional economist, the answer is, "Just fine." These principles are the basis of most modern economic theory, and so to the extent that modern economics works (and it does), this theory can be said to be supported. However, a psychologist might respond, "Au contraire, mon frere." Because of a psychological emphasis on experiments testing individual behavior as opposed to the long-term study of markets, the conclusion of psychologists (and many behavioral economists) has been that subjective expected utility does not, in fact, describe human decision-making very well.

A major criticism of utility theories stems from their claim that people make decisions based on their values of outcomes. While this seems pretty straightforward, it leaves out the essential role that context plays in making decisions. Any poker player can tell you that a twenty-dollar win seems huge after a losing streak, while he's numb to a twenty-dollar loss at that same point in the game. Another way of expressing this idea is to think about "found money," like in the episode "Boy Scoutz 'N the Hood," when Bart and Milhouse find Homer's twenty-dollar bill and use it to buy an all-syrup Squishee. According to utility theory, the decision of how to spend that money shouldn't be affected by the source of the money. However, we see they use it to go crazy, Broadway-style! This squandering happens as a result of the way the money is accounted for mentally. It is tallied as a gain, and not as part of their current state of wealth. Their subsequent choices are dependent on the boys' point of reference.

The research laboratory version of this effect is called *gain-loss framing*. It is difficult for utility theory to explain these effects. Gain-loss framing occurs when people demonstrate irrationality by changing their preferences for identical decisions based on the way they are described. As you might imagine, the two possible descriptions are as gains or as losses. For example (from Tversky and Kahneman, 1981):

Imagine that the U.S. is preparing for the outbreak of an unusual Asian disease, which is expected to kill 600 people. Two alternative programs to combat the disease have been proposed. Assume that the exact scientific estimate of the consequences of the programs is as follows:

Program A$_1$: If this program is adopted, 200 people will be saved.
Prospect B$_1$: If this program is adopted, there is 1/3 probability that 600 people will be saved and 2/3 probability that no people will be saved.

or

Program A$_2$: If this program is adopted, 400 people will die.
Program B$_2$: If this program is adopted, there is 1/3 probability that nobody will die and 2/3 probability that 600 people will die.

Hopefully, it is clear that prospect A is the same in both cases—200 people live, 400 die. The same is true for prospect B: 1/3 of the time everyone lives, 2/3 of the time everyone dies. However, if you are like most people in Tversky and Kahneman's original study, you chose A$_1$ and B$_2$ (seventy-two percent of people chose A$_1$ and seventy-eight percent of different people chose B$_2$). This pattern is called gain-loss framing and clearly violates the rules of rationality, since according to those rules we must be consistent. It turns out that we tend to prefer risky choices when faced with losses and sure things when dealing with gains. This is an example of how our reference point can influence preferences, since losses and gains must be relative to something.

When we first meet the Simpson family in their own show ("Simpsons Roasting on an Open Fire"), Homer needs money for Christmas presents and looks at his options based on *prospect theory* (Tversky and Kahneman, 1981). In other words, he evaluates his wealth state not based on the fact that his mall Santa job left him wealthier than not having the job at all, but based on the point that he is poorer than if he had gotten his regular Christmas bonus.

Prospect theory is a variant of subjective expected utility theory that accounts for some deviations from the rational rules. It is also used when people are dissatisfied with using algorithms to describe decision-making and are looking for something different. Prospect theory has three important principles that differentiate it from utility theories. First is the inclusion of a reference point. Under prospect theory, we judge options based not on the final result, but on how that result compares to some basis for comparison. That comparison point is usually our current state, but it isn't always.

The reference point is important because it creates a dividing line between gains and losses, which prospect theory says we treat very differently. This brings us to the second element of the theory, which is that gains of increasing size are valued less and less, by the law of diminishing returns, and losses of increasing size are more and more unpleasant. There is diminishing pain for losses just as there is diminishing joy for gains.

As we saw with the Asian disease problem, this causes people to tend to avoid risk when dealing with gains and seek risk to avoid losses. Returning to Homer at the track, we see that going Christmas shopping with his meager earnings would have seemed like a sure loss, because it was less than his reference point. Under these circumstances, it's not surprising that he was risk-seeking in his attempt to avoid the sure loss, because the pain of the even bigger loss isn't that much greater. If he saw his earnings as a sure gain, as the audience mostly did, he would not have gambled, because the increased gain wouldn't bring as much joy and the risk wouldn't be worth it. Of course, Homer being Homer, he chooses to ignore the advice he is given about the sure thing and decides to listen to Bart and risk his money on Santa's Little Helper.

Another attribute of the reference point in prospect theory is that losses are felt more acutely than gains. This means that you would be unhappier about losing twenty dollars than you would be about winning twenty dollars. This explains why most people won't bet one dollar on a fair coin toss. The win won't feel as good as the loss would feel bad. This aspect of prospect theory explains the *endowment effect*. Once we own an item, it's part of our total wealth, even if we've just acquired it. Selling feels like trading money for a loss and buying feels like trading money for a gain. In this context, it's easy to see why we need more money for the loss than for the gain—we need to be paid more for the more unpleasant loss.

At the bottom line, prospect theory does a much better job of explaining what decisions people will actually make than subjective expected utility theory. Does this mean that people aren't rational, at least in the economic sense we described earlier? Some have argued that this is true, and it certainly seems likely in Springfield. One of the strongest arguments against rationality has been the existence of heuristic decision-making. These shortcuts seem to ignore the issue of rationality entirely and use our mental resources as the basis for decision-making.

## Heuristic (Homer/Bart-Type) Decision-Making

As we've said, heuristics are guidelines or rules of thumb for making decisions. They've been called "fast and frugal" by some (Gigerenzer and Goldstein, 1996) for this reason. Malcolm Gladwell has praised heuristic decision-making in his book *Blink*, in which he provides dozens of real-life examples where people's unconscious, automatic judgments turn out better than their reasoned, algorithmic ones. One of those examples is of art experts who can immediately judge the authenticity of ancient artifacts and decide not to buy them. The experts may not know exactly what bothers them at first glance, but the artifacts don't "look right." This automatic, heuristic way of making judgments can be very accurate, but does have its problems. The catch is that heuristics can lead to systematic errors in decisions that are referred to as biases. These biases are not always important, but in some cases lead to real problems. The three most researched heuristics are *availability*, *representativeness* and *anchoring and adjustment*. All three were discovered and named by Amos Tversky and Daniel Kahneman in the 1970s. The heuristics have a few commonalities that are important to notice. First, they are indeed efficient. Second, they all rely on basic cognitive processes like memory retrieval or putting things into categories; and third, they are prone to the biases we mentioned earlier.

Turning first to the availability heuristic, try to remember as many episodes of *The Simpsons* as possible that include Patty and Selma. No doubt you can think of many, including such classics as "The Way We Was" (when Homer meets Marge), "A Fish Called Selma" (when Selma marries Sideshow Bob), and "Homer vs. Patty and Selma" (when Homer borrows money from the menacing twins). Now, try to think of as many episodes as you can that do not include Maggie. Not as many probably come to mind, since most people don't categorize episodes based on which characters are not in them. You might therefore estimate that there are fewer of those episodes. This is the concept of availability, which says that some events are much easier to retrieve from memory than are others. This is not surprising, but what might be is the idea that we sometimes make decisions about future probabilities based on availability, and not on past probabilities. This naturally leads to a bias toward over-predicting events that are similar to memorable events in the past. We leave it to our readers to figure out whether there are more episodes with Patty and Selma than without Maggie.

A classic example goes like this: Are there more words in English that (1) start with the letter "k" or (2) have the letter "k" as their third letter? Many people answer (1), because those words are easier to think of (are more available). However, there are actually three times more words with "k" as the third letter. This is an example of availability affecting one's judgment.

Representativeness is a different sort of heuristic. It is used to judge whether or not a person or object belongs to a particular category or not. These judgments are often crucial in making decisions. For example, when deciding to gamble, you'd like to look at the roulette wheel and tell whether or not it falls in the category of really random (and thus fair). If you meet a new kid on the playground, you must quickly determine whether he's more like Milhouse or Nelson so you can react accordingly. How do we make these decisions? By using representativeness, or the rule of thumb that says that the more representative something is of the category, the more likely it is to be in the category.

Suppose Maggie starts school in a few years. We know from Lisa and Bart's experiences that there are roughly three nerds for every one bully in Springfield Elementary. Maggie meets a new boy, Max. He fits the stereotype of a bully—big, goofy teeth, wears a vest, says "ha ha" often. Representativeness tells us that Max is likely to be a bully, since he fits the category. However, it's important to remember that there's only a one in four chance that he is a bully. This means that we might make an error here by ignoring the makeup of the school population. The technical term for this is "ignoring the base rate" and will reappear later when we discuss biases.

The classic experimental example of the representativeness heuristic is Linda the bank teller. In Tversky and Kahneman's 1974 paper, they presented subjects with this description of Linda:

Linda is thirty-one years old, single, outspoken and very bright. As a student she was deeply concerned with issues of discrimination and social justice, and participated in anti-nuclear demonstrations. Which of the following statements about Linda is more probable?

(1) She is a bank teller.

(2) She is a bank teller who is active in the feminist movement.

In the original study, eighty-five percent of participants judged statement two as more likely. This has been explained by their use of the representativeness heuristic. Again, this is a problem, because the second statement contains the first, and so it has to be less (or equally) likely, because just one non-feminist bank teller would make statement one more likely. This was termed the "conjunction" fallacy, and the blame was laid at the feet of the representativeness heuristic.[1]

Anchoring and adjustment is our last and most generally applicable heuristic. As you'll see, it can be applied to any situation where one

---

[1] Later research has disputed this claim (Gigerenzer and Goldstein, 1996).

is required to make a numerical judgment. Anchoring and adjustment describes the process by which we generate some number as an estimate and adjust based on our beliefs about the accuracy of our initial estimate. The term "anchor" is really appropriate, though, since our final guesses are dragged toward our initial estimates. We usually fail to adjust enough, even when we know our initial estimates are useless. In one of the best psychology experiments of all time, Kahneman and Tversky (1974) asked students to spin a wheel of fortune to generate a random number (they actually rigged the wheel so that half of the students got a low number and half got a high number). Afterward, they asked them what percentage of countries in the United Nations are from Africa. If you think about it, there is no reason whatsoever to think that subjects in this study would allow their estimates of U.N. countries from Africa to be influenced by the spin of a wheel, but they did. The people who saw the wheel land on ten guessed twenty-five percent of countries and those who saw it land on sixty-five guessed forty-five percent. This shows that even when we know the anchor is meaningless, we fail to adjust our estimates appropriately.

Closely related to heuristics are a set of biases that we often bring to our decisions. You see them in everyday life both in the "real world" and in Springfield. Some of these biases, like the so-called *gambler's fallacy*, or base rate errors, are clearly related to the heuristic decision methods we've been talking about. Others, like the *overconfidence bias*, are caused by other aspects of the decision-making process. What all of these biases have in common is the effect of making our choices less effective than they could be.

Representativeness causes the gambler's fallacy, which comes into play whenever someone is trying to predict the future outcome of some random process. Naturally, casinos provide a perfect example of this, but this way of thinking can influence our judgments of people's behavior, the weather or anything else that seems random to us. Here's how it works, using roulette as a simple example: If you've ever been to a casino (don't take Flanders, and don't end up married if you can help it) you may have noticed that roulette wheels frequently list the previous results in lights above the table. This is to help bettors find patterns in the rolls. Assuming that the casino keeps the wheel fair and even, this list is there to play into the gambler's fallacy, which is that the output of a random process should look random at all times. That means that for a fifty-fifty (roughly) proposition like red or black on a roulette wheel, there should never be a large number of reds without a corresponding number of blacks.

This is silly, of course, since each spin of the wheel is random and independent. The wheel can't see the list above it, and certainly doesn't remember what was rolled. After ten or twenty or a hundred rolls of black, the chances on the next roll are still the same as they were on the first roll. The wheel is not "due" for a red. If anything, one might believe that the wheel is biased toward black.

It's clear from spending five minutes in a casino that people do believe that the wheel is "due." This happens, according to heuristic theory, because a set of spins that has lots of blacks and reds alternating is more *representative* of a random process than one with many runs of red and/or black. People are using representativeness to predict future rolls rather than their understanding of how the wheel actually works.

Another bias that has a substantial effect on our decision-making is overconfidence. While most people would express overconfidence as a mistaken belief in one's ability to jump Springfield Gorge on a skateboard, psychologists talk about overconfidence in decision-making as an inappropriate belief in the accuracy of our own judgments. In the laboratory, this is often expressed numerically. Imagine that I bring in a weather forecaster every day and ask her whether or not it will rain the next day and how confident she is in her prediction on a one to one hundred percent scale. We can then look at all of the fifty percent days, sixty percent days and so on. What we'll find is that the actual percent of rainy days is consistently lower than her estimate. In other words, she was more confident in her prediction than she ought to have been, given the weather. We call that overconfidence. This happens in all walks of life, and it has wide-ranging consequences.

One of them is the *self-fulfilling prophecy*. In "Bart the Genius," when Bart's school aptitude test shows that he is a genius, overconfidence in that assessment causes his life to be turned upside-down as he is shipped off to the nerd class. Of course, Bart isn't able to live up to this prophecy, but in many situations people behave as they are treated, and so overconfidence in snap judgments can be important. A real-life example plays itself out on poker tables every day. There are many players out there who are overconfident in their assessments of the hands that others are holding. They wager based on those assessments and often lose money to other players who have compensated for their overconfidence.

What we've seen from these examples and explanations is a view of decision-making that emphasizes our intuition and how our automatic thought processes cause us to make decisions that don't seem to match up with the "correct" answers. From this point of view, it's easy to conclude that people are stupid. While this holds true for Clancy and Ralph Wiggum, it's unfair to paint all of us with this broad brush.

The psychologist Gerd Gigerenzer and his group have been arguing that the reason people are so bad at these decisions is because the decisions are too artificial. The laboratory examples we've been discussing all require people to make decisions about probabilities, like the chance it will rain tomorrow, or carefully constructed situations, like Linda the bank teller's. In real life, we see events as part of a set of similar circumstances, and so consider frequencies rather than the probability of a single event. If when talking about "Linda," you ask, out of 100 people like her, "How many are bank tellers?" and then, "How many are feminists?" And then, "How many are both?" people don't make nearly as many errors. Why? Because this version of the problem uses frequency and not probability, and many of the biases we've discussed disappear when the problems are reframed using frequencies. Does this mean that we should then abandon the heuristic viewpoint? We would argue not. Many of these biases do occur frequently outside of these examples, and people do, in fact, make decisions about probabilities at times. It is therefore useful to remember these heuristics and biases when making our own decisions and evaluating those of our friends and neighbors in Springfield.

## Conclusions

To review, there are two major types of decision theory: heuristic and algorithmic. Heuristics are simple rules of thumb designed to get quick and efficient answers. In Homer's or Bart's hands (or minds), they are tools of laziness, but many consider them to be necessary for our mental efficiency. Algorithms are formulas or rules we use to calculate our preferences and make sure we get what we want. We've called this Marge or Lisa-type decision-making, but it's a basis for thinking about all decisions. Utility and prospect theories are the examples of algorithmic decision-making discussed here.

## References

Bernoulli, D. "Exposition of a new theory on the measurement of risk." *Econometrica, 22,* 1954: 23–36. Original work published 1738.
Gigerenzer, G. and D. Goldstein. "Reasoning the fast and frugal way. Models of bounded rationality." *Psychological Review, 103(4),* 1996: 650–669.

Hastie, R. and R. Dawes. *Rational choice in an uncertain world*. Thousand Oaks, CA: Sage, 2001.

Kahneman, D., J. J. Knetsch and R. Thaler. "The endowment effect, loss aversion and status quo bias." *The Journal of Economic Perspectives*, 5(1), 1996: 193–206.

Kahneman, D., P. Slovic and A. Tversky. *Judgment under uncertainty: Heuristics and biases*. Cambridge: Cambridge University Press, 1982.

Tversky, A. and D. Kahneman. "The framing of decisions and the psychology of choice." *Science*, 211, 1981: 453–458.

Tversky, A. and D. Kahneman. "Judgment under uncertainty: Heuristics and biases." *Science*, 185, 1974: 1124–1131.

David A. Rettinger is assistant professor of psychology at Yeshiva University in New York City. His research interests focus on the cognitive processes of decision-making and students' academic integrity decisions. James Rettinger is a recovering attorney and New Yorker in San Diego. He likes to barbeque and loves the Mets. The brothers were raised on a steady diet of high and low culture growing up, and find *The Simpsons* the perfect TV show for them. If only you could eat it. They wish to thank their wives and AOL IM for supporting the writing of this chapter.

# (a) None of the Below

Psychology Testing
on *The Simpsons*

Harris Cooper

THERE'S NOTHING LIKE a good old-fashioned paper-and-pencil test to separate the idiots from the geniuses, the good lovers from the bad, the sane from the rest of us. And once you know your score, you can adjust your self-image, dress and behavior to reflect your test results.

This is the operating principle in the Simpsons' Springfield, at least when it comes to psychological testing. Like many important aspects of modern life, psychological testing is mercilessly skewered in multiple episodes. In fact, you only have to wait until the series' second episode to see intelligence tests used as the central plot device ("Bart the Genius," season one).

In Springfield, test results are overvalued, misinterpreted and misapplied. The tests themselves are poorly written and poorly administered by psychologists whose misanthropy rivals that of C. Montgomery Burns—okay, maybe not that bad. But Springfield's psychological testers do inflict their abuse with a level of dispassion that even Monty admires and exploits ("Stark Raving Dad," season three).

In fact, I can imagine that there is a committee of Springfield psychologists, perhaps ensconced deep in the bowels of the New Bedlam Rest

Home for the Emotionally Interesting or perhaps in Proctorville, Iowa, home of the National Testing Center (where the entrance sign reads "Controlling Your Destiny since 1925"), who have gleefully prepared....

---

### The Springfield Psychological Association's
### Manual for Constructing Tests Guaranteed to Cause Mental Distress

Welcome, Mental Health Professionals! This manual will introduce you to the exciting and lucrative practice of constructing psychological, intelligence and achievement tests for the citizens of Springfield.

In the world of testing, test-makers are required to ask the question, "How well does the test measure what it is supposed to?" This is referred to as test validity. Many of the tests people take, especially the important ones like standardized achievement tests, have high test validity. Others, including the types you often find in magazines, are much less valid. Test validity is highly overrated, even counterproductive. This guide will help you develop tests that have very low test validity. That is, any resemblance between Springfieldians' scores on a test constructed using this manual and where they actually stand on the psychological characteristic being tested will be purely coincidental. Defective testing, random error and test-taker confusion and anxiety can help erode the mental health of the test-taker, thereby requiring the need for further testing (and your services)!

Throughout the manual, we will illustrate the principles of distress-causing test construction by reference to a family case study: the Simpsons of Evergreen Terrace. Ethical psychologists would obtain the Simpsons' permission, called informed consent, before revealing their test scores or the content of our secret surveillance tapes. Of course, because we are Springfield psychologists, we did not do this. This is **Rule #1**.[1] (You can view the surveillance tapes yourself by referring to the tape descriptions in parentheses.)

---

[1] In the spirit of full, unauthorized disclosure, here is a list of the IQ scores of some of Springfield's more prominent citizens:

| | |
|---|---|
| Martin Prince | 216 |
| Professor Frink | 199 (197 after hitting his head) |
| Comic Book Guy | 170 |
| Maggie Simpson | 167 (with a little help from her big sister) |
| Lisa Simpson | 159 |
| Dr. Julius Hibbert | 155 |
| Homer Simpson | 105 (after a crayon is removed from his brain) |

(Seymour Skinner and Lindsy Naegle are Mensa members, but their IQ scores are unknown to us.)

**Rule #2:** Make up questions that are confusing, ambiguous and preferably incomprehensible.

Here is an example of an excellent Springfield IQ test question:

At 7:30 A.M. an express train traveling sixty miles an hour leaves Santa Fe bound for Phoenix, 520 miles away. At the same time a local train traveling thirty miles an hour and carrying forty passengers leaves Phoenix bound for Santa Fe. It's eight cars long and always carries the same number of passengers in each car. An hour later, the number of passengers equal to half the number of minutes past the hour get off but three times as many plus six get on. At the second stop, half the passengers plus two get off, but twice as many get on as got on at the first stop.... ("Bart the Genius")

This is the first question on an IQ test given to Mrs. Krabappel's fourth grade class. In order to throw test-takers into a state of panic, it is always good to start a test with a very difficult question. This is a very rare strategy in testing outside of Springfield. However, it is true that some questions on good IQ and achievement tests will contain information that is irrelevant to their answers. Test-makers do this to raise the difficulty of the question and determine whether the test-taker is capable of separating relevant from irrelevant information. But this type of question typically comes toward the end of a test and always has a unique solution.

A Springfield IQ test question should be so full of useless information, while suggesting that numbers incalculable from the description are needed, that the test-taker is driven to a state of high anxiety. In Bart Simpson's case, this question leads him to fall off his chair, upon which his teacher admonishes him (Mrs. Krabappel: Bart, there are students in this class with a chance to do well!), thereby raising his anxiety even more, and ultimately causing him to cheat on the test. Good Springfield question![2]

Here's another excellent Springfield question, sure to confuse, developed by Miss Hoover, Lisa Simpson's teacher: "Mr. Blank needs a blank in order to blank his blank" ("Lisa Gets an 'A'," season ten).

This question leads Lisa (who admittedly hasn't completed the relevant assignment) to think out loud, "Oh, I am in deep blank," and fantasize that the president of Harvard told her the "doors are now closed to you" but she could still go to Brown (an institution where Otto the bus driver almost got tenure). Questions that generate irrelevant thoughts are sure to lower test performance.

---

[2] And don't forget to consider recruiting others to heighten test anxiety. For example, you can ask Groundskeeper Willie to say, "I got a zero once and my life turned out just fine," while he's cleaning a toilet ("Lisa Gets an 'A'").

Lisa doesn't like the question because it contains no clues about where in the assignment the right answer might be found. This makes for an excellent Springfield test question. However, a caution here, test-makers! This question is so ambiguous that multiple answers might be correct. Such questions can lead hostile test-takers to claim their answer is in fact true, even if it is not the one you were looking for (for example, "Mr. Blank needs a cartoon character in order to develop his voiceover"). Creating such confusion is good because it will anger and frustrate the Springfield test-taker, but it also requires the test proctor to spend time justifying the question and actually talking to test-takers, perhaps finding out what they really know. In Springfield, this should be avoided at all costs. Remember, the sole purpose of psychological tests is to increase the demand of psychological services.

**Rule #3:** Don't worry about whether a question is relevant to the issue, as long as it looks like it's relevant.

Makers of good psychological tests spend much time and effort constructing valid test questions. The validation process involves developing more questions than you need, pre-testing and rewriting them and discarding ones that fail to distinguish among test-takers on the psychological characteristic of interest. This can be a difficult and painstaking process. Therefore, we suggest that Springfield test-makers simply construct questions that have what is called face validity. These are questions that look like they measure the right thing but really may not. Constructing such questions is much easier and many people, including poorly trained test-makers, are fooled by them.

An example. One of Springfield's most successful tests is the Career Aptitude Normalizing Test, or CANT ("Separate Vocations," season three). It contains these two questions:

If I could be any animal I would be (a) a carpenter ant, (b) a nurse shark, or (c) a lawyer bird.

I prefer the smell of (a) gasoline, (b) french fries, or (c) bank customers.

Many career tests are constructed by asking people who are happy in their profession what their interests and attitudes are. Then, these are matched with the interests and attitudes of test-takers. What a waste of time! In Springfield, you can simply tell a student who answers (c) to the first question and (a) to the second question to grow up to be an Ambulance Chaser. The questions have face validity and it is easy to see how the career prescription was drawn from them. But is the prescription a valid prediction of what career the test-taker will succeed at and find rewarding in the future? Beats us! Of course, people unhappy with their careers are great candidates for our services. So either way, we win!

**Rule #4:** Make up confusing answers.

If you are having trouble constructing a confusing, ambiguous or incomprehensible question, take heart. You can still inflict much mental distress on your test-taker by constructing bad answers. For example:

> HOMER SIMPSON (while completing a test from *Self Test Monthly*)**:** "There's a black widow at your door, a rattlesnake at the window, and a scorpion on the phone. Do you (a) none of the below, (b)...("Kill the Alligator," season eleven)

"None of the below" is the perfect answer option to befuddle the Springfield test-taker! When the test-taker first reads this answer option, it is impossible to know if it is right or wrong. Of course, "None of the above," "All of the above" and their variants are already a part of any test-maker's bag of tricks, not just those of us who reside in Springfield. These answers are meant to increase the difficulty of questions by not permitting the test-taker to simply pick the answer that looks most correct. (They also help test-makers who have run out of clever answer options.) But, "None of the below," why didn't we think of it sooner! This answer option is unique to Springfield and guaranteed to increase the test-taker's confusion. In fact, we recommend using both "None of the below" and "All of the above" as answers to the same question.

**Rule #5:** Exploit the power of the test proctor.

The Springfield test proctor can be key to inflicting mental distress on a hapless test-taker. Most importantly, a test proctor can heighten anxiety by imbuing the outcome of a test with life-determining importance. For example, while handing out an IQ test, Mrs. Krabappel, one of our favorite proctors, utters what fourth graders fear most: "Now, I don't want you to worry, class. These tests will have no effect on your grades. They merely determine your future social status and financial success...if any" ("Bart the Genius"). In fact, IQ test scores correlate moderately well with grades in school, less well with job performance (and only when a person has little experience on the job) and not well at all with the likelihood of obtaining a prestigious occupation. But Springfield fourth graders don't need to know that!

Proctors can also confuse test-takers while administering projective tests. Unlike paper-and-pencil tests, projective tests are designed to reveal what's going on in the test-taker's unconscious mind. The most frequently used of these is the Rorschach Test with its well-known inkblots. Several years back, the inkblots were administered to Homer Simpson, at New Bedlam, and our hidden cameras picked up the following exchange ("Stark Raving Dad"):

*Psychiatrist holds up the first inkblot.*
**HOMER:** The devil with his fly open.
**PSYCHIATRIST:** Right.
*Psychiatrist holds up the second inkblot.*
**HOMER:** That's a spill on the floor with bugs goin' after it. They're gonna eat it.
**PSYCHIATRIST:** Good.

Sounds innocent enough, yes? No! This psychiatrist has violated a cardinal rule of administering projective tests. Simply by saying "Right" and "Good" after Homer's answers, the Springfield head-shrink has communicated that there are correct and incorrect interpretations of the inkblots. In fact, none exist. While a projective test might reveal that the test-taker is crazy, there really are no right or wrong answers, since only the content of the unconscious is at issue. How can this be labeled correct or incorrect? It can't. By suggesting that some answers are right and some better than others, the psychiatrist guarantees that Homer will become confused and apprehensive because he cannot possibly know what the right answers might be. Perhaps Homer will think it is good to simply continue to give answers similar to those he has already given (and been rewarded for). This will further erode the validity of the test. Outside of Springfield, psychologists who administer projective tests are trained to be aware of and minimize how they can influence responses. In Homer's case, the psychiatrist actually verbalizes reactions to his answers. A nice Springfield touch. But Springfield inkblot-administrators who really want to show off might choose to use more subtle cues, such as a head nod, smile, or upbeat voice inflection.[3]

---

The manual continues, but you get the idea.

The Springfield Psychological Association shows us how to construct invalid test questions and how to present them in ways that will interfere with test-takers' ability to answer honestly and show their stuff. Each of these flaws in tests and the testing process exists in the real world. How-

---

[3] When Homer exclaims about the inkblot test, "This isn't fair! How can you tell who's sane and insane?" the psychiatrist answers Homer's question by saying, "Well, we have a very simple method. (Stamps "insane" on Homer's hand.) Whoever has that stamp on his hand is insane." Talk about a simple test with face validity!

ever, as is its way with all, in Springfield the foibles of testing are exaggerated into caricature. The standardized achievement and IQ tests we all take have undergone rigorous and thoughtful development to ensure they are valid, and not just face valid. Proctors are trained and their interactions with test-takers are scripted so as not to influence the test-taking process. As we move down the psychological testing food chain, away from the high-stakes standardized tests and into the realm of classroom and pop culture tests, the issues raised in *The Simpsons* episodes become more real. Homer believes that his test results from *Self Test Monthly* are never wrong because "they're put together by the finest scientists in the magazine business" ("Kill the Alligator"). That may be true, but many magazine scientists probably didn't ace their final exam in their *Tests and Measurements* course. And yes, the Mrs. Krabappels of the world (and, dare I say even the Professor Frinks) certainly have written a clunker or two.

Thankfully, the citizens of Springfield are not nearly as helpless as the Springfield Psychological Association's members might wish. True, the Simpsons don't question the lack of validity of the tests they take or the insensitivity in the way they are administered. Instead, they strike back in the way they know best—by subverting the test-taking process itself and treating the testers as being just as foolish as the Simpsons are taken to be.

In fact, I can imagine that, feeling so abused, a poorly mimeographed flier circulates through the Springfield underground. . . .

---

### The Springfield Citizen's Association Manual for Subverting Psychological Tests

Tired of getting pushed around by pointy-headed pencil-pushers? Us too! So, here are some proven strategies for the citizens of Springfield to strike back at the psychologists and educators who probe our minds and pigeon-hole us. We say proven because they have all been tried out by our "test family," the Simpsons of Evergreen Terrace, who have graciously provided us with access to their secret surveillance tapes, recorded WITHOUT the permission of the test-givers, of course.[4] (You can view the surveillance tapes yourself by referring to the tape descriptions in parentheses.)

---

[4] Turnabout is fair play. For instance, Lisa Simpson was admitted to Mensa based on Principal Skinner sharing her standardized test scores with the other members. When Lisa inquires, "Aren't those supposed to be confidential?" Skinner replies, "Welcome to Mensa!" ("They Saved Lisa's Brain," season ten).

**Rule #1:** Befuddle and beguile the test proctor or scorer.

It's always good to throw a Springfield test proctor off guard. That way, they are more likely to lose track of time or have their attention diverted when you cheat!

One way to flummox a test-giver is to start taking the test before the test actually begins. For example, if you have an important final exam in an adult education class, consider this strategy, skillfully employed by Homer Simpson ("The Front," season four):

**INSTRUCTOR:** All right, here are your exams, fifty questions, true or false.
**HOMER:** True.
**INSTRUCTOR:** Homer, I was just describing the test.
**HOMER:** True.
**INSTRUCTOR:** Look, Homer, just take the test and you'll do fine.
**HOMER:** False.

Clearly, the instructor was thrown off his best game. Mission accomplished! But be careful: some testy test-givers might disqualify you for talking out of turn!

Another strategy is to turn the tables on the test-giver ("Kill the Alligator"):

**PSYCHOLOGIST:** You hate your father, don't you?
**HOMER:** Sometimes, but the guy I really hate is your father.
**PSYCHOLOGIST:** I shouldn't have brought that up. I was just venting.

Few trained psychologists will fall for this ruse but, after all, psychologists are people, too.

A tactic related to befuddling the proctor is sweet-talking your test-grader into giving you good grades. For example, in an effort to get grades good enough to spend his summer at camp ("Kamp Krusty," season four), Bart Simpson resorts to (a) pointing out to Mrs. Krabappel that his textbooks have been returned in excellent condition (some still in their original wrappings), (b) telling Mrs. Krabappel that her beauty resembles that of an angel and, when these don't work, he (c) just begs. Still doesn't work.

But it is worth a try because, after all, teachers are people, too.

**Rule #2:** Have someone help you answer the test questions.

Springfield tests of mental health can be tricky. So, if you think you may in fact be insane, get some help answering them. Of course, this works best with certain types of tests, such as Dr. Marvin Monroe's Take Home Personality Test, which contains twenty simple questions that determine how crazy, or "meshuggenah," someone is ("Stark Raving Dad"). Anyone who believes twenty simple questions can evaluate mental health deserves to have his head examined! So, turn these tests into an opportunity for a night of family fun and bonding. One evening, Bart helps his dad complete Dr. Monroe's test while they watch TV together:

BART: Hey, Dad. Do you hear voices?
HOMER: Yes, I'm hearing one right now while I'm trying to watch TV!
BART: Yes. Are you quick to anger?
HOMER: Bart! Shut up or I'll shut you up!
BART: Yes. Do you wet your pants? Well, even the best of us has an occasional accident.

Note how, by taking the first question at its most literal meaning, the Simpsons can render the test score meaningless. Of course we all hear voices. (A better question would have asked, "Do you hear voices when no one else is around?"—but don't let the test-makers know this.)

Okay, so maybe this isn't the best example, at least not if you want to come off looking normal. Remember, if you seek help in completing a test of mental health, find someone saner than you are.[5]

Here's a better example. Sometimes, intelligence tests are given using tasks that don't require verbal responses. Typically, this is done to avoid what is called *language or cultural bias*. If an IQ test's questions are asked in Swahili, people who don't speak Swahili as their native language might score lower, not because they are less smart but because they are at a disadvantage decoding the questions.[6] But nonverbal responses are visible, as are the actions of others present when the test is given. This opens a myriad of ways to subvert the test.

The Simpson family wants their youngest, Maggie, to go to Wickerbottom's Pre-Nursery School; after all, according to Apu Nahasapeemapetilon, "the fast track begins at birth" ("Smart and Smarter," season fifteen). Because Maggie

---

[5] It's always good to know the questions before taking the test. We don't have a complete version of Marvin Monroe's Take Home Personality Test but we did sneak a peek at the last part of several questions. Here's what we got: ...oudly to thin air? ...ren't really there? ...circles for hours? ...our father and mother? ...verything in red? ...o apparent reason? ...its of violence? ...eeping down food? ...nsist on rewards?

[6] Lisa Simpson knows that Albert Einstein didn't speak until he was three years old. And Marge Simpson knows that even then he could only speak German.

doesn't talk, she is given a nonverbal intelligence test to see whether she qualifies for admission. She does remarkably well and is admitted. However, a videotape later reveals that whenever Maggie was asked a question she looked over at her sister, Lisa. Lisa signaled the correct answers by holding up two fingers when Maggie was asked how many eyes she had, signaling "no" to another question, making a square with her arms for another question, and even making a perfect shadow puppet of a California condor. All unknowingly, of course. Once these nonverbal communications between sisters are discovered, Maggie is no longer welcome at Wickerbottom's.

Lisa's technique for helping her sister, conscious or otherwise, has been known about for over a hundred years. In the late nineteenth century, Clever Hans was a horse who responded to questions from humans by tapping his hoof. For example, if Clever Hans was asked what the sum of one plus two was, he would tap his hoof three times. People came to believe the horse could understand human language, do math calculations, tell time and so on. However, even before the invention of videotape but only after many years, it was discovered that Clever Hans was responding to slight physical cues from the questioner, such as changes in body position or head movements, that "told" the horse when to stop tapping.

So, if you want to use this technique to help someone on a Springfield nonverbal test, make your motions very subtle, and keep your back to any surveillance cameras!

**Rule #3:** When all else fails, just cheat.

Here are a few ways the Simpson family has cheated on tests over the years:

### 1. Steal someone else's paper and change the name.

After being stumped by an IQ test, Bart changes the name on Martin Prince's test to his own ("Bart the Genius"). Thus Bart is identified as a gifted child. The mislabeling works for a while because, according to Dr. J. Loren Pryor, Bart does exhibit numerous traits in common with gifted children, such as being bored in school and dreaming of leaving class to pursue his own intellectual development on an independent basis. Ultimately, though, Bart is rejected by his gifted class peers and returns to the regular fourth grade. Moral: If you're going to switch papers with someone smarter than you, don't shoot too high![7]

---

[7] Even Homer, not known for his critical thinking skills, is incredulous about Bart's test score, leading him to query, "Doc, this is all too much. I mean, my son is a genius—how could it happen?" to which Dr. Pryor replies, "Well, genius-level intelligence is usually the result of heredity and environment...although in some cases it's a total mystery."

### 2. Change your grade on the bus ride home.

On the bus ride home from school, Bart changes his grade from D- to A+ ("Kamp Krusty"). A good strategy, but Bart is admonished by Lisa for not forging more plausible grades. Sure enough, even Homer, probably a veteran of this strategy himself, sees through Bart's plan, proclaiming, "A+! You don't think much of me, do you, boy?....You know a D turns into a B so easily. You just got greedy." Again, Springfieldians, when you cheat, don't get greedy.

### 3. Purchase the answer sheet.

Even Springfield's most moral citizen can be driven to use this strategy. After spending several days at home vegging out before a test, Lisa Simpson purchases a test's answers from Nelson Muntz ("Lisa Gets an 'A'"). If you are generally an upright person, though, don't lose your nerve after committing the deed. Lisa discovers that her grade brought the entire school's GPA up to the state's minimum standard. When she admits to Principal Skinner that she cheated, it was only his own convoluted moral standards that saved the day: "As long as we handle this in a mature and, above all, quiet manner we'll still get that grant money....It's not the money's fault you cheated."

### 4. Remember the answers when you get left back.

When Bart gets held back to third grade, he simply remembers the test answers from the year before ("Bart vs. Lisa vs. Third Grade," season fourteen). In Springfield, getting held back is a good way to get smarter without having to work hard.

---

So, the battle rages on between Springfield's test-makers and test-takers.

In their own convoluted way, the Springfield test-makers know the basic rules of good test construction. They just don't employ them.

Instead, the rules are turned on their head. This shows how psychological tests are sometimes flawed and invested with unwarranted meaning that can lead to misuse. *The Simpsons* tells us people feel that too much in their lives can hinge on pencil scratches and brief utterances made in response to test questions. Whether it's the preschool fast-track, school funding, future social status and financial success, or even how long you will live,[8] the ethos of the Simpson family is that placing undue weight on occasionally flawed and always fragile measurements

---

[8] HOMER: According to this [test] I'll live to be . . . 42!!! Oh, that's horrible, I won't even live to see my children die! ("Kill the Alligator")

is, well, insane. The point is an important one but, certainly in Springfield, the point is exaggerated for comic purposes.

And, as is true in so many *Simpsons* plot lines, our favorite cartoon family finds its own way to subvert the asymmetric power relationship between the tester and the tested. But our heroes don't take on the testers directly. They don't expose the lack of validity of Springfield tests, citing the differences between the invalid tests they take and what valid tests might look like. That would be no fun at all. Instead, Homer and family opt for sillier and more subtle subversions. In doing so, they reveal a deep intelligence and full humanity that endears them to us all.

Harris Cooper is professor of psychology and director of the program in education at Duke University. He studies research methodology and applications of social psychology to educational policy and practice. Dr. Cooper was raised by Friz Freleng, Hanna Barbera, MGM and the Warner Brothers, while his mother must have been doing something more important. When not watching *The Simpsons*, he is editor of the *Psychological Bulletin*, the premiere journal publishing research syntheses in the social sciences.